PUBLIC THEOLOGY IN LAW AND LIFE

Edited by Brian Edgar, Paul Babie and David Wilson

PUBLIC THEOLOGY IN LAW AND LIFE

Edited by Brian Edgar, Paul Babie and David Wilson

ATF THEOLOGY

Adelaide

2012

Interface: A Forum for Theology in the World
Volume 15, Number 1&2 2012
Interface is an ecumenical and interdisciplinary theological journal dealing with issues of a social and cultural nature.
Interface is an independently refereed journal.

Mailing address:
Interface, PO Box 504, Hindmarsh, SA 5007 email: hdregan@atf.org.au
ATF Home Page: www.atf.org.au

Subscription Rates (2012)

Australia:	Individual Aus $55 p/a (includes GST)
	Institutional Aus $85 p/a (includes GST)
Overseas:	Individual and institutions Aus $95 p/a

Electronic subscriptions available.

Send all subscriptions to:
Interface
PO Box 504 Hindmarsh SA 5007

Interface is published by the ATF Theology an imprint of ATF (Australia)Ltd (ABN 90 116 359 963) and is published in May and October of each year.
Interface is indexed in the *Australasian Religion Index*
ISSN 1329-6264

www.atfpress.com

Table of Contents

B. PUBLIC THEOLOGY AND SOCIAL LIFE

C. PUBLIC LECTURES

Introduction: Public Theology Today

Brian Edgar, Paul Babie and David Wilson

Christian theology, properly understood, is always *public* theology. As Dutch journalist, theologian, politician and Prime Minister, Abraham Kuyper (1837–1920) famously declared, 'No single piece of our mental world is to be hermetically sealed off from the rest, and there is not a square inch in the whole domain of our human existence over which Christ, who is Sovereign over *all*, does not cry: "Mine!"'[1]

But the reality is that Christians have not always thought in this way and the contemporary term 'public theology' reflects the need to overcome the privatised form of faith that became dominant in modern society. Maybe one day the designation 'public' will become redundant, but at present it serves a useful function as a reminder of the proper role of theology. This edition of *Interface* primarily focuses on the role Christian theology plays in society but a distinctly public enterprise will welcome theological contributions from other perspectives and so we are pleased to include an article on the role of public theology in Islam.

Christian public theology involves the application of biblical and theological principles outside the confines of the church and assesses their implications for wider society. It examines both the theoretical structures of society (the nature of secularity, government, globalisation, pluralism and so forth) and the myriad specific issues involved in daily life (everything from sport to work-place relations to economics). Public theology is also, very importantly, a discipline that is practiced by the 'ordinary' Christian as well as the academic, and it is done in public (with all the scrutiny that

1. Abraham Kuyper, 'Sphere Sovereignty', in James D Bratt, *Abraham Kuyper, A Centennial Reader* (Grand Rapids: Eerdmans, 1998), 488.

entails) and in such a way that it communicates to non-Christians (although it remains a theological endeavour). In a real sense it is theology for the world, from the Word, by the people of God.

Today the term 'public' theology is found in many places. There is a Global Network for Public Theology (including several Australian universities), an *International Journal of Public Theology* (and too many other journals dealing with the topic to mention) and numerous centres of research into public theology. Within Australia there is an Australian Public Theology Network, the Centre for Public Christianity (focusing on media analysis and presentations), the ecumenical, Canberra-based Australian Centre for Christianity and Culture, the Centre for Public and Contextual Theology (of Charles Sturt University), the Ethos Centre for Christianity and Society (which combines the previous work of the Australian Evangelical Alliance department of Public Theology and the Zadok Institute), the Sophia Think Tank (connected with the Bible Society), the Tinsley Institute (the public theology focus of Morling College) and The Public Square (of the Australian Catholic University). These are merely illustrative of the interest (and so our apologies to all those other centres, networks, institutions and individuals with an intentional focus on public theology who have not been mentioned).

One of the areas where theology most plays a role in influencing public debate is in relation to the structures of governance generally, and legal structures and law specifically. Four essays in this volume take up the task of exploring the place of theology in law. In the first of these, '*Public Theology, Justice and Law: A Preliminary Note*', Benny YT Tai sets out, in simple terms, the role of public theology as a discourse having three aspects: (1) it is theologically informed; (2) it is about public issues, and (3) it uses public reason. For Tai, if public-ness is a part or even a core component of Christian faith, one still needs to know what the Bible teaches about the scope and content of that public-ness and what is therefore expected of Christians. Returning to the Old and New Testaments, Tai argues that the Bible displays a concept of justice that provides one of the justifications and guides for public theology. As law is also mainly about dispensing justice, that concept offers the bridge for Christian lawyers to engage in public discourse in the capacity of a public theologian in pluralistic societies.

The second essay of this section provides a glimpse of the sorts of issues that fall within the conception of justice as understand in secular-liberal law, but with which theology may need to come to terms if it is to enter into dialogue with such legal structures. In '*What Lies Beneath: A Brief Introduction to the Issues Underlying the Development of the Law in the*

Context of Medical Treatment', Bernadette Richards argues that because we live in an increasingly complex world, ideals of 'right' and 'wrong' may no longer be as simply defined as perhaps they once were. For that reason, in order to understand the law, and the nature of humanity, lawyers must master many disciplines and doctrines. Yet, in the attempt to ensure that society as a whole can flourish, individual rights and interests may, at times, be compromised. This is particularly so in the context of medical treatment. Richards offers a brief reflection on the ongoing struggle to reconcile these diverse interests and considers whether or not an appropriate balance has been struck in the case of medical treatment. And it is here, Richards suggests, that theological discourse can add to the diversity of considerations, enriching, enlivening and informing the debate.

Taking another approach to what theology might have to offer the broader political-legal world in which we live, *'The Australian Legal Academy and the Concept of Property'*, by Paul Babie, picks up on Tai and Richards' point that what both law and theology seek to achieve is morality and justice, and sets out to demonstrate how those who currently inhabit our Australian legal academy would do well to re-discover that simple fact. Yet, law schools fail to study this largely because, it is claimed, there is no rationality to religious belief (theology) and, therefore, it clearly has no role in the make-up of law. Australian law schools and universities overlook the relationship between theology and law at their peril. At best, it leaves impoverished our understanding of contemporary Australian social life and, at worst, leads to serious misinterpretations of the sociology of law. Thus, Babie concludes with a brief reflection on what an engagement of legal thought and theology might look like in the case of a Christian perspective on private property, and what that might mean for the account of property advanced in secular liberal legal systems, including Australia's.

The final essay in the section, Nadirsyah Hosen's fascinating *'Public Theology in Islam: A New Approach?'*, demonstrates that public theology is not simply a Christian endeavour. Rather, as Hosen argues, while the global discourse of Islam after 9/11 focused on the radical side of Islam, other, positive aspects of Islam have been ignored. Hosen's article seeks to redress this imbalance by responding to the question 'how should Islamic theology respond to the real and practical issues facing Muslims?' While clearly not questioning the five pillars of Islam, Hosen engages with Islamic theology as *kalam* (discourse) and *falsafa* (philosophy), seeking an understanding of theology through dialectic. His overarching argument is that making Islam a living religion that deals with public issues in the modern world requires a new approach to Islamic theology; and for Hosen, this involves the union of *kalam* and *falsafa*.

The second section of the journal contains four articles that deal with very different areas of life: education, economics, business and technology. Brian Edgar argues that the convergence of a number of new technologies (from stem cell technology to genetic engineering to the extreme extension of life-span) has the potential to lead to a form of self-directed evolution of human functioning that is so radical that it will challenge our understanding of the nature of humanity. In *'On the Future of Humanity: Enhancing the Image of God?'* he discusses the theological issues surrounding the nature of humanity as a physical species and as a part of creation that is made in the image of God. In the light of scientific developments he discusses the role of human creativity, the possibility of new forms of humanity (and the danger of de-humanisation) and the nature of the future destiny of human life.

In *'Is there a Theology of Values Education?'* Brian V Hill, Emeritus Professor of Education at Murdoch University, Western Australia shows how the growing religious pluralisation of society in the present day obliges us to revisit some of our basic assumptions concerning the nature of Christian involvement in education. This is a topic complicated by denominational differences and the needs of both public and private education. He discusses issues related to the place of values in education and argues for the need for there to be an organised study of world-views. He identifies some central theological concerns which bear directly on the way that it is possible to conceptualise and work on values education and fashions a form of discourse that can enable Christian educators to communicate across denominational and other divides about such issues.

Then in *'Biblical Ethical Principle and Its Critics'* Clive and Cara Beed demonstrate how contemporary Christian ethical thought has deduced normative ethical principles from the Bible in order to apply them to social and economic issues. They evaluate the criticism that has been directed at the principle approach (which endeavours to reveal the relevance of the Bible to the modern world, while conceding that the Bible does not speak directly to the burning issues of today) and conclude that it is not compelling, and then they show that it has been relatively neglected in socio-economic matters when it ought to be a constituent element of it.

Alasdair MacIntyre's concept of virtue is applied to professions and the world of business in Chris White and Gordon Preece's *'Professions,*

Business and MacIntyre—Fellow Travellers?' They outline the origins of the idea of a profession and discuss the changes that have taken place more recently in terms of its relationship with contemporary business practice. They consider the importance of ethics in business and whether, on the one hand, professional practice is anything more than a business and, on the other hand, whether business management can be a profession. They show that a nuanced version of MacIntyre's theory of virtue can be beneficially applied to contemporary businesses and professions.

In addition to the preceding articles all of which were written specifically for publication in an academic context there is a third section with two articles that were originally given as verbal presentations for a more general audience. These two public lectures also deal with public theology and, apart from the value of their specific content they have the virtue of reminding us that theology is properly done in the public arena. The first, *'The Bible Hits the Streets'* is by David Wilson and it deals with the question of what the wisdom contained in the Bible would call out to the various sectors of Australian society if given half a chance. The second, '*Wisdom and Transformational Leadership*', is by George Savvides who looks at what transformative leadership looks like in the worlds of business and education and draws some challenging conclusions.

The purpose of this collection of articles is to demonstrate the way that public theology can function. Hopefully the various contributions will provoke thought, stimulate conversation and even facilitiate a work of transformation within society.

PART A
PUBLIC THEOLOGY, LAW AND JUSTICE

Public Theology, Justice and Law: A Preliminary Note

Benny YT Tai

Associate Professor of Law
University of Hong Kong

According to Jürgen Moltmann, *'[a]s the theology of God's kingdom, theology has to be public theology . . . [i]ts public character is constitutive for theology, for the kingdom of God's sake'*.[1] David Tracy echoed that, *'all theology is public discourse'*.[2] Harold Breitenberg understood public theology to be *'theologically informed descriptive and normative public discourse about public issues, institutions, and interactions, addressed to the church or other religious body as well as the larger public or publics, and argued in ways that can be evaluated and judged by publicly available warrants and criteria'*.[3] In short, public theology[4] is a discourse that has three aspects: (1) It is

1. Jürgen Moltmann, *God for a Secular Society: The Public Relevance of Theology* (Fortress Press, 1999), 5.
2. David Tracy, *The Analogical Imagination: Christian Theology and the Culture of Pluralism* (New York: Crossroad, 1981), 3.
3. E Harold Breitenberg Jr, 'What is Public Theology?', in *Public Theology for a Global Society: Essays in Honor of Max L Stackhouse*, edited by Deidre King Hainsworth and Scott R Paeth (Grand Rapids: Eerdmans, 2010), 5.
4. This article is about public theology but not political theology though both concern with the relationship between Christian faith and the Church with politics. (See E Harold Breitenberg, Jr 'To Tell the Truth: Will the Real Public Theology Please Stand Up', in *Journal of the Society of Christian Ethics*, 23/2 (2003): 55–96, 59.) However, public theology, unlike political theology, gives priority to the civil society believing that the civil society, of which religious faith and organisation is inevitably the core, is more determinative of and normatively more important for politics than politics is for society and religion. As Stackhouse has written, 'public theology differs from political theology . . . because public theology tends to adopt a social theory of poli-

theologically informed; (2) It is about public issues; and (3) It uses public reason.[5]

All advocates for public theology assume that 'publicness' is a part of Christian faith but that may not be self-evident to many Christians.[6] If publicness is a part or even a core component of Christian faith, we still need to know what the Bible has taught us about the scope and content of that publicness and what is expected from Christians. The aim of this article is to go back to the Bible, both the Old Testament and the New Testament, to trace the biblical sources of the public dimension of Christian faith. Through that, the scope and content of the public dimension of Christian faith can also be identified.

It is argued that justice, as understood in the Bible, is an overarching concept and a principle that provides one of the justifications and guidances for public theology.[7] As law is also mainly about dispensing justice,[8] justice provides the bridge for Christian lawyers to engage in public discourse in the capacity of a public theologian.[9] Therefore, this is an article specifically written for Christian lawyers and Christians who have an interest in seeing how the law can be used to advance justice in contemporary pluralistic societies.

The Public Dimension of Christian Faith as Reflected in the Old Testament

I start with a famous verse from the Old Testament, Micah 6:8:

---

tics, and political theology inclines to have a political view of society.' (See Max L Stackhouse, 'Civil Religion, Political Theology and Public Theology: What's the Difference?', in *Political Theology* 5/3 (2004): 275–293, 285 and 288.) In another words, public theology advocates gradual change in the political culture rather than revolutionary change in the political system.

5. The criteria in determining what constitutes public reason may be debatable. The discussion will be left to later parts.
6. Oliver O'Donovan gave an explanation on the separation between politics and theology. See Oliver O'Donovan, *The Desire of Nations* (Cambridge: Cambridge University Press, 1996), chapter 1.
7. The other principles may include 'to love kindness' and 'to be the salt of the earth and the light of the world'.
8. David A Funk, 'Major Functions of Law in Modern Society', in *Case IS. Res. L. Rev.*, 23 (1972): 257–306.
9. Andries van Aarde, 'What is "theology" in "public theology" and what is "public" about "public theology"?', in *HTS Teologiese Studies/Theological Studies*, 64/ 3 (2008).

He has told you, O man, what is good;
And what does the Lord require of you
But to do justice, to love kindness,
And to walk humbly with your God?

There are two reasons for choosing this verse.[10] First, the verse is expressed in a form of general command to all people of God. Second, the themes covered in the verse can be found throughout the Old Testament.[11] One can identify four core components of Christian faith from the verse. They are: (1) to do justice; (2) to love kindness; (3) to be humble; and (4) to walk with your God.[12]

Both the first and the second component demand a social dimension, meaning that it can only be practiced in one's relationship with others. This social dimension is the public nature of Christian faith. The third component concerns the building of a believer's character and the fourth component is about relationship with the divinity. The four components overlap with each other and are interconnected. However, one can still argue that the first two components belong to the public dimension of Christian faith and the following two components belong to the private dimension of Christian faith.

I admit that the public/private division is sometimes misleading as the two dimensions intertwine with each other. However, there are still some practical reasons for using this distinction to illustrate the scope and relevance of Christian faith. The private dimension basically is about building the character of a believer and her relationship with God. This can happen, in theory, without interaction between the believer and other

10. The author is well aware of the warning of not to build a theology out of a verse but has to be based on the Bible in its entirety. See Oliver O'Donovan, *The Desire of Nations* (Cambridge University Press, 1996), 22.
11. Hays has provided a diagnostic checklist to assess a theological claim. (See *The Moral Vision of the New Testament: A Contemporary Introduction to New Testament Ethics* (San Francisco: Harper One, 1996).) The criteria included: (1) the accuracy/adequacy of the exegesis of the texts used; (2) the comprehensiveness of the scope of texts employed; (3) the selection of specific text as the guiding canon; (4) the way texts that are in tension with the claim are being handled; (5) the mode of appeal to the text; (6) the other sources of authority relied upon; and (7) the fruit of the claim. I have this checklist in mind in formulating my theological claim.
12. Most commentaries on this verse merge the 'being humble' and the 'walking with God' commands as a single command. I prefer to separate the two though this does not affect the major arguments in this article.

persons.[13] One major difference between the public dimension and the private dimension is that the public dimension cannot be practiced without interaction between a believer and other persons. This may be the key aspect of the public dimension of Christian faith.

To do justice or to love kindness assumes that there are people to act upon according to the command of the biblical verse. Later on I will illustrate the differences between doing justice and loving kindness whichmay show the different ways to practise the public dimension of Christian faith.

I will now focus the discussion on 'to do justice' or 'justice'. The Hebrew words for justice are *šāpaṭ* (verb) and *mišpāṭ* (the related noun). According to Christopher Wright, it means 'to put things right' or 'to intervene in a situation that is wrong, oppressive or out of control and to fix it'. [14] In the Old Testament, justice very often comes together with righteousness in a pair.[15] To understand the meaning of justice, one also has to ascertain the meaning of righteousness. The word in Hebrew for righteousness is *ṣĕdeq* and *ṣĕdāqâ* and the meaning is 'a norm—something by which other things are measured'.[16] Putting justice with righteousness means that, *mišpāṭ* is 'what needs to be done in a given situation if people and circumstances are to be restored to conformity with'[17] the norm or the standard. Wright asserted that the nearest English expression to the double word phrase of justice and righteousness would be 'social justice'.[18]

We will postpone further discussion on the exact meaning of justice until later. What we need to illustrate here is that the Old Testament discourse about justice is very often connected with the treatment of widows, orphans, resident aliens, and the poor.[19] With this understanding of justice in the Old Testament, it means that people of God have a religious duty to act in a particular way to put things right as to the wrongs done to

13. To most Christians, it is very clear that it will be difficult to talk about character building and walking with God in a totally isolated situation. One can build one's character better in one's relationship with others and one can see God more in one's interaction with others. However, for the sake of distinguishing the public and private dimensions of Christian faith, it is argued that the last two components of Christian faith in theory can be practiced without any interaction with other people.
14. Christopher JH Wright, *Old Testament Ethics for the People of God* (Golders Green: IVP Academic, 2004), 255–257.
15. An example is Psalm 33:5.
16. *Wright, op cit*, 256.
17. *Ibid*, 257.
18. *Ibid*.
19. Deuteronomy 24:17, Deuteronomy 27:19, Exodus 22:21–22, Isaiah 1:17.

widows, orphans, resident aliens, and the poor.[20] The public dimension of faith demonstrated in the Old Testament can now be clearly seen because this part of the faith can only be practiced in one's interaction with other people.

We may further ask what the scope of this 'public' is. Must it be limited to only people of the same faith or people belonging to the same religious community? The four categories of people suffering injustice include resident aliens which indicates that the Old Testament writers had a much wider 'public' in mind—including all people on earth. Our duty toward widows, orphans and the poor should not be limited to those in our own religious community. The public for Christians should not be limited to the church, though it is an integral part of the 'public' that Christians have to face.[21]

A wider understanding for the 'public' can be furthered confirmed by two observations from the Old Testament. First, Israelites were commanded to love the strangers residing among them because they themselves had been aliens in Egypt.[22] The people of God had also themselves been aliens, therefore the golden rule is that you should 'do to others as you would have them do to you'.[23] Second, in the Book of Ruth, Boaz, an Israelite, was commended for treating Ruth, a Moabite woman, justly by allowing her to glean and gather after the reapers in his fields,[24] which is a way recommended by the Bible for doing justice.[25]

The Public Dimension of Christian Faith as Reflected in the New Testament

The verse from the New Testament that I will use to illustrate the public dimension of Christian faith is equally famous, Matthew 22:39:

---

20. Put in a positive sense, the duty to do justice is to act rightly. One should treat widows, orphans, resident aliens, and the poor in ways that they deserve. See the discussion below on the level of care should be provided to them.
21. David Tracy mentioned that the three publics of public theology are the society, academy and the church. (See David Tracy, *The Analogical Imagination: Christian Theology and the Culture of Pluralism* (New York: Crossroad, 1981), chapter 1: A Social Portrait of the Theologian: The Three Publics of Theology–Society, Academy, Church.
22. Leviticus 19:34.
23. Matthew 7:12.
24. Ruth 2.
25. Leviticus 19:9.

You shall love your neighbor as yourself.[26]

The reasons for choosing this verse as the overarching verse for the New Testament are similar. First, it is a general command from Jesus Christ to all believers. Second, the theme of this verse can be found throughout the New Testament and is connected also with the Old Testament.[27] At first sight, one may question how this verse could have a public dimension. Is it not about a character that Jesus Christ wants Christians to have?

Indeed, to love is a personal character or a fruit of the Holy Spirit[28] but there must be some people beyond oneself for one to express one's love because Jesus commands us to love our neighbors. One then may agree that Christian faith has a public dimension under the New Testament but it is still not the same as the Old Testament.

This may be a place for us to draw a difference between 'to do justice' and 'to love kindness' referred in Micah 6:8. The 'love your neighbor' command seems to be very similar to the 'to love kindness' command. The Good Samaritan parable[29] is used to illustrate their difference.[30] In the parable, the good Samaritan was commended by Jesus for his good deeds to the man being robbed and wounded. His compassion included having his wounds bandaged, pouring oil and wine on them, taking him to a place of safety for someone to take care of him and making a payment to the innkeeper for taking care of him. To 'love your neighbour' is to have mercy upon a person in need and provide actual and immediate assistance to the person by satisfying his needs. However, to do justice is different. It may require one to take action to get the people who had done wrong to that person, that is, the robbers, to take responsibility for their wrongful acts. They would have to be punished or to pay compensation to the wounded person. Even though Christian faith, as described in the New Testament has a public dimension, some may not consider that it is not the same as

26. Mark 12:31, Luke 10:27.

27. See the discussion below.

28. Galatian 5:22–23.

29. Luke 10:30–37.

30. Here I am not suggesting a new reading to the parable and the central messages of the parable should be seen as relating to the command to 'love your neighbour' and the question 'who is my neighbour?' I use the parable as just a familiar example to illustrate the differences in the essence of the 'to do justice' and the 'to love kindness' commands.

the Old Testament because it does not put the command to do justice in the highest priority.[31]

I will delay the discussion of the different means to do justice until later. What we need to answer in this part is whether the 'love your neighbor' command also contains the 'doing justice' component as referred in Micah 6:8. We have to look at the context in which Jesus issued that command. Jesus was asked by a lawyer, who was an expert in Mosaic Law, on which was the greatest commandment in the Law. In answering this question, he referred to this 'love your neighbor' command.

The 'love your neighbor' command originated from Leviticus 19:18. However, in Leviticus 19, there are also many examples of just actions including: one should not reap every corner of one's field and gather every gleaning of one's harvest in order to leave them for the needy and the stranger,[32] one should not oppress one's neighbor or rob him, one should not delay in paying wages to one's hired workers. One should not ill-treat a disabled person[33] or a stranger,[34] one should also judge fairly and should not give preference to the poor or to the rich.[35] In other words, Jesus would have known that his answer would be read by the lawyer in the literal context of the 'love your neighbor' command in Leviticus. Therefore, the 'love your command' clearly contains the same element of justice as in Micah 6:8.

We may also refer to Jesus himself, the person who issued the command. At the beginning of his ministry, he read from the book of Isaiah:[36]

> The Spirit of the Lord is upon me,
> because He anointed me to preach the gospel to the poor.

31. Nicholas Wolterstorff in his book on Christian conceptions of justice, *Justice: Rights and Wrongs* (Princeton: Princeton University Press, 2008), used two chapters to analyse the concept of justice in the New Testament. My understanding on justice is strongly influenced by the view of Wolterstorff. He noted that there has long been a powerful strand of thought in the Christian tradition that de-justicises the New Testament. This strand of thought believes that justice is the theme of the Old Testament but love is the theme of the New. It is believed that Christians should put considerations of justice behind love and love supplants justice. Before he explained his view on justice in the New Testament, he used a whole chapter to rebut this strand of thought that de-justicises the New Testament.
32. Leviticus 19:9–10.
33. Leviticus 19:13–18.
34. Leviticus 19:33.
35. Leviticus 19:15.
36. Luke 4:16–19.

He has sent me to proclaim release to the captives,
and recovery of sight to the blind, to set free those who are oppressed,
to proclaim the favorable year of the Lord.[37]

He, himself, provides an example on how to love one's neighbor, that is, by doing justice. Nicholas Wolterstorff argued that, 'doing justice is an example of love'.[38] He proposed 'an understanding of love such that the imperative to act justly is not in conflict with the law of love'[39] Following this understanding, the New Testament also clearly contains a public dimension and that dimension includes both doing justice and loving kindness as in the Old Testament.

What we have argued up to this point is that Christian faith has a public dimension. If one agrees then a public theological discourse is is significant to all Christians. The core components of our faith include a public dimension but is often overlooked by Christians. What we can know also is that the public dimension of our faith is comprised at least of two elements: to do justice and to love kindness.[40] In the following parts, I will further illustrate the differences between these two elements with regard to their exact meanings and the specific acts needed for one to comply with the commands. That can then bring us closer to reflect on the role of law and of Christian lawyers in this project of public theology.

Justice: What is It?

If we accept that 'to do justice' is a core component of Christian faith, then it is important to clarify the meaning of justice, as it will determine what are the legitimate concerns and acts of Christians in fulfilling their

37. Isaiah 61:12.
38. Nicholas Wolterstorff, *Justice in Love* (Grand Rapids: Eerdmans, 2011), 84.
39. *Ibid.*
40. The central argument of this article is not that the publicness of Christian faith is limited to 'doing justice'. What we want to assert is that 'doing justice' must be a core component of the Christian faith. 'Loving kindness' is an equally important aspect of the public dimension of Christian faith. There may be another biblical basis to support another aspect of the public dimension of Christian faith and that is to be the salt of the earth and the light of the world (Matt 5:13–16, Luke 14: 34–35, Mark 9:50). (See below footnote 70.) The reason that the 'to do justice' aspect is emphasised in this article is only because this is an aspect that is often overlooked by many Christians even if they see that their religious faith incorporates a public dimension and it is also an aspect most relevant to Christian lawyers, who are the targeted readers of this article.

religious duty.[41] As mentioned above, the discourse about justice in the Old Testament is often connected with the treatment of widows, orphans, resident aliens and the poor. A possible understanding of justice is to ensure that widows, orphans, resident aliens and the poor are not being oppressed by others and are given sufficient care.

Before I proceed further to ascertain whether the concern of justice is applicable to people beyond these four groups and the standard to be used in determining the level of care that should be provided to widows, orphans, residents aliens, the poor or other vulnerable groups, I will look at some other possible understandings of justice in the Old Testament suggested by others.

Wolterstorff in advancing his biblical understanding of justice,[42] which I find very inspiring, referred to Oliver O'Donovan's understanding of justice in his book, *The Desire of Nations*.[43] According to Wolterstorff, O'Donovan's understanding of justice in the Old Testament is that justice should only be limited to juridical judgment or to the claim of a plaintiff before a judge. [44] In Wolterstorff's terms, O'Donovan's understanding of justice in the Old Testament refers only to rectifying justice and the procedures for achieving it.[45] In another words, O'Donovan's understanding of justice is about how to rectify a wrong after the wrong has been done on some persons especially through a judicial process.

41. I agree with Duncan Forrester that the understanding of justice from a Christian perspective as presented in this article may only be theological fragments and there is no intention to present a comprehensive theory of Christian justice. See Duncan B Forrester, *Christian Justice and Public Policy* (Cambridge: Cambridge University Press, 1997).
42. Nicholas Wolterstorff, *Justice: Rights and Wrongs* (Princeton: Princeton University Press, 2008).
43. Cambridge University Press, 1996.
44. Oliver O'Donovan's political theology is rich, thick and dense. His theological concern does not focus on justice but the political act of making judgment. The views of Oliver O'Donovan on justice in this article are based on Wolterstorff's reading of O'Donovan's work, especially, *The Desire of Nations*. For other critical reviews of the different aspects of Oliver O'Donovan's political theology, see Craig Bartholomew, Jonathan Chaplin, Robert Song and Al Wolters, *A Royal Priesthood? The Use of the Bible Ethically and Politically A Dialogue with Oliver O'Donovan* (Grand Rapids: Zondervan, 2002).
45. Nicholas Wolterstorff, *Justice: Rights and Wrongs* (Princeton: Princeton University Press, 2008), 71.

Wolterstorff referred also to Walter Brueggemann's understanding of justice in the Old Testament.[46] According to Wolterstorff, Brueggemann's understanding of justice is mainly about distributive justice. In Wolterstorff's terms, Bruggemann's understanding of justice concerns primary justice.[47] In other words, Brueggemann's understanding of justice is about how goods should be distributed in the society to prevent anyone from suffering.

Wolterstorff advanced his own position that 'a place midway between Bruggemann's emphasis on primary justice in Israel and O'Donovan's on rectifying justice' seems to be the right place to be.[48] In arguing his case, he hinted that political rights, the right to be heard, and the right to security of person should also be covered by the concern of justice.[49]

Translated into modern terms,[50] O'Donovan's version of justice seems to be procedural justice like the right to fair trial; Wolterstorff's version of justice is civil or political justice like the right to personal liberty and other civil and political rights;[51] and Bruggemann's version of justice is social justice emphasising economic rights.[52] From an exegetical perspective, there is no reason that all three versions cannot be adopted together as

46. Walter Brueggemann, *Theology of the Old Testament* (Minneapolis: Fortress Press, 1997).
47. Nicholas Wolterstorff, *Justice: Rights and Wrongs* (Princeton: Princeton University Press, 2008), 78.
48. *Ibid.*
49. *Ibid*, 77–78.
50. This seems to be a suggestion that the biblical concept of justice can be translated into the modern language of human rights. Some Christians may have the reservation that the language of human rights may not be appropriate for Christianity as it carries with a too strong tone of individualism. Indeed, the language of human rights, at least in its more popular use, may not be totally compatible with Christianity but it is not static. Connecting the Christian understanding of justice with the language of human rights may provide new insights into the conception of human rights, transforming it to be more communitarian and less individualistic. This will be more consistent with Christianity and can also be taken as a possible contribution of Christianity to the human rights discourse. See Max L Stackhouse and Stephen E Healry, 'Religion and Human Rights: A Theological Apologetic', in *Religious Human Rights in Global Perspectives: Religious Perspectives*; edited by John Jr Witte and Johan D r van Vyver (Hague: M Nijhoff, 1996); Max L Stackhouse, 'Human rights and Public Theology: The Basic Validation of Human Rights', in *Religion and Human Rights: Competing Claims?*, edited by Carrie Gustafason and Peter Juviler (Armonk, NY; London, England: ME Sharpe, 1999); and John Jr Witte, 'Law, Religion and Human Rights', (1996) 28 *Columbia Human Rights Law Review* 1, at 31–32.
51. See the International Covenant on Civil and Political Rights.
52. See the International Covenant on Economic, Social and Cultural Rights.

they are not mutually exclusive but are multi-perspective or accumulative, providing more or deeper protection to those who should be protected.[53]

I now have to consider whether the concern of justice is applicable to people other than widows, orphans, resident aliens and the poor. In Isaiah 1:17, Isaiah of Jerusalem says,

> Seek justice,
> Rescue the oppressed,
> Defend the orphan,
> Plead for the widow.

In Isaiah 10:1–2, the prophet says,

> who make iniquitous decrees,
> who write oppressive statutes,
> to turn aside the needy from justice,

53. One possible comment is that this understanding of biblical justice is too broad. It is argued that the duty to do justice is only a negative duty. It only requires Christians not to inflict harm upon others, that is; not to be involved in acts oppressing or depriving the social vulnerable groups. It does not require Christians to take positive actions to right the wrongs done upon the social vulnerable groups. I will argue that this understanding of justice is too thin and Christians will be encouraged to tolerate or show indifference to unjust phenomenon in the society. Even if we are not directly causing the suffering of the social vulnerable groups, our inaction or omission may have contributed to their sufferings indirectly as the wrongdoers are not being challenged or not stopped from continuing their wrongful acts. I will further argue in this article that very often we, as members of the community, may find ourselves also to be one of the wrongdoers even if we have not consciously or directly participated in acts oppressing or depriving the social vulnerable groups. Even if we have fulfilled the negative duty of doing justice, I assert that we may still have failed important aspects of doing justice expected from God.

However, some might argue that this understanding of biblical justice is too narrow. Some assert that the loving kindness aspect should not be separated from the doing justice aspect. As argued in this article, I have no difficulty in accepting that the two aspects are interconnected. What I want to emphasise is that Christians should not dilute the doing justice command by over-emphasising the loving kindness command. Some other people assert that the concept of justice in the Bible incorporates also a Christian understanding of humanity, which may be different from versions of humanity based on pure humanism or secular theories. To do justice will then also include acts to promote this 'proper understanding of humanity in the society. I will argue that this view may be conceptually clearer to be put under another aspect of the public dimension of Christian faith, 'to be the salt of the earth and the light of the world', rather than 'to do justice'.

and to rob the poor of my peoples of their right,
that widows may be your spoil,
and that you may make the orphans your prey!

A reasonable reading of these verses on justice is that the beneficiaries of the 'to do justice' command include all people in society who are being oppressed or who are in need. The four categories of widows, orphans, resident aliens and the poor are just examples of the most vulnerable groups at the time of the Old Testament on the basis of the social customs at that time and at that place. In different societies, traditional or contemporary, there may be other social vulnerable groups beyond these four categories who are also being oppressed and are in need, like the outcasts in India, women in Muslim societies, blacks in the Apartheid South Africa, etc. There is no reason that the Bible should be read in such a rigid way to allow only the four categories as the only legitimate beneficiaries of the 'to do justice' command.

Another question is whether we should care about the injustice suffered by people other than socially vulnerable groups? How about the rich who may also suffer unjust treatment? In Leviticus 19:15 we have referred to above, it is said,

Do not pervert justice;
do not show partiality to the poor or favoritism to the great,
but judge your neighbor fairly.

It seems that justice should also apply to the more affluent in society. Whether they will in fact suffer unjust treatment depends on the understanding of justice. It is unlikely that they will suffer social injustice as they have the sufficient means to satisfy their basic needs, but in theory they may still be treated by the more powerful in society in a procedurally unjust manner, or their civil and political rights can also be oppressed. However, this situation may be more unlikely to happen than in the case of socially vulnerable groups, and the hurt suffered by socially vulnerable groups in similar situations may be more pronounced. Therefore, we will assume that the beneficiaries of the 'to do justice' command include the rich in appropriate circumstances.

What we have arrived at up to this point is only that Christians have a religious duty to do justice by ensuring that socially vulnerable groups are not being oppressed and can have their needs satisfied. However, the level of care that should be provided to the vulnerable groups in the society is still not clear. The level of care may determine whether a person is actually being oppressed or whether her specific need should be satisfied. The question is beyond the kind of needs necessary for human survival, yet, what additional needs must also be satisfied in doing justice? Take this example: in the past only those who are very resourceful can have a computer at home. One cannot say that a person is being oppressed if his family is not provided with a computer. However, at this digital age computers become a necessary good especially for children to learn. Should then computers not also be provided to children of poor families as an act of doing justice?

Does the Bible provide any guidance on the level of care that should be provided to socially vulnerable groups? Would it be limited only to satisfying procedural fairness in treating a person or a minimal level of subsistence to be provided to a person? Wolterstorff suggested that it is determined by 'the worth of a human being'.[54] But what exactly is the worth of a human being?

Many verses in the Bible refer to the human as being created in the image of God. Genesis 1:27 says,

> So God created mankind in his own image,
> in the image of God he created them;
> male and female he created them.

Genesis 9:6 says,

> Whoever sheds human blood,
> by humans shall their blood be shed;
> for in the image of God
> has God made mankind.

What gives worth to human beings as an image of God, *imago dei*? Wolterstorff argued that 'being loved by God gives a human being great worth'. 'And if God loves equally and permanently each and every creature who bears the *imago dei*, then the relational property of being loved by God is

54. Wolterstorff, *Justice: Rights and Wrongs, op cit,* 301.

what we have been looking for'[55] to determine the level of care that should be provided to socially vulnerable groups.

Adopting this understanding, we as Christians have a religious duty to do justice by preventing socially vulnerable groups in our society from being oppressed and providing them with goods to satisfy their needs to match their worth as the image of God who are being loved equally and permanently by God. Still, while those goods that need to be provided may not be clear, at least we have set an overarching standard.

To do Justice: How?

What then can be the concrete acts to be done by Christians to fulfill this duty to do justice? To recall the previous discussion on doing justice and loving kindness, we know that there is a difference between providing relief and seeking redress. Providing relief is a way to loving kindness. We, ourselves, will not act in an oppressive manner disrespecting the worth of socially vulnerable groups. Out of our own resources, we may satisfy the needs of the needy. However, these acts cannot provide redress as socially vulnerable groups are still being wronged even if they are loved by us and their needs are satisfied.

To do justice requires us to find ways to undo the wrong. The Psalmist in 82:3–4 said:

> Vindicate the weak and fatherless;
> Do justice to the afflicted and destitute.
> Rescue the weak and needy;
> Deliver them out of the hand of the wicked.

All the verbs related with doing justice—'vindicate', 'rescue' and 'deliver'—require some concrete actions to be taken for the oppressed and deprived. Harm has been done to the person hurt by the wrongful act and undoing the wrong requires the wrongdoer to be accountable for his wrong either by being punished for the wrong or compensation of the hurt person for the harm she has suffered. This involves two issues. First, we have to and can identify the wrongdoer. Second, there is a platform, a channel or a way, which can allow us to cause the wrongdoer to be accountable for the wrong he has done to the hurt person. This is not to say that the Bible ex-

55. *Ibid*, 352.

pects us to be always successful in making the wrongdoer accountable for his wrong but it does expect us to at least take positive steps to bring forth justice even if our acts may at the end fail.

For the first issue, if the wrongdoer is an actual person who has inflicted the harm to the hurt person, that will not be a big difficulty at least in theory. For example, a government official has treated a widow in a procedurally unjust manner depriving her of the benefits she should have received. The government official is the wrongdoer. Another example: a member of the local community discriminated against a foreign worker by not allowing her to enter a park that is often visited by local residents. That member of the local community is the wrongdoer. For procedural and civil injustice, it is not too difficult to identify the wrongdoer in individual cases of injustice. However, it may be more difficult for social injustice. Goods are not provided to socially vulnerable groups to satisfy their basic needs who has the responsibility to provide?

If the whole community has the duty, then we, as part of the community, may also be one of the wrongdoers. We then may have to do justice by providing them the goods. But we have already provided them with the goods under our duty to loving kindness. Yes, that is exactly the reason why the 'love your neighbor' command must have a justice dimension as we have argued above. Under certain situations, we may be the wrongdoer ourselves and to do loving kindness is the same way for us to do justice. Or, to do justice is also to do loving kindness. Nevertheless, there may be situations that we provide the goods to the needy not because we are one of the wrongdoers but just out of love.[56]

How about other members of the community if the whole community is responsible? Even if we have done our part, justice still may not have been realised, as there are still wrongdoers at large not yet accountable for the wrongs they have done. How then can we do justice to make the others also accountable for their own part of the wrong? What we have provided may also be insufficient to undo the wrongs committed by the whole community. Some may even say that the state is responsible if the

56. For the relationship between love and justice, see Reinhold Niebuhr, *Love and Justice* (Louisville, Kentucky: Westminster/John Knox Press, 1957); Paul Tillich, *Love, Power and Justice* (New York: Oxford University Press, 1960); Linda Woodhead, 'Love and Justice', in *Studies in Christian Ethics* (1992) 5: 44–61.

specific person cannot be identified to be directly or solely responsible. How can we make the state accountable for the wrong in seeking justice?[57]

Even if we can identify the wrongdoer in an individual case of injustice, we still have to find a proper platform or channel to cause the wrongdoer to be accountable for his wrong, such as having him be punished or making compensation to the one being wronged. We assume that such a platform or channel is available but it might not be used by the one being wronged out of different reasons like ignorance or incapacity. So in fulfilling our role to do justice, we assist the person to seek redress. However, if that platform or channel does not exist at all, what can we do then in order to do justice in that particular case of injustice? There may be little we can do. I will come back to this point later in this part.

This takes us to another situation or cause of injustice. There may be no malice on part of the person responsible for inflicting the harm to the vulnerable person. The so-called 'wrongdoer' is just complying with laws or orders given in accordance with laws legitimately made. It may not be right to call the 'wrongdoer' a wrongdoer, as he may be an innocent civil servant performing a duty conscientiously.

In Isaiah 10:1–2, the prophet also condemns 'iniquitous decrees' and 'oppressive statutes' which 'turn aside the needy from justice' and 'rob the poor of my peoples of their right'. The wrongdoers are the lawmakers but not the one who implements the laws. How can we do justice if there are unjust laws? Punishing the lawmakers or asking them to compensate for the harm inflicted will not be sufficient. Even if we can make them do so, the unjust laws are still there. Injustice will continue to be inflicted on vulnerable groups. Until the laws are changed, there will be no justice. Then, to do justice may have to involve acts to cause unjust laws to be changed.

Replacing unjust lawmakers with just lawmakers may be a way. However, this assumes that there are some kinds of democratic elections. Assuming there is, Christians may put pressure on the lawmakers to reform the laws. They may choose to vote against persons who advocate to make or refuse to undo the unjust laws and support those who promise to enact laws that can bring justice to the vulnerable groups. These lawmakers may or may not be Christian themselves. Not many Christians will do justice for this purpose by becoming lawmakers themselves, though there is nothing preventing Christians from doing so if that is their calling from God.

57. See the following discussion on acts of doing justice in bringing changes to the political institutions so that systemic injustice can be prevented.

In many cases, we may not be able successfully to change the lawmakers because we may not command the majority or our cause may not be supported by sufficient numbers of other voters. In some cases, to win over more people to our cause, we may have to do something extraordinary (even that is prohibited by law though violence should in most cases be avoided) in order to expose the injustice of the existing laws. Doing something illegal may be necessary if justice in that case demands.[58] Nevertheless, that still assumes the existence of democratic elections.

Several notes have to be made here. First, this duty is for each and every Christian but not necessarily for the Church as an associative entity. Second, to take action to cause laws to be changed is only limited to making laws that bring justice, that is, preventing socially vulnerable groups in the society from being oppressed or ensuring basic goods are provided to those in need. This action should not be taken for the purpose of making laws that are more compatible with Christian values, especially on sexual morality matters. At least, this is not within the command of doing justice.[59] This is also in line with the reactive principle advocated by Oliver O'Donovan.[60] Third, the above actions may not be available if there is no democratic election. There is no way, at least no easy way, for us to do justice by pressuring or changing the lawmakers so as to change the unjust laws. Then, how can we change the unjust laws?

Like doing justice in an individual case of injustice, not much can be done if there is no effective platform or channel to bring the wrongdoer to justice. The same is true for changing unjust laws: not much can be done if there is no effective mechanism to put pressure on the lawmakers for changing the unjust laws or for changing the lawmakers. The cause of the injustice may be systemic. To do justice then will have to target the systemic cause of injustice. Institutional reform or even revolutionary changes to the political order may be needed.[61] This may take us to the third level of doing justice in addition to bringing the wrongdoer to justice in a particular case of injustice and changing the unjust laws.

---

58. Charles Villa-Vicencio, 'Theology, Law and State Illegitimacy: An Agenda for Theologians and Lawyers', *Journal of Law and Religion* (1987): 241–257, at 247.
59. Owing to the coercive nature of law, the goal of law in many occasions should be limited to prevent wrong rather than to promote a particular understanding of good.
60. Oliver O'Donovan, *The Ways of Judgment* (Grand Rapids, Michigan, Cambridge, UK: Eerdmans, 2005), 59–66.
61. The burden to prove that a system is so unjust that it has to be overthrown must be high.

We may have to redesign and reconstruct the constitutional order, political institutions and legal systems. A constitutional order designed and operated in accordance with the principle of constitutionalism may serve this purpose of doing justice. In simple terms, constitutionalism aims to limit powers of government through the rule of law, separation of powers and democracy so that human rights are protected.[62] This principle of constitutionalism is arguably originated or incubated[63] by Christianity through its cultural influence in Western societies though it is now secularised[64] and universalised.[65]

If doing justice involves institutional changes to cure the systemic diseases in the society, it is not just about institutional design or structure building. A kind of constitutional order requires an appropriate kind of constitutional culture for maintenance.[66] Effort to change or reform the political institutions will also be inefficient or ineffective if the political culture sustaining the political institutions is missing or only piecemeal.

Therefore, we can also do justice through changing the system by incubating a culture that is needed for constitutionalism.[67] Cultivating a right culture is not the same as evangelism. If Christianity contains those values needed for constitutionalism, then converting the population to Christianity should generate the needed culture. However, that may not be necessary. One may have to distinguish doing justice from proselytisation. It

62. See Louis Henkin, 'Elements of Constitutionalism', in *The Evolving African Constitutionalism: Special Issue, ICJ Review*, edited by Adama Dieng (International Commission of Jurists, 1998).
63. Brian Tierney, *Religion, Law and the Growth of Constitutional Thought 1150–1650* (Cambridge: Cambridge University Press, 1982) and Quentin Skinner, *The Foundations of Modern Political Thought: Volume 2 The Age of Reformation* (Cambridge: Cambridge University Press, 1978), Part Two.
64. Walter F Murphy, 'Constitutions, Constitutionalism, and Democracy', in *Constitutionalism and Democracy: Transitions in the Contemporary World*, edited by Douglas Greenberg, *et al* (New York: Oxford University Press, 1993).
65. Nwabueze, Bo, *Constitutionalism in the Emergent States* (London: C Hurst 1973), chapter 1.
66. Daniel P Franklin and Michael J Baun, 'Introduction: Political Culture and Constitutionalism', and 'Conclusion' in *Political Culture and Constitutionalism: A Comparative Approach*, edited by Daniel P Franklin and Michael J Baun (New York: ME Sharpe, 1995).
67. See Larry Diamond, 'Political culture and Democracy', and 'Causes and Effect', in *Political Culture and Democracy in Developing Countries;* edited by Larry Diamond (Boulder: L Rienner Publishers, 1993).

may also be our duty to make 'disciples of all nations',[68] but that should not be mixed with doing justice.

From the above outline of how to do justice, in particular by connecting the acts needed for the 'doing' with the aims of the acts, that is, the purpose of justice under the Bible, I hope I have not only explained what should be done for Christians to fulfill their duty of doing justice but also the boundary of our acts in realising the public dimension of Christian faith in the public square. In another words, I hope I have also clarified what should not be done in the name of doing justice.

Our duty to do public acts for the sake of justice is owed to the oppressed and deprived but not to advance the Christian position in the society.[69] Acts to reform unjust laws are not done for the purpose to replace them with laws based on Christian values[70] but by laws that are just to the oppressed and deprived. Acts to reform the institutions are also not done for the purpose of establishing structures for Christians to dominate but structures that can bring justice to the oppressed and deprived. The culture to be cultivated is also not necessarily a 'Christian culture' as such but a culture that can incubate and sustain just structures for the sake of the oppressed and deprived, who may not be Christians.

Another note I want to make here is that Christians, in fulfilling this duty, should not act merely like a soldier following a general's command without reflecting on the meaning of the command.[71] We do justice because God himself loves justice[72] and we would very much like to fulfill the

68. Matthew 28:18–20.

69. To be more accurate, our duty to do justice to socially vulnerable groups is not owed to socially vulnerable groups directly but to God as it is God's command upon us to do justice.

70. There are Christians who believe that the presence of Christian faith in the public square demands actions to cause the laws of the land to be consistent with Christian faith and values. In contemporary pluralistic and secular societies, these actions have generated heated debates. The hottest controversies surround laws on homosexuality, same sex marriage, abortion, euthanasia, and stem cell research. It is arguable that actions taken on these issues are not within the scope of doing justice or the public dimension of Christian faith if they are not directly related to justice, that is, a concern with seeking justice for the oppressed and deprived in the society. An alternative biblical basis has to be sought. One source may be Jesus's command to the disciples at the Sermon of the Mount that they are to be the salt of the earth and the light of the world (Matt 5:13–16, Luke 14:34–35, Mark 9:50).

71. Miroslav Volf, *A Public Faith: How Followers of Christ Should Serve the Common Good* (Grand Rapids: Baker Publishing Press, 2011).

72. Christopher JH Wright, *Old Testament Ethics for the People of God* (IVP Academic, 2004), 254–265.

purpose of the One who loves us and whom we also love. We would also like to co-work with God in doing justice as we could have the privilege to participate in God's plan in the world as well as in us.

One final point: doing justice does not always need to be involved with law, whether in its design, making, implementation or adjudication, though law must be an important aspect of the project. There are needs to do justice as much in and through law as in many other social interactions like education, economic activities, medical care, community relationships, etc.

The Role of Law in Public Theology

As I have argued above, it is the duty of every Christian to do justice, which may involve three levels of action: to stand up and seek for justice for the oppressed and deprived in specific cases of injustice; to cause unjust laws to be changed; or to cause the unjust legal, constitutional and political institutions, which may be the systemic causes of the injustice mentioned, to be reformed by redesigning the structures of the institutions and to cultivate a cultural formation and orientation in the society so as to incubate and sustain the structural forms of those institutions.

This is a duty for all Christians but Christian lawyers, owing to their training and position in the society, seem to be the most appropriate persons to take up the particular Christian duty to do justice. To be an advocate for the oppressed and deprived, to be a law reformer, and to be a constitutional architect,[73] are the roles for which lawyers are trained. Even non-Christian lawyers are using their knowledge, skills and experience to do justice, Christian lawyers not doing justice will be evading their duties even more than others. They may be criticised as faith idling.[74] I am not saying that every Christian lawyer should be doing acts at all three levels or must be actively involved in doing justice on every occasion. But what a Christian, including a Christian lawyer, should do must still be determined by the calling received directly from God.[75] It is just that the

73. Yash Ghai, 'A Journey Around Constitutions—Reflecting on Contemporary Constitutions', *South African Law Journal,* 122 (2005): 804–831.

74. Volf, above n 71.

75. A Christian lawyer may have a calling not in doing justice but in other aspects of Christian faith. The same is for every Christian one may not have a calling to do justice. A calling means that this is a burden God has put in the heart of a Christian for how one's work should be mainly focused on at a particular stage of one's life. Identifying 'doing justice' as a core component of Christian faith means that every

chance will be higher for God to call a person to do things He has already equipped with the appropriate gifts.[76]

Two Old Testament passages illustrate. Esther, an Israelite girl, was prepared to be chosen as the Queen of the Persian King Xerxes to fulfill God's saving plan for the Jewish nation from being destroyed.[77] Esther was brought to a position for a certain purpose set by God. Christian lawyers are trained to be lawyers and are brought to their present positions by God. Be it a practicing lawyer, a judge, a legislator, a prosecutor, a public administrator, or a legal academic (like myself), Christian lawyers acquire their legal knowledge, skills and the experiences in using them from a special plan from God for each of us.

Nehemiah was sent by the Persian King Artaxerxes to rebuild the Wall of Jerusalem and to fulfill the plan of God. The responsibilities for rebuilding different sections of the Wall were assigned to different families. Jedaiah, son of Harumaph was responsible for making repairs to the section of the Wall opposite his house.[78] Hashabiah, ruler of half the district of Keilah carried out the repairs for his district.[79] Benjamin and Hasshub made repairs in front of their houses.[80] For the section above the Horse Gate, the priests made repairs, each in front of his own house.[81] If dispensing justice is the main function of law,[82] it is at least arguable that doing justice is similar to being responsible for repairing the part of the Wall in front of a Christian lawyer's house or in the district that a Christian lawyer is ruling.

Christian has a duty to find ways to practice this aspect of their faith in their life just like the other components of their faith. However, that does not mean that they must take 'doing justice' as their Christian calling.

76. Fulfilling this duty does not mean that Christians must be involved in 'radical' or 'great' acts. There are many opportunities for us to fulfill this duty in our daily life: that may include being a witness for victims in cases of injustice, writing an opinion to the government on possible reform in certain unjust laws, voting in an election supporting candidates who promise to bring justice to laws and policies, or participating in a public and peaceful procession putting pressure on the ruling regime to introduce institutional reforms to make the constitutional or political system a more just system.
77. Cf of Esther.
78. Nehemiah 3:10.
79. Nehemiah 3:17.
80. Nehemiah 3:23.
81. Nehemiah 3:28.
82. David A Funk, 'Major Functions of Law in Modern Society', 23 *Case W Res L Rev* (1972): 257-306. See also: Dennis Lloyd, *The Idea of Law* (London: Penguin Books, 1984), chapter 6: Law and Justice.

Not only are Christian lawyers fit for the role of doing justice for God because of their legal training and experiences, but also doing justice needs Christian lawyers. In many cases, a command in the language of law is required. The language of law is the 'second language' spoken by lawyers.[83] Here, we are talking about the reasons, arguments and expressions that are considered to be legitimate according to the disciplinary requirements of law.

Speaking on behalf of the oppressed and deprived before courts of law, administrative tribunals or public hearings require the command of legal language. Making suggestions to reform law needs to be expressed in the form of legal arguments. Even supporting civil disobedience to alert the general public about the injustice inflicted on the oppressed and deprived by certain laws, the injustice of the laws must be articulated in a legally relevant manner. Institutional change does require knowledge or skills more than law, but the knowledge of law at least is needed in writing a new constitution for the newly designed structures to satisfy the requirements of justice. Legal culture[84] constitutes an important part of the culture needed for incubating and sustaining just structures. This again needs someone who is fluent in legal language to plant the seeds of the needed cultural values and orientations in the society.

In order to fulfill their duty to do justice, if that is their specific calling from God, how then should Christian lawyers prepare themselves to perform this duty? I assert this article that Christian lawyers can play the role of a public theologian. Doing the above act seeking justice, should be within Andries van Aarde's understanding of being a public theologian.[85] To recall the three aspects of public theology: it must be theologically informed, it must be about public issues and it must use public reason.[86]

83. Jonathan Sacks, *The Persistence of Faith: Religion, Morality and Society in a Secular Age* (London, New York: Continuum, 1991, 2005).

84. Lawrence Friedman, 'The Concept of Legal Culture: A Reply', in *Comparing Legal Cultures*, edited by David Nelken (Aldershot: Dartmouth, 1996).

85. Andries van Aarde, 'What is "theology" in "public theology" and what is "public" about "public theology"?', *HTS Teologiese Studies/Theological Studies*, 64/3 (2008).

86. Here I am not saying that Christians cannot use religious language and religious reasons in the public sphere; I am saying that if Christians want people in the public square who are not Christians to accept their viewpoints, the use of public reason may be a strategic move. For further thoughts, see Kent Greenawalt, 'Religious Convictions and Political Choice: Some Further Thoughts', *De Paul L Rev* 39 (1990): 1019; Robert Audi and Nicholas Wolterstorff, *Religion in the Public Square: The Place of Religious Convictions in Political Debate* (London: Rowman & Littlefield Publishers,

The discourse of law is surely public reason expressed in public language. Christian lawyers should have no problem with this. No question that laws involve public issues but doing justice concerns only certain kinds of public issues, ie those related to people being oppressed and deprived. Christian lawyers need to learn to discern and identify those public issues for which they are responsible for under their biblical duty. This will demand an understanding of the theological basis of justice for Christian lawyers, who also need to know how this understanding of biblical injustice informs the standards, reasoning, arguments and expressions to be raised in their work of doing justice. This includes acting for the oppressed and deprived, reforming unjust laws, raising public concern of the injustice embedded in existing laws, restructuring the legal, constitutional and political systems and planting the appropriate values and orientations in the culture of the society.

The theological understanding of justice may not be something that can be applied directly in contemporary pluralistic societies, but may be a source of inspiration for Christian lawyers to creatively develop their thinking on how to realise social justice.[87]

I would like to thank Professor Phee-Seng Kang and Dr Wai-Hang Ng of the Department of Religion and Philosophy, The Hong Kong Baptist University, Dr Kin-Yip Louie of The China Graduate School of Theology and Professor Nicholas Aroney of the TC Beirne School of Law, The University of Queensland for their critical comments on this article.

1997); and Robert Audi, *Religious Commitment and Secular Reason* (Cambridge: Cambridge University Press, 2000).

87. Villa-Vicencio, above n 58.

Interface Vol 15 1&2/2012

What Lies Beneath: A Brief Introduction to the Issues Underlying the Development of the Law in the Context of Medical Treatment

Bernadette Richards

Senior Lecturer
Law School
University of Adelaide
South Australia

> Lawyers and ethicists need to be anthropologists, and anthropologists need to be neuroscientists, archaeologists, sociologists, Shakespeare scholars and classicists. It would also help if they had a nodding acquaintance with the Torah, Talmud, New Testament, Koran, Upanishads, the myths of Old Iceland, and the Walmart catalogue. From these texts, as well as from their own experience of testy judges, departmental bickering, broken marriages, sick children, red wine, mountains, and celebration, they would get some idea about what humans are; what makes humans tick and what makes them tick well: what makes them thrive.[1]

We live in an increasingly complex world where ideals of 'right' and 'wrong' are no longer as simply defined as perhaps they once were. As suggested by Foster, to understand the law, and the nature of humanity, one would have to be a master of many disciplines and doctrines. The law is interested not only in the nature of individuals but also in the manner in which individuals interact, and must look beyond the question of what makes each individual thrive. Indeed, the law must strive to ensure that

1. C Foster, *Human Dignity in Bioethics and the Law* (Oxford: Hart Publishing, 2011), 4.

society as a whole can thrive and in aiming for this ideal, individual rights and interests may, at times, be compromised.

The law represents an intricate web of rights, interests, beliefs, wishes, ideals and needs: and not all of these can be met. This is particularly so in the context of medical treatment where we see the individual rights and needs of the patient sitting alongside those of the health-carers within the confines of their professional roles. These potentially conflicting rights and interests are found within the broader framework of public policy, needs and accepted social norms. This brief discussion will reflect on the ongoing struggle to reconcile these diverse interests and consider whether or not an appropriate balance has been struck. The question to be addressed is: can these disparate interests co-exist or must it be that in each situation a different right (or interest) must prevail? The questions raised here touch on wide-ranging issues including (but not limited to), the nature of humanity, the role of private interests in the public arena, the principles of autonomy and sanctity of life and how they sit alongside the ideals of beneficence and non-maleficence and the question of what constitutes not only life, but a life worth living.[2] It is the raising of these questions that makes my discussion relevant to this collection. Theological discourse can add to the diversity of considerations and enrich, enliven and inform the debate. A comprehensive consideration of these issues cannot realistically be attempted here, instead I will simply sketch the landscape of the complexities that can underlie lawmaking in the context of medical treatment. I will aim to do that through two somewhat different discussions. The first will introduce the issues underlying the regulation of assisted reproductive technology and the second will briefly explore the process of judicial decision-making when the court is asked to assist in life or death decisions.[3] This modest analysis will not attempt to cover the field, nor will it propose any solutions, rather it will merely serve to dip a thoughtful toe

2. The four principles of autonomy, beneficence, non-maleficence and justice are explored in depth by T Beauchamp and J Childress in *Principles of Bioemedical Ethics*, fifth edition (Oxford: Oxford University Press, 2001) and are introduced as four clusters or principles that provide an analytical framework underlying common morality (12). The phrase 'a life worth living' is most commonly identified with the ethicist Peter Singer and his work *Practical Ethics*, second edition (Cambridge University Press, 1993).
3. This will cover three different legal conundrums: ceasing life sustaining treatment, determining whether or not parents who killed their son out of love and mercy deserve to go to jail and deciding whether or not conjoined twins ought to be separated when the result will be the certain death of one.

into the murky waters of the law surrounding medical treatment, swirl them around a little and raise the question of what truly lies beneath.

Assisted Reproductive Treatment: Whose interests?

The law in the context of medical treatment represents a delicate balancing act between different interests and it follows from the complex nature of the interplay of these interests that a neat balance is rarely struck. Often the rights of one party will outweigh the interests of another. It is important at the start of this discussion to highlight the correlative nature of the relationship between rights and duties. A right to cannot exist (or be measured) without reference to a related duty. Hohfeld reduced the law to 'eight jural conceptions',[4] and explained the specific relationship between a right and a duty: 'A duty or a legal obligation is that which one ought or not to do. "Duty" and "right" are correlative terms when a right is invaded, a duty is violated.'[5] In the context of assisted reproductive treatment the different parties include those who provide the treatment, the child to be born as a result of the treatment, the future parents of that child and any person donating reproductive material. To complicate matters further, the rights of the parents can become intertwined with those of the future child and can exist simultaneously as a right to be protected by the duty of the clinic to provide appropriate treatment and a duty to the future child to seek appropriate treatment. If we throw into this mix the vexed question of when does human reproductive material become worthy of legal protection or attain the rights of a human being (that is, the philosophically and legally impossible question of when does life truly begin) we find a quagmire of rights and interests which require a clear statement of priority. And it is here, in this complicated array of rights, duties and interests that we see a firm statement of principle: at all times the rights and interests of the future child are paramount. The problem is determining how these are to be identified and measured.

Turning first to the current regulatory regime in Australia there is a clear starting point: the future child. Given the brevity of this discussion I will only provide an overview of the existing legislation and guidelines but it is necessary to begin with a recognition that we have incomplete

4. WN Hohfeld, *Fundamental Legal Conceptions* (New Haven: Yale university Press, 1964), 38.
5. *Ibid*, citing *Lake Shore & MSR Co v Kurtz* (1984) 10 Ind App, 60.

legislative coverage[6] which is supplemented by the National Health and Medical Research Council (NHMRC) Guidelines.[7] Significantly, according to these guidelines, clinical decisions must be made with a primary focus on the 'interests and welfare of the persons who may be born'.[8] The interesting point here is that unlike other areas of the law, there is a focus on what something *may* become, not on what it is now. The rights of an individual yet to be conceived can outweigh the interests of those who are actually receiving the treatment and making reproductive choices. This position is echoed in the legislation in South Australia and Victoria whilst the legislation in New South Wales and Western Australia seeks to recognise the rights of all parties.[9] It is clearly rights based legislation that aims to set specific limits on what can and cannot be done in the name of reproductive technology and a brief examination of those limits provide some insight into what lies beneath the regulation of assisted reproductive treatment.[10]

The NHMRC Guidelines specifically prohibit two activities: sex selection for nonmedical purposes and commercial surrogacy. They draw a clear line around a third: preimplantation genetic diagnosis. Each of these represent the potential to interfere with what it is that makes us human, to commodify reproductive material and perhaps to undermine the diversi-

---

6. There are four jurisdictions with specific legislation: *Assisted Reproductive Technology Act 2007* (NSW), *Assisted Reproductive Treatment Act 1988* (SA), *Assisted Reproductive Treatment Act 2008* (Vic) and *Human Reproductive Technology Act 1991* (WA).
7. NHMRC *Ethical Guidelines on the Use of Assisted Reproductive Technology in Clinical Practice and Research* (2007), http://www.nhmrc.gov.au/guidelines/publications/e78, 19 March 2012. In addition to this, the Reproductive Technology Accreditation Committee (RTAC) oversees a code of practice and the accreditation of ART clinics in Australia. RTAC requires compliance with the NHMRC Guidelines for accreditation, therefore all licensed clinics must comply not only with the legislation (where relevant) but also with the Guidelines.
8. *Ibid*, 5.1.
9. NSW and WA both specifically refer to all involved parties, *Assisted Reproductive Technology Act 2007* (NSW) s(3) explains the objects of the Act as including protection of the interests of the future child, those providing gametes and a woman undergoing the treatment and *Human Reproductive Technology Act 1991* (WA) s23(e) provides that in determining whether or not reproductive treatment will be given the welfare and interest of the participants and any child likely to be born as a result of the procedure must be considered. The other two jurisdictions with legislation focus primarily on the child: *Assisted Reproductive Treatment Act 1988* (SA) s4A, *Assisted Reproductive Treatment Act 2008* (Vic) s5(a)
10. This discussion is specifically focussing on reproductive treatment as opposed to research using embryos which raises a broader set of issues outside of the scope of this paper.

ty that makes our society thrive. The Guidelines recognise sex selection as being an 'ethically controversial issue' and defer to the Australian Health Ethics Committee (AHEC) position that 'admission to life should not be conditional upon a child being a particular sex'.[11] Equally prohibitive language is used with respect to commercial surrogacy. The Guidelines unequivocally state that 'it is ethically unacceptable to undertake or facilitate surrogate pregnancy for commercial purposes. Clinics must not undertake or facilitate surrogacy arrangements'.[12] Noncommercial surrogacy on the other hand is described as 'a controversial subject' and whilst it is not prohibited, caution is counselled.[13] A similar approach is advocated for the complex question of pre-implantation genetic diagnosis (PGD).

In 1992 Chloe O'Brien was born after her parents, both carriers of the cystic fibrosis gene, accessed the new technology of PGD which enabled fertility specialists to screen embryos for the disease.[14] It is thus a relatively new technology and one that has provoked a strong instinctive reaction. The NHMRC Guidelines acknowledge that PGD is a valuable tool in the provision of assisted reproductive treatment but caution that it must be carefully evaluated. The role of PGD in the detection (and prevention) of serious genetic conditions, the improvement of treatment outcomes and, in 'rare circumstances to select an embryo with compatible tissue for a sibling' are all acknowledged in the Guidelines,[15] yet caution is advocated and clear lines are drawn. In referring to the 'profound ethical significance'[16] of PGD the Guidelines specifically prohibit the use of PGD to:

- prevent conditions that do not seriously harm the person to be born,
- facilitate sex selection except to reduce the risk of the transmission of a serious genetic condition, or
- select in favour of a genetic defect or disability.[17]

11. NHMRC *Ethical Guidelines on the Use of Assisted Reproductive Technology in Clinical Practice and Research* (2007), http://www.nhmrc.gov.au/guidelines/publications/e78, 19 March 2012, 11.1. This does not include sex selection based on medical need.
12. *Ibid*, 13.1.
13. *Ibid*, 13.2.
14. C Gavaghan, *Defending the Genetic Supermarket: Law and Ethics of Selecting the Next Generation* (London: Routledge-Cavendish, 2007), 6.
15. NHMRC *Ethical Guidelines on the Use of Assisted Reproductive Technology in Clinical Practice and Research* (2007), http://www.nhmrc.gov.au/guidelines/publications/e78, 19 March 2012, 12.1
16. *Ibid*.
17. *Ibid*, 12.2.

In summary whilst assisted reproductive treatment is a valued medical service, there are clear and emphatic lines across which we cannot step. The interests of the unborn child are paramount and reproductive autonomy and choice are abrogated in favour of other, broader interests. It is interesting to note here that an early scholar commenting on the issues, lamented what he viewed as the inappropriate focus on the parents as opposed to the child and referred to the 'cacophony of sound and fury regarding women and reproductive technology' which overlooked the interests of the children. [18] However, he had earlier argued that 'a society without rights would be morally impoverished.'[19] How then are the rights of the parents to be balanced against those of the potential child? And why do the rights of the potential child outweigh those of the existing adults? This is an issue raised and argued by Gavaghan when he defends the 'genetic supermarket'.[20] Gavaghan argues for more rather than less individual choice and less rather than more regulation.[21] It is his position that the 'notion that state regulation is invariably "safer" than individual choice is not a self-evident, universal truth'[22] and that some of the worst human atrocities in the name of eugenics have historically been committed under the auspices of state intervention in individual reproductive choice.[23] Persuasively he asks why we, as a society, view it as acceptable to step in and prohibit behaviour simply because we find it personally unacceptable. He challenges us to 'bold[ly] recognise that, in a complex, diverse society such as ours, some people will want to do things that most of us find odd, unsettling, or which we cannot imagine ever wanting to do ourselves but that, absent very good reasons to the contrary, we should not prevent them from doing'.[24]

Why then do we accept state intervention in reproductive treatment? Why do we as a society draw such clear boundaries around what is acceptable? Perhaps Gavaghan himself provides the answer to this when he argues that 'unless some likely harm to other parties can be shown, the most likely course of action to maximise good outcomes lies in respect-

---

18. M Freeman, 'The New Birth Right? Identity and the child of the reproduction revolution', in *The International Journal of Children's Rights,* 4 (1996): 273, 273.
19. M Freeman, 'Taking Children's Rights Seriously', in *Children and Society,* 4 (1987–88): 299, 306.
20. Gavaghan, above n 13.
21. *Ibid*, 2.
22. *Ibid*, 3.
23. *Ibid.*
24. *Ibid*, 12.

ing liberty'.[25] Is it the notion of harm and our broad acceptance of what constitutes a potential harm that lies beneath regulation in this sphere? The image of a *Gattaca* like society looms large in our consciousness,[26] perhaps it is not harm to an individual but harm to a functioning society that drives this regulation. In regulating intervention in the reproductive process we are protecting a complex and diverse society that thrives on that diversity. To intervene in what makes us human is perhaps a step too far and has been found to outweigh the individual rights of reproductive autonomy and choice.

What happens, however, when individual situations are so out of the ordinary that they potentially undermine broader societal interests but warrant an exception? Is there any role for overriding the collective interest in protecting such ideals as the sanctity of life and making an individual exception? And if there is, what principle lies beneath such exceptions?

Overriding the Sanctity of Life?

A foundational principle of the law is the sanctity of life. This is clearly represented in the criminal offence of murder and, in Australia and many other countries, the illegality of assisted suicide and euthanasia. The sanctity of life is embraced by most religious groups, accepted by most societies and reflected in our law. But what happens when the sanctity of life conflicts with the equally foundational principle of autonomy? What if an individual wishes to cease life-saving treatment? Or if medical intervention is needed to save one person but will almost certainly result in the death of another? And if two loving parents who have cared for and nurtured a profoundly ill child for twenty-nine years see no option but to end his life of suffering and kill him, are they guilty of murder? Based upon the sanctity of life principle all of these actions would be untenable but, thanks to some judicial discretion they have, to some degree, been sanctioned. An exploration of the judicial processes in these three situations will further reveal the complexities of the interest that lie beneath the law in the context of medical treatment.

25. *Ibid*, 17.

26. *Gattaca* a 1997 science fiction movie explores a world in which all children are selected using PGD and what happens when a 'genetically inferior' individual wants to excel.

Drawing distinctions

The potential for a clash of interests underpinning the law and medical treatment was demonstrated in the difficult decision of *Ms B v An NHS Hospital Trust* [2002] 2 All ER 449. Ultimately the presiding judge, Dame Elizabeth Butler-Sloss, solved the conflict of interests by drawing fine but significant distinctions. The background facts are that Ms B suffered a haemorrhage of the spinal column in her neck in 1999. At this time she was diagnosed with an underlying condition that could cause further complications. In response to this she made a 'living will' or advanced care plan stipulating that she wished treatment to be withdrawn if she was suffering from a life threatening condition. In 2001 further complications did arise and Ms B was rendered a tetraplegic, meaning that she suffered from total paralysis from the neck down. At this time she informed the doctors of her 'living will' and that she did not wish to be ventilated. She was informed that this was not sufficient to authorise withdrawal of the ventilation and her current capacity to make a decision was challenged. Ms B turned to the courts to meet her needs and argued that not only did she have capacity to make the decision but that the continued ventilation constituted an unlawful trespass.[27]

Clearly this case represents a clash of the personal interest of autonomy and the sanctity of life. In determining how to balance these two key principles Dame Elizabeth emphasised that the question before her was not about whether or not Ms B was going to live or die but whether she was legally competent to make a treatment decision.[28] In exploring the issues before her she acknowledged that the general law on mental capacity is clear and easily understood by lawyers but its application in the context of a 'hospital ward and especially an intensive care unit is infinitely more difficult to achieve'.[29] Of significance to our discussion here was the manner in which Dame Elizabeth addressed the potential conflict of interests. She began by acknowledging the importance of the fundamental principle of sanctity of life to both society and the medical profession and noting the fact that 'the interface between the two principles of autonomy and sanctity of life is of great concern to the treating clinicians in the present case'.[30] Her Honour went on to recognise the conflict of autonomy and

27. This statement of facts is drawn from the judgment.
28. *Ms B v An NHS Hospital Trust* [2002] 2 All ER 449, [12].
29. *Ibid*, [14].
30. *Ibid*, [22].

beneficence in this particular situation but concluded that 'the right of the competent patient to request cessation of treatment must prevail over the natural desire of the medical and nursing profession to try to keep her alive'.[31]

It is important to note that despite acknowledging the conflict between the underlying principles, Dame Elizabeth specifically retreated from this conflict in arriving at her decision to respect Ms B's treatment choices. It was of importance to Her Honour that she was not being asked to make a determination about the quality of the decision, rather she was considering the validity of it. This conclusion was similar in its rationale to Gavaghan's exhortation (discussed above) to respect the decision rather than challenge its appropriateness. Disagreement with, even abhorrence of, a decision does not validate prohibition.[32] In her conclusions Dame Elizabeth made some further important points. She warned against the temptation of 'beneficent paternalism'[33] and emphasised that the treatment decision was Ms B's to make. Of note, however, were her final points which were to respect the efforts of all associated with the treatment of Ms B and to direct Ms B that she was not bound by her earlier decision but merely free to make it.[34] In short, Dame Elizabeth, in an unusual judicial move, recognised a plaintiff's right to make a decision but asked her to exercise her discretion not to.

Binding principles

A second situation that highlights the issues raised here is the sad case of the Sutton family. On the evening of the 22 April 2001 Mr and Mrs Sutton sedated their much loved twenty-nine-year-old son with the intention of killing him. Later that night, Mr Sutton did, indeed kill his son and the Suttons subsequently faced charges of murder.[35] But should they have been held culpable for their actions and should other principles besides the sanctity of life prevail? In addressing these questions it is relevant to sketch a brief background picture of the Sutton's life prior to taking this drastic step. Matthew Sutton was born profoundly disabled–he had no eyes, a large, oddly-shaped nose and a cleft lip and palate. He was subsequently diagnosed with Trisomy 13 Syndrome which is incurable and

31. *Ibid*, [27].
32. Gavaghan, above n 14, 12.
33. *Ms B v An NHS Hospital Trust* [2002] 2 All ER 449, [94].
34. *Ibid*, [95] and [97]-[99].
35. *R v Sutton* [2007] NSWSC 295, 4 April 2007.

has other, significant symptoms. As he grew older Matthew underwent attempts to repair his palate and nose and it became evident that he was profoundly developmentally disabled (he developed to the mental age of a child of three or four). In addition to this he was completely deaf in the right ear and had only thirty or forty per cent hearing in the left. He had limited speech.[36]

Life with Matthew was difficult. In delivering his judgment Barr J carefully emphasised the burdensome nature of caring for Matthew and the fact that his parents faced up to and accepted their responsibility for Matthew. His honour noted that 'the burden upon them was enormous and they began to suffer the effects of the unrelenting demands placed on them.'[37] By 2001 Matthew's condition had remained constant for a number of years but a decline became evident. At this point the Suttons were informed that he would need invasive surgery which would impact on his limited hearing. In addition he would probably lose the limited speech that he had. He might also suffer paralysis of one side of the face and his sense of taste. Without the treatment Matthew was likely to die.[38] His parents were devastated and well aware that this proposed treatment would be something beyond Matthew's comprehension causing him deep distress and removing from him the few faculties that he had and enjoyed.[39] They could not countenance inflicting such misery on their son and it was this that led them to take matters into their own hands and end Matthew's life on the 22nd of April.

Did the Suttons violate the sanctity of life principle? The answer is a clear yes. Were they guilty of the crime of murder? Again the answer is a clear yes. Ought they go to jail and suffer for this? Here, the answer was not quite so clear but the response from the judge was a carefully reasoned no. Whilst the sanctity of life is a foundational principle, clearly there are other matters to be taken into account when assigning culpability. In reaching his decision to impose a suspended sentence on the Suttons, Barr J paid close attention to the facts of the case. He carefully considered the life of emotional and physical demand faced by the Suttons, noted their dedication to their son and his welfare and concluded that whilst criminal responsibility was clear, a custodial sentence would serve no purpose. His Honour returned to the basic principles of sentencing which were, as

36. These facts are drawn from the decision of Barr J, [2] ff.
37. *R v Sutton* [2007] NSWSC 295, 4 April 2007, [8] (Barr J).
38. *Ibid*, [11] (Barr J).
39. Matthew enjoyed his food and listening to music.

outlined by the Sutton's representative, to punish offenders, prevent crime by deterring them and others from committing similar offences, protect the community from them, promote their rehabilitation and make them accountable for what they have done. Furthermore, sentencing serves to denounce the criminal conduct and recognise the harm that they have done to the victim and the community.[40] In these limited and very particular circumstances His Honour concluded that none of these purposes were relevant to the Suttons. He asserted that he could not possibly punish them any further[41] and that community interests were better served here by caring for the health and continued treatment of the Suttons.[42] Of importance to His Honour was the fact that the Suttons had devoted their lives to Matthew and his welfare and even their 'last act was one born of love for him'.[43] Their act was clearly wrong and not one to be encouraged or condoned but neither was it one worthy of further punishment. In His Honour's view the narrow interests of the Suttons mirrored the broader societal interest of supporting and rehabilitating them through healthcare and counselling as opposed to a 'cruel' custodial sentence.[44]

Thus the balancing act continues and the swirl of interests underneath the decisions becomes ever more complicated. Clearly the sanctity of life principle stands but it must, at times, be tempered by the recognition that other factors can impact on an individual's chosen course of action. This perhaps begins to turn towards the issue of what constitutes a life worth living and how society is to thrive if we are seen to value one life over another.

Can the needs of one prevail over the needs of another?

The tragic case of a hospital seeking permission to separate conjoined twins is the third and final situation to be discussed here. It is relevant to this discussion because it draws into sharp relief the almost impossible nature of situations which represent not only conflicting rights and duties but also pits the interests of one individual against those of another. The facts of the case are straightforward enough. The parents were of modest means and strong religious conviction. They learned during the preg-

40. *R v Sutton* [2007] NSWSC 295, 4 April 2007, [32] (Barr J).
41. *Ibid*, [38] (Barr J).
42. *Ibid*, [39] (Barr J).
43. *Ibid*, [42] (Barr J).
44. *Ibid*.

nancy that the twins were conjoined and travelled from their homeland to the United Kingdom to seek the best possible treatment for the twins. It became apparent in the latter stages of the pregnancy that not only were the children conjoined but that there were significant health issues. Termination of pregnancy was illegal in their country of origin and it was not something that they would personally countenance due to their strong religious conviction that everyone has a right to life.[45] Lord Justice Ward neatly summarised the conundrum facing the hospital and now, the court. The twins, Jodie and Mary, each had their own brain, heart, lungs and other vital organs. The also had their own limbs. They were joined at the lower abdomen and whilst they could be surgically separated, this would kill Mary whose lungs and heart were deemed to be incapable of supporting life. Mary was only alive because Jodie was sustaining her, which itself placed an untenable load on Jodie's heart. Eventually it would fail and both twins would die within three to six months. The parents were unable to place a value on the life of one twin over another and refused permission to separate them. In their eyes it was God's will that the children live their brief lives this way. But the hospital argued that it could intervene and provide Jodie with a life that was worthwhile and sought a declaration that the operation could be carried out.[46]

As we saw in the decision of Ms B outlined above, the Court found it necessary to draw lines and distinctions around their judgment. This approach was clearly represented in the thoughtful judgment of Lord Justice Walker where he emphasised the respect that must be accorded to the feelings and wishes of the parents but focussed his concluding remarks on the rights and interests of the children. He pointed to the right of Mary to life and stipulated that to intentionally undertake an operation with the primary aim of killing her would be unlawful. This reality had to sit alongside Jodie's right to life and to bodily integrity. In his Honour's view a fine but significant line had to be drawn here between the primary purpose of the operation (the saving of Jodie) and its 'rare and tragic' consequence of Mary's death. Significantly, the death of Mary was not the purpose or intention of the surgery, she would die because her own body could not sustain her.[47]

---

45. These facts are drawn from the parents' statement, reproduced in the judgment of Lord Justice Ward. *A (Children)* [2000] EWCA Civ 254, [2].
46. *Ibid*, Introduction to the decision.
47. *Ibid*, conclusion to the judgment of Walker LJ.

Of interest in this judgment is the insistent referral to 'evil'. The Law Lords repeatedly refer to the need to avoid the evil of both twins dying, to choose between the lesser of two evils and the necessity to protect from an 'inevitable and irreparable evil'.[48] If we set these references alongside Lord Justice Ward's claim in the introduction to the judgment that 'this court is a court of law, not of morals, and our task has been to find, and our duty is then to apply, the relevant principles of law to the situation before us - a situation which is quite unique'[49] we see a deeply conflicted court. The eddies and swirls of individual rights and interests threatened to swamp this particular court with reference to 'evils' but in the end, lines were drawn, and principles were identified and applied: and in the eyes of the court the lesser of two evils was chosen and the separation sanctioned.

So What does Lie Beneath?

It is clear therefore that the application of principles, rights, ideals and duties in the context of medical treatment is unclear. Under the surface of the law lies a complex mix of rights and duties sitting alongside individual views of what is right in the circumstances. At times the legislature and government bodies have been prepared to draw clear and significant markers and assert that we will go no further. This is evidenced in the regulation of assisted reproductive treatment and PGD. In other areas, despite apparently insurmountable obstacles (such as the clear legal prohibition of intentional killing) decisions can be made that will ultimately result in the death of someone, so long as it is the quality and process of the decision that is scrutinised and not the ultimate result. And finally, even when a clear wrong is identified (the murder of a son for example) there may be circumstances where understanding and support is sanctioned rather than pointless punishment.

Perhaps the reality is that whilst Lord Justice Ward would have us believe that the courts and the law deal with the law and not murky morals, what lies beneath is human understanding, instinct and beliefs. And perhaps it is the fact that this understanding and instinct is occasionally permitted to intrude on judicial decision-making is what makes us thrive as individuals and thus as a society. And surely, the issue of what makes us thrive, individually and collectively, is central to theological discourse and

48. This final reference was to Sir James Stephens discussion of necessity in *Digest of the Criminal Law* (1887).
49. *A (Children)* [2000] EWCA Civ 254, Introduction (Ward LJ).

the modern theologian can add to the eddies and swirls that lie beneath the development and application of the law.

Interface Vol 15 1&2/2012

The Australian Legal Academy and the Concept of Private Property

Paul Babie

Adelaide Law School
Research Unit for the Study of Society, Law and Religion
The University of Adelaide
South Australia

Introduction

In every aspect of modern life, from the moral to the political, religion seems to matter to more and more people in Australia.[1] And, in one way or another, it seems to structure the way that people interact socially. Overlooked in the influence of religion in Australian social life, though, is the relationship between *theology* and law. While there is a paucity of Australian legal literature on that relationship, engaging the two disciplines might give a fuller understanding of Australian life.

The absence of Australian scholarship does not mean that the relationship between theology and law has been entirely forgotten. The American scholarship, for instance, demonstrates a number of possible dimensions to this relationship.[2] Among other things, this work emphasises the fact

1. See Paul Babie, 'Religion and Australian Socio-Legal Interaction: A Preliminary Account of the Need for Empirical Research', *UNSW Law Journal*, 34 (2011): 255–280; *UNSW Law Journal FORUM* 17 (2001): 4–18. See also William Twining, *General Jurisprudence: Understanding Law from a Global Perspective* (Cambridge, UK: Cambridge University Press, 2009), 6–7 and 125; John Micklethwait and Adrian Wooldridge, *God is Back: How the Global Rise of Faith is Changing the World* (New York, NY: Penguin, 2009).
2. The seminal work in this area, and that which masterfully summarises the historical evidence, is that of Harold J Berman, *The Interaction of Law and Religion* (Nashville,

that the earliest courts in England were not common law but ecclesiastical. Thus, the

> . . . basic institutions, concepts, and values of Western legal systems have their sources in religious rituals, liturgies, and doctrines of the eleventh and twelfth centuries, reflecting new attitudes toward death, sin, punishment, foregiveness, and salvation, as well as new assumptions concerning the relationship of the divine to the human and of faith to reason. Over the intervening centuries, these religious attitudes and assumptions have changed fundamentally, and today their theological sources seem to be in the process of drying up. Yet the legal institutions, conceptions, and values that have derived from them still survive, often unchanged. Western legal science is secular theology, which often makes no sense because its theological presuppositions are no longer accepted.[3]

This is especially true of the Australian legal academy, which seems to have forgotten—and perhaps overlooks in favour of a more secular account—the historical relationship between theology and law.[4] And therein lies the problem which this essay addresses: the failure of theology and law to speak to and learn from one another, as they did historically.[5] This essay takes the position that the interdisciplinary study of theology and law really aims at the same goal—morality and justice—and how, in that common pursuit, they might offer insights to one another and better explain

---

Tenn: Abingdon Press, 1974); Harold J Berman, *Law and Revolution: The Formation of the Western Legal Tradition* (Cambridge, Mass: Harvard University Press, 1983); Harold J Berman, *Faith and Order: The Reconciliation of Law and Religion* (Grand Rapids, Mich: Eerdmans, 1993). See also *Religion, Morality, and the Law*, edited by J Rowland Pennock and John W Chapman (New York, NY: New York University Press, 1988).

3. Berman, *Law and Revolution*, above n 2, 165.
4. See for example Alex C Castles, *An Australian Legal History* (Sydney, NSW: Law Book Company, 1982), the authoritative legal history of Australia, which makes no explicit reference to the role played by Christianity in the development of the common law.
5. A problem identified by Berman, *The Interaction of Law and Religion*, above n 2, 49–76, and Berman, *Law and Revolution*, above n 2, generally.

modern social life.[6] Simply, the argument advanced here is that Australian legal science stand in need of a re-discovering the theological background to Anglo-Australian law necessary to a full understanding of the world in which we live. This paper, then, is an exercise in public theology in the sense that if theology is to engage with society, it must engage with the political and legal structures of a society. That can only happen when theology can demonstrate what it might offer.

To achieve that objective, this essay considers three matters. First, in Part II, it briefly outlines the importance of religion, or theology, in contemporary Australian life. Yet, in Part III, we see that the Australian legal scholarship tends to downplay, or not pay enough attention to the place of religion/theology in public life. This has the potential to end the engagement before it has even begun. Still, while seeking to maintain the strict liberal separation of religion when it comes to the development of law, it does not reject the study of the way that religion might nonetheless remain significant in the way that Australians interact with one another through law. If that is true, then, the legal academy is best placed and therefore ought to explore the place of religion in modern Australian life. Having argued that such an engagement is not only useful but necessary as part of the public theology project, Part IV of the essay offers a brief reflection on what such an engagement might offer: a Christian perspective on private property.

Religion in Australian Life

This Part demonstrates, using Gary Bouma's *Australian Soul*,[7] that religion is important to Australians.[8] This Bouma divides into the 'qualities' and the 'quantities' of Australian religion and spirituality.

Qualities[9]

For Bouma, Manning Clark's 'a shy hope in the heart'[10] best summarises the quality of Australian religion/spirituality, which can be broken into

6. See Berman, *Law and Revolution*, above n 2, 33–45; Berman, *Faith and Order*, above n 2.
7. Gary Bouma, *Australian Soul: Religion and Spirituality in the Twenty-first Century* (Cambridge, UK: Australia: Cambridge University Press, 2006).
8. I outline this much more extensively in Babie, above n 1.
9. This title is taken from Bouma, above n 7, chapter 2.
10. John Thornhill, *Making Australia: Exploring Our National Conversation* (Newtown, NSW: Millennium, 1992), 172, as cited in Bouma, above n 7, 32.

twelve themes: (i) a serious but light touch in dealing with religion; (ii) a wariness of enthusiasm in religion, and especially high demand religion; (iii) a wariness of imported, mass culture religion and spirituality; (iv) serious distancing from authoritarian leaders promoting sacred causes or sacrifice for principle; (v) a serious commitment to living for now, not sacrificing for the future; (vi) an antipathy to empty formality; (vii) a serious mateship grounded in shared experience; (viii) serious tolerance of difference flowing from a commitment to seeking a fair go for everyone and keeping an even keel; (ix) a serious readiness for humour and to laugh at oneself; (x) a serious quiet reverence, a deliberate silence, including comfort with an inarticulate awe and a serious distaste for glib wordiness; (xi) a serious wariness and intolerance of the 'gate-keepers', the 'straighteners' and 'God's police'; (xii) a preference to live and let live tolerance grounded in mutual respect as opposed to enforcing one group's viewpoint on others as a primary mode of acceptable inter-religious group relations.[11]

While it may be understated and wary of excessive public displays, and while at the personal level it may be typified by a rejection of religious organisations, the principal conclusion to be drawn from the evidence, though, is that religion/spirituality is present in the lives of Australians. In addition to its quality, Bouma also examines the quantitative dimension of Australian religion/spirituality.

Quantities[12]

Using data compiled in recent Australian censuses, Bouma identifies four quantitative elements of Australia's religion/spirituality. First, the available data indicates that migration and conversion continue to produce greater Australian diversity in the number of religious groups, the number of religions represented and the range of difference between and within religious groups.[13] Of greatest interest here is the shift of people to 'no religion' and the growth in numbers in major world religions other than Christianity, such as Buddhism, Islam, Hinduism and Sikhism.[14]

Second, in relation to Christianity itself, while still the largest religious group in Australia, its numbers as part of the overall Australian population continue to shrink, the numbers of Anglicans and other British

11. Bouma, above n 7, 45-7.
12. This title is taken from Bouma, above n 7, chapter 3.
13. Bouma, above n 7, 52.
14. *Ibid*, 55–6, figures 3.2 and 3.3.

Protestant groups shrank, matched by a growth in charismatic Christian groups, and the emergence of Catholicism as the largest Christian group.[15]

Third, the evidence indicates both an increase in spirituality among Australians as well as increasing membership in multiple religious groups; Australia's religious identity is increasing plural and diverse.[16]

Finally, two interrelated demographic trends emerge from the 2001 census data.[17] First, rather than being characteristic of the poor, Australian religion/spirituality remains the province of the educated middle classes. Second, and related to this, the migration of the 1960s and 1970s brought people to Australia who were more religious than they would have been if they had stayed were they were raised—and while their children and grandchildren may have ceased to practice the religion of their forebears, they have not discarded religion altogether.[18] Far from 'God being dead', a substantial majority of Australians continue to identify with a religious group and spirituality is on the rise: '[r]eligious belief, participation and denomination are far from inconsequential in Australian life'[19] and 'it cannot be ignored, nor can it be privatised, and nor can it be relegated to the margins.'[20]

Theology in Australian Legal Scholarship

The focus of the Australian legal academy remains the study of the wall of separation between church (religion) and state (law) and between the personal (theological) and public (liberal/secular) spheres of life.[21] There is little if any analysis, however, of the sociological role played by theology in the development of law. This Part, therefore, first, outlines why the Australian legal academy has forgotten about the study of theology as part of the development of law and, second, offers an argument for why it *should* study that relationship.[22]

15. *Ibid*, 65–8.
16. *Ibid*, 61–5.
17. *Ibid*, 68–72.
18. *Ibid*, 73–4 (footnotes omitted).
19. *Ibid*, 84.
20. Australian Human Rights Commission, *Freedom of religion and belief in 21st century Australia* (Sydney, NSW: Australian Human Rights Commission, 2011) 80.
21. See, for example, Denise Meyerson, 'Why Religion Belongs in the Private Sphere, Not the Public Square', in *Law and Religion in Theoretical and Historical Context*, edited by Peter Cane, Carolyn Evans, and Zoë Robinson (Cambridge, UK: Cambridge University Press, 2008).
22. I outline this in my earlier work: Babie, above n 1.

Legal development

This section briefly considers the work of Ngaire Naffine on the place of religion/theology in law and its development.[23] While adopting a solidly liberal stance that religion offers little to our understanding of law and, indeed, that it ought to be constrained as a source of legal change, Naffine nonetheless argues, along sociological lines, that the legal academy ought to study the role of religion in social life.

In *Law's Meaning of Life*, for instance, a seminal and important piece of scholarship exploring the meaning of the legal person, Naffine presents the fullest Australian exposition of scepticism concerning the place of religion in law. For Naffine, there are three ideal types of personhood in Western thought: those involving reason, such as law, those involving the sanctity of life, such as religion, and those involving value placed on our species nature, such as biology. These are further grouped into five metaphysical approaches: legalism, rationalism, religionism, naturalism, and social relational.[24] The first is hived off and the next three are grouped under the banner of 'metaphysical' approaches, within which some are said to take a 'strong metaphysical approach' and in so doing, 'tend to communicate poorly with those of different mentalities'.[25] That seems also to include those falling within the fifth category, the 'social relational person' favoured by legalists, who insist that '[t]he legal person . . . is defined by their relations and only by their legal relations.'[26]

Naffine posits that the various ways of understanding personhood demonstrate a range of incommensurable worldviews or mentalities. And the religious has little place in the 'rationalist philosophy of liberal individualism' in '. . . which any academic necessarily participates.'[27] Thus, '[t]he sceptic can perhaps understand the striving to find meaning in our lives, but faith in a personal God may be entirely alien. The believer and

---

23. See especially Ngaire Naffine, 'Law's Sacred and Secular Subjects', in Cane, Evans, and Robinson, above n 21, 268; Ngaire Naffine, 'How Religion Constrains Law and the Idea of Choice', *Adelaide Law Review*, 30 (2009): 15; Ngaire Naffine, *Law's Meaning of Life: Philosophy, Religion, Darwin and the Legal Person* (Oxford, UK: Hart Publishing, 2009).
24. Naffine, *Law's Meaning of Life*, above n 23, 167–8.
25. *Ibid*, 167.
26. *Ibid*, 168–9.
27. *Ibid* 173.

the non-believer have incommensurable positions.'[28] Naffine concludes that

> Although law may have (historically determined) metaphysics, law is not the same as philosophy and it is not a form of natural science and it is not theology. The highly practical and diverse tasks of social regulation and dispute resolution, which are given to law, also give it its own distinctive nature.[29]

For this reason, Naffine '. . . is critical of [religious] interventions [in law], regarding them as constraining of human choice and against human interests, and tends to be critical of jurists who permit them'.[30] This analysis therefore suggests that incommensurable mentalities ought to be confined to the private sphere; law ought to be left to get on with its work free of such encumbrances, while people live their lives under the law, although in the private sphere relying upon their metaphysical worldviews.

Yet, if it is people living their lives that matters, then it is these incommensurable mentalities that the legal academy ought to study, for that is where the law operates. And Naffine recognises this. Rather than a complete break of the tie between legal persons and real human beings,[31] Naffine, recognising the competing myths, mentalities or belief systems that constitute our nature, argues that '. . . this is not to say that the myths are false or meaningless or ineffectual or without social and moral value. We live our legal lives according to them and they may well be doing very good work for us.'[32] Any attempt to keep the legal strictly closed to metaphysical considerations '. . . cannot succeed because, one way or another, community and even sectarian beliefs about what makes a person a person find their way into law'.[33] Naffine seems implicitly to suggest that the legal academy ought to study the work that these metaphysical considerations do in relation to law:

28. *Ibid.*
29. *Ibid.*
30. Naffine, 'How Religion Constrains', above n 23, 15 (footnotes omitted).
31. Naffine, *Law's Meaning of Life*, above n 23, 180.
32. *Ibid*, 181.
33. Naffine, 'Law's sacred and secular subjects', above n 23, 288.

> [p]erhaps the critical task of the reflective judge and scholar is to attend quite openly to the beliefs, religious and otherwise, that enter and shape law, especially those beliefs about our very being which are multiple and often in tension. The burden is to consider the precise nature of those beliefs as well as their logic, their degree of congruence, their contemporary relevance, their representativeness, their practical implications for all the different parties affected and perhaps most importantly their compatibility with justice.[34]

If theology is important to Australians, if it plays a role in the way they interact with law and with each other, then the legal academy ought to study it.

Sociologically

C John Sommerville argues that it is the university's mission to attempt to make sense of society and its human meanings and so to foster wisdom; as such, the academy ought at least attempt to study the social dynamics taking place in the broader society in order to understand the role religion plays in people's lives.[35] In relation to law specifically, we might identify four reasons to heed Sommerville's call. First, exploring this relationship might allow us better to understand the underlying motivations for and the historical background to the liberal tradition[36] and the western legal tradition founded upon it.[37] Second, religion and faith influence and form our values and behaviour, which become and are reflected by law.[38] Third, plural and communitarian approaches to understanding human existence tell us that many social inputs construct law, each making a valid contribution. Understanding them allows us to critique the legal order.[39] Finally,

34. *Ibid*, 290.
35. C John Sommerville, *The Decline of the Secular University* (Oxford, UK: Oxford University Press, 2006) 13–5 and 141.
36. Elizabeth Mensch, 'Christianity and the Roots of Liberalism', in *Christian Perspectives on Legal Thought,* edited by Michael W McConnell, Robert F Cochran, Jr, and Angela C Carmella (New Haven, Conn: Yale University Press, 2001) 54, 54–72.
37. Berman, above n 2, 33–45.
38. David S Caudill, 'Law and Belief: Critical Legal Studies and Philosophy of the Law-Idea', in McConnell, Cochran, Jr, and Carmella, above n 36, 109; Phillip E Johnson, 'Do You Sincerely Want to Be Radical?', *Stanford Law Review,* 36 (1984): 247, 288–329.
39. Michael W McConnell, Robert F Cochran, Jr, and Angela C Carmella, 'Introduction', in McConnell, Cochran, Jr, and Carmella, above n 36, xvii–xxii.

by failing to recognise the place of religion in any of these debates, those in the academy and beyond it who study legal, political, and social structures, fail to address and connect with an increasingly important part of contemporary social life.[40]

In the last thirty years, relying on a combination of these four reasons, some in the American legal academy have begun to study the relationship between law and religion. Their work reveals three positions. First, that law itself exhibits theological dimensions, and may even be a dimension of theology influencing the development, application and operation of 'secular' law.[41] Second, and related, theology might historically and dialectically inform—crossing-over and cross-fertilising[42]—the development of the contemporary Western legal tradition.[43] And third, some religions have their own law, which operates within the broader secular tradition of some Western systems.[44]

If it is the mission of the university, and the legal academy specifically, to explore the relationship between law and theology, what might an engagement between the two yield? By way of a preliminary and partial answer, the final Part of this essay offers a brief reflection on the concept of private property seen through Christian eyes.

Theology Engaging with Law

In my own work, I have characterised the standard secular liberal account of private property as being the liberal vehicle which permits the atomistic liberal individual rights that allow choices in relation to goods and resources. Those choices are typically said to arise within the context of relationship, but only insofar as that relationship ensures autonomy and liberty, and ultimately human flourishing, through protecting the rights held by the individual at the expense of those who do not hold such rights. Thus, the choices made are self-serving or self-seeking, rarely taking account of their consequences either for the environment in which we live, or others, both locally and globally. And liberalism provides no answers

40. Sommerville, above n 35, 3–22.
41. *Ibid*, 273–519.
42. John Witte, Jr, 'Introduction' in John Witte, Jr, and Frank S Alexander, *Christianity and Law: An Introduction* (Cambridge, UK: Cambridge University Press, 2008) 1.
43. Berman, above n 2, 1–45 and 520–58.
44. H Patrick Glenn, *Legal Traditions of the World* (Oxford, UK: Oxford University Press, fourth edition, 2010), 99–132, 133–80, 181–236, 288–318, and 319–60.

for how one ought to exercise that choice or regulation of the choices people actually make. Thus, the consequences, or as economists might refer to them, the externalities, of those choices are visited indiscriminately on the environment and others the world over. The obvious examples of this are no less than the two most significant moral crises facing humanity today: global climate change and the effects of global finance.[45] And because it constructs a worldview which exalts not the atomistic liberal individual but the connection to other humans and ultimately to a transcendent God, religion generally, and Christianity specifically, rejects the

45. See my earlier work: Paul Babie, *Climate Change, Private Property, and the Children of Abraham* (Vancouver, BC: UBC Press, 2012 forthcoming); Paul Babie, 'How We Control the Environment and Others', in *An Invitation to Wild Law,* edited by Peter Burdon (Adelaide, SA: Wakefield Press, 2011), 279; Paul Babie, 'Why Should I Do This? Private Property, Climate Change and Christian Sacrifice', in *Law and Religion in Public Life: The Contemporary Debate,* edited by Nadirsyah Hosen and Richard Mohr (Oxford, UK: Routledge, 2011),165; Paul Babie and Mark Brindal, 'Australian Water Law: Property, the Constitution and an Anticommons Tragedy', in *Water: A Matter of Life and Death,* edited by Norman Habel and Peter Trudinger (Adelaide, SA: ATF Press, 2011) 19; Paul Babie, 'Climate Change and the Concept of Private Property', in *Revelling in the Wilds of Climate Law,* edited by Rosemary Lyster (Brisbane, Qld: Australian Academic Press, 2010) 7; Paul Babie, 'Climate Change: Government, Private Property and Individual Action', *Sustainable Development Law & Policy: Climate Law Reporter 2010,* 11 (2011): 19; Paul Babie, 'Choices that Matter: Three Propositions on the Individual, Private Property and Anthropogenic Climate Change', *Colorado Journal of International Environmental Law and Policy,* 22 (2010): 323; Paul Babie, 'Idea, Sovereignty, Eco-colonialism, and the Future: Four Reflections on Climate Change and Private Property', *Griffith Law Review*, 19 (2010): 527; Paul Babie, 'Private Property: The Solution or the Source of the Problem?', *Amsterdam Law Forum,* 2 (2) (2010): 17, http://ojs.ubvu.vu.nl/alf/article/view/124/231; Paul Babie, 'Is Private Property the Solution or Part of the Problem?', *BraveNewClimate,* 2010 http://bravenewclimate.com/2010/02/12/climate-and-property-law/#more-2334; Paul Babie, 'Looking East to the Concept of Property: A Review Essay of Witte and Alexander, *Christianity and Law: An Introduction*', *Adelaide Law Review*, 30 (2009): 175; Paul Babie, 'Two Voices of the Morality of Private Property', *Journal of Law and Religion,* 23 (2007): 271; Rachael Oliphant and Paul Babie, 'Can the Gospel of Luke Speak to a Contemporary Understanding of Private Property: The Parable of the Rich Man', in *Colloquium: The Australian and New Zealand Theological Review,* 38 (2006): 3; Paul Babie, 'The Ukrainian Catholic Church and Moral Theology: The Pastoral Writings of Metropolitan Andrei Sheptyts'kyi on Private Property', *Australian EJournal of Theology*, 6 (2006): http://dlibrary.acu.edu.au/research/theology/ejournal/aejt_6/babie.htm; Paul Babie, 'Private Property and the Gospel of Luke', *Australian EJournal of Theology,* 3 (2004): http://dlibrary.acu.edu.au/research/theology/ejournal/aejt_3/babie.htm; Paul Babie, 'Private Property, the Environment and Christianity', *Pacifica*, 15 (2002): 307.

liberal edifice of unfettered and self-interested choice,[46] although choice itself makes possible sacrifice, to choose for others, for the community. Thus, the fact of choice made possible by private property becomes the place for a Christian understanding of obligation and duty.

What Christianity tells us about the way in which the choices conferred by liberalism though private property ought to be exercised begins with a re-conceptualisation of the person. Beginning not with the liberal individual, but the Christian person, we can make sense of Christian (biblical and Patristic) admonitions regarding the use of possessions (private property).

The Christian person[47]

Liberalism treats the individual, the empowered, atomistic, rights-bearing entity, as paramount to community and separate from society. A new reading of Patristic Christian thought offered by John Zizioulas,[48] however, provides a tool for a reconciliation of the individual and the community achieved, paradoxically, by *separating* the meaning of 'person' from that of 'individual'.[49]

For Zizioulas, the Patristic synthesis of Christian theology and Greek philosophy conceives of the person as possible only *within* and capable of ontological existence only *through* relationship.[50] This is not to deny the liberal project and its understanding of the person as an individuated entity, nor is it to say that persons are *only* relations with no substance.[51]

---

46. Stephen L Carter, 'Liberal Hegemony and Religious Resistance: An Essay on Legal Theory', in McConnell, Cochran, Jr, and Carmella, above n 36, 25, 47.
47. This section draws upon the work of John Zizioulas—John D Zizioulas, *Being as Communion: Studies in Personhood and the Church* (Crestwood, NY: SVS Press, 1985); John D Zizioulas, *Communion & Otherness: Further Studies in Personhood and the Church* (London, UK: T&T Clark, 2006)—and that of Christos Yannaras, *The Freedom of Morality* (Crestwood, NY: SVS Press, 1984). See also Douglas H Knight, 'Introduction', in Douglas H Knight, *The Theology of John Zizioulas* (London, UK: Ashgate, 2007) 1; Colin Gunton, 'Persons and Particularity', in Knight, *ibid*, 97; Douglas Farrow, 'Person and Nature: The Necessity-Freedom Dialectic in John Zizioulas' in Knight, *ibid*, 109.
48. Zizioulas, *Being as Communion*, above n 47, 27-65; Zizioulas, *Communion & Otherness*, above n 47. See also Knight, 'Introduction', above n 47, 3, who writes that Zizioulas' work '. . . represents one of the most rigorous expressions of the neglected themes of the Christian faith'.
49. Knight, 'Introduction', above n 47, 1–14.
50. Yannaras, above n 47, 22; Knight, 'Introduction', above n 47, 2.
51. Knight, 'Introduction', above n 47, 4–5.

Rather, this conclusion stresses the relational nature of the individuated entity. Indeed, it stresses that the individuated entity can only *be* a person as a consequence of relationship. Kallistos Ware summarises this ontological model for human existence this way:

> [p]ersonhood in turn implies *relationship* . . . it is no coincidence that the Greek word for person, *prosopon*, should have the literal meaning 'face': each of us is authentically a person only in so far as he or she 'faces' others and relates to them in love. Thus [a] key term . . . is *koinonia*, which in Greek signifies equally 'communion' and 'society'.[52]

From the conclusion of personhood as relationship, three anthropological implications for the human person emerge.[53] First, Zizioulas' reading of the early Christian understanding of the Trinity leads to the further conclusion that the human person, who is otherness in communion and communion in otherness, emerges as an identity through relationship—an 'I' that can exist only as long as it relates to a 'thou' which affirms both its existence and its otherness. Isolating I from thou results in the loss not only of otherness, but of being. The I simply cannot be without the other. This distinguishes a person from an individual.

Second, both anthropologically and theologically, personhood is freedom. While this implies the freedom to have different qualities, above all it is the freedom to be oneself: absolute uniqueness, not subject to norms and stereotypes, not classifiable in any way. And because a person depends for existence on relationship—'one person is no person, [thus] freedom is not *from* the other but . . . *for* the other. Freedom thus becomes identical with *love*'.[54] God is love, we know, because God is Trinity. We, on the other hand, as persons, can only love if we allow the other to be truly other, and yet remain in communion, in relationship with us. For Zizioulas, 'only a person is free in the true sense',[55] which means that '[i]f we love the other not only in spite of his or her being different from us but *because* he or she is different from us, or rather *other* than ourselves, we live in freedom as love and in love as freedom'.[56]

52. Bishop Kallistos of Diokleia, 'Foreword' in Yannaras, above n 47, 9, 11.
53. Zizioulas, *Communion & Otherness*, above n 47, 9–11.
54. *Ibid*.
55. *Ibid*, 9.
56. *Ibid*, 11.

Finally, personhood is creativity. Because freedom is not from but *for* someone or something other than ourselves, the person is ec-static, going outside and beyond the boundaries of 'self'; and rather than moving towards the unknown, this affirms the other. Although usually limited to the other that already exists, it may also extend to affirming the other that does not yet exist.[57]

What are the implications of personhood as relationship for a better understanding of the exercise of choice contained within the liberal conception of private property?

Implications for private property

When viewed from the perspective of the relationally constituted Christian person, the liberal concept of private property, freed from the atomism and absolutism of its associations with the individual, becomes a tool of freedom, not simply the freedom to choose one's own preferences in relation to a given resource, but freedom to choose both *for* others and what is *best* for others.[58] In short, private property ceases to be self-serving, self-centred and egotistical and becomes other-focussed. To choose for oneself and so deny the community is in fact to negate one's very personhood, one's very existence. This shifts the focus from protecting choice so that property may exist to how best to exercise choice, at the level of personhood. And that is true freedom.

This final section concludes with an examination of early Christianity admonitions concerning choice, a set of guidelines that retain their value today. Moreover, they demonstrate what theology might offer law in a reconceptualisation and a redeployment of the concept of private property. The work of two Patristic writers in two distinct periods contains the core of this early Christian writing on private property: St Clement of Alexandria in the pre-Constantinian period (prior to 325 CE)[59] and St John Chrysostom, writing in the post-Constantinian period. Together, they

57. *Ibid*, 10.

58. A rudimentary outline of this conception of private property forms the core of some recent Eastern Christian scholarship: see, for example, Kyriakos Dounetas, *Beyond Wealth: Orthodoxy, Capitalism, and the Gospel of Wealth* (Etna, CA: Center for Traditionalist Orthodox Studies, 2009).

59. Jaroslav Pelikan, 'Stewardship of Money in the Early Church: A Close Reading of *Who Is the Rich Man that Shall Be Saved?* By Clement of Alexandria', in *Good and Faithful Servant: Stewardship in the Orthodox Church*, edited by Anthony Scott (Crestwood, NY: SVS Press, 2003), 15–6, citing Franz Xavier Funk, 'Clemens von Alexandrien über Familie und Eigentum', *Theologische Quartalschrift*, 53 (1871): 427, and L Paul,

provide an early Christian framework with which to consider the nature and exercise of choice conferred by private property.

For Clement, correct choice meant:

> It is unbecoming that one man live in luxury when there are so many who labor in poverty. How much more honourable it is to serve many than to live in wealth! How much more reasonable it is to spend money on men than on stones and gold! How much more useful to have friends as our ornamentations than lifeless decorations! Who can derive more benefit from lands than from practising kindness.[60]

For Chrysostom:

> Now when poor people sit, with feet that have been amputated, seeing you running by, since they are unable to follow you on foot, as though with a kind of hook they think they will detain you by the fear of an oath, and, stretching out their hands they adjure you that you give them only one or two coins. But you run on by, though adjured by the name of your Lord. And indeed if by the eyes of your husband who is out of town, or your son or your daughter, you are adjured, immediately you give in, and your mind leaps up and you are warmed. But if he adjures you in the name of the Lord, you run on by.[61]

'Welcher Reiche wird selig warden?', *Zeitschrift für wissenschaftliche Theologie,* 44 (1901): 504.

60. St Clement of Alexandria, *Christ, the Educator of Little Ones*, translated by Simon P Wood (New York, NY: Fathers of the Church Inc, 1954) book 2, chapter 12, 193.
61. St John Chrysostom, *Homilies on First Thessalonians*, 11.3, in *Patrologia Graeca,* edited by J Minge 161 vol (1857–1866) 62.465–6 (the translations of Chrysostom's writings used in this essay are those of Margaret M Mitchell, 'Silver Chamber Pots and Other Goods Which Are Not Good: John Chrysostom's Discourse against Wealth and Possessions', in *Having: Property and Possession in Religious and Social Life,* edited by William Schweiker and Charles Mathewes (Grand Rapids, Mich: Wm B Eerdmans Publishing, 2004) 88). One continues to find similar Christian statements today, both Western and Eastern, that explore this understanding of 'stewardship' first taught by Christ and spread widely by the Patristic tradition. For the Christian East see the collection of essays found in Scott, above n 59. On the Christian West see Frank S Alexander, 'Property and Christian Theology', in Witte, Jr, and Alexander, above n 42, 205.

In allowing one to exercise choice in the freedom of love and creativity for the other, private property therefore serves an instrumental purpose: '[i] f no one had anything, what room would be left among men for giving?'[62] Without the choice conferred by private property, in other words, there can be no opportunity, at least as concerns goods and resources, to remain in relationship with others.[63] There can therefore be no opportunity to constitute one's self.

Two questions arise. First, who does one 'face' in relationship; in short, for whom is one exercising these choices? And, second, what is the proper attitude that one must take to one's possessions given the 'other' that we face?

To answer the first question, one must understand the classical world in which Christianity emerged. There, wealthy citizens, the rich, bore a civic responsibility to provide benefactions for the community (comprised of many strata). In a radical move, however, Chrysostom inserted the poor, previously unrecognised both as a concept and as a group, into this established world-view.[64] The concept of the poor served a very significant theological purpose. Because they share the same human body as the rich, those who would give, it established the poor as legitimate objects of concern and thus philanthropy.[65] In *On Lazarus* Chrysostom wrote that poverty and wealth tell us nothing of the true human person. Rather, because both are masks, these notions hide the fact that rich and poor are created equal.[66] As such, the choice conferred by private property ought to be exercised in favour of the poor and, in so doing, in the service of God and so for one's own personhood and salvation. For those who have possessions, the art of Christian life is to 'learn in what way and how to use wealth and obtain life'.[67]

---

62. St Clement of Alexandria, above n 60, para 13.
63. *Ibid.*
64. Mitchell, above n 61, 100. On St John Chrysostom and the poor see also Peter Brown, *Power and Persuasion in Late Antiquity: Towards a Christian Empire* (Madison, Wis: University of Wisconsin Press, 1992); Blake Leyerle, 'John Chrysostom on Almsgiving and the Use of Money', *Harvard Theological Review*, 87 (1994): 29.
65. Mitchell, above n 61, 100–1; Brown, above n 64, 91. See also St Clement of Alexandria, above n 60, para 16. And see Pelikan, above n 59, 24.
66. St John Chrysostom, *On Lazarus*, 6, in Migne, above n 61, 48.986, as cited by Mitchell, above n 61, 101, n 39.
67. St Clement of Alexandria, above n 60, para 27. See also Pelikan, above n 59, 21; Mitchell, above n 61, 102.

How, then, can one exercise the freedom of love and creativity for the other as concerns goods and resources?[68] Clement provides the answer in this penetrating statement:

> he who holds possessions, and gold, and silver, and houses, as the gifts of God; and ministers from them to the God who gives them for the salvation of men; and knows that he possesses them more for the sake of the brethren than his own; and is superior to the possession of them, not the slave of the things he possesses; and does not carry them about in his soul, nor bind and circumscribe his life within them, but is ever labouring at some good and divine work, even should he be necessarily some time or other deprived of them, is able with cheerful mind to bear their removal equally with their abundance. This is he who is blessed by the Lord, and called poor in spirit, a meet heir of the kingdom of heaven, not one who could not live rich.[69]

Three principal components of the proper attitude toward private property follow: asceticism, almsgiving and solidarity.[70] Margaret Mitchell identifies asceticism as 'the seabed' from which almsgiving and solidarity rise.[71] This prioritisation is already evident in Clement's statement above that one who is 'superior to the possession of' private property and is able to deal with the resources and goods conferred by private property in such a way as to be 'able with cheerful mind to bear their removal equally with their abundance' is the one who is saved.[72] In fact, Clement denounced the rich person who 'carries his riches in his soul, and instead of God's Spirit bears in his heart gold or land, and is always acquiring possessions without end, and is perpetually on the lookout for more'.[73] And from inner ascetic conversion follows its outward sign: almsgiving.[74] And this brings into play solidarity of the rich with the poor as a key attribute of the prop-

68. This section draws upon Mitchell, above n 61, 111–4.
69. St Clement of Alexandria, above n 60, para 16.
70. This division is taken from Mitchell, above n 61, 111–4.
71. Mitchell, above n 61, 111.
72. St Clement of Alexandria, above n 61, paras 16 and 39.
73. *Ibid*, 17. See also Pelikan, above n 59, 24.
74. Mitchell, above n 61, 111. See also Pelikan, above n 59, 23.

er attitude towards possessions. In solidarity, Chrysostom combines into one virtue the requirements of asceticism and almsgiving:[75]

> Let us go down via almsgiving into the furnace of poverty, let us see the people who walk in it, philosophising and treading on the hot coals, let us see the strange and paradoxical marvel of a person in a furnace singing praise, a person amid flames giving thanks, a person bound in the most extreme poverty and yet bearing great praise to Christ . . . Now, let's not stand outside the furnace, with no mercy toward the poor . . . But if you go down to them . . . no longer will the fire be harmful to you. But if you sit above, disregarding those in the flames of poverty, the flames will burn you up. Come down, then, into the fire, so that you might not be burned up by the fire. Don't sit outside of the fire, lest the flames snatch you up. But if it sees you with the poor, then it will stay away from you. But if you are alienated from the poor, the fire will chase you down quickly and snatch you up. Therefore don't stand apart from the ones who are being thrown into the furnace. For when the devil orders those who have not worshipped money to be thrown into the furnace of poverty, do not be with the ones who are throwing, but rather with those thrown, so that you might be among the saved, and not the burned.[76]

In explaining solidarity Chrysostom alludes here to community—the relationship between rich and poor—within which the proper attitude towards possessions operates and achieves its fullest expression.

Conclusion

An engagement with theology, then, has much to offer law. In the case of private property, it can provide a model of community perhaps unknown or at least not fully developed in secular liberal legal thought. And, private property is but one aspect of law where theology may provide such fertile ground for growing new ways of looking at the world around us.

75. Mitchell, above n 61, 114.
76. St John Chrysostom, *Homilies on the Gospels of Saint Matthew*, 4.20, as translated by Mitchell, above n 61, 114.

Restorative justice,[77] professional ethical responsibility of lawyers,[78] corporate social responsibility,[79] and alternative dispute resolution[80] are but four of many other possibilities explored in the American literature in recent years.[81]

More than this, it may even be that such engagements and dialogue will reveal that what was has always viewed as 'secular' law is not really secular at all, but that which is '... increasingly being recognised as varied, plural, and overlapping, dependent on religious anthropologies and cosmologies, as well as sharing symbols, ideas, and institutions with religion'.[82] All that is required is that the Australian legal academy overcome its antipathy towards theology, allowing the models of human relationship it offers to be taken seriously in a truly liberal marketplace of ideas.

---

77. Christopher D Marshall, 'Satisfying Justice: Victims, Justice and the Grain of the Universe', *Theology and Law: Partners or Protagonists?*, edited by Christine Parker and Gordon Preece (Adelaide, SA: ATF Press, 2005) 35; Paul Babie, 'Expanding the Scope of Restorative Justice: Some Thoughts on Private and Public Law', *International Perspectives in Victimology*, 5 (2011): 72.
78. Adrian Evans, 'Encouraging Lawyer's Values in a Faith Conscious World', in Parker and Preece, above n 77, 6; Christine Parker, 'Christian Ethics in Legal Practice: Connecting Faith and Practice', in Parker and Preece, above n 77, 23.
79. Steve Rundle, 'Corporate Social Responsibility in a Globalizing World: What's a Christian Executive to Do?', *Business & Professional Ethics Journal*, 23 (2004): 171.
80. Ken Sande, *The Peacemaker: A Biblical Guide to Resolving Personal Conflict* (Grand Rapids, Mich: Baker Books, third edition, 2004).
81. See McConnell, Cochran, Jr, and Carmella, above n 36; *Recovering Self-Evident Truths: Catholic Perspectives on American Law*, edited by Michael A Scaperlanda & Teresa Stanton Collett (Washington, DC: Catholic University of America Press, 2007); Witte, Jr, and Alexander, above n 42.
82. Winnifred Fallers Sullivan, Robert A Yelle, and Mateo Taussig-Rubbo, 'Introduction', in *After Secular Law*, edited by Winnifred Fallers Sullivan, Robert A Yelle, and Mateo Taussig-Rubbo (Stanford, CA: Stanford Law Books, 2011), 7.

Public Theology in Islam: A New Approach?

Nadirsyah Hosen

Senior Lecturer
Faculty of Law
University of Wollongong
New South Wales

The discourse of Islam around the world after 9/11 has been focused on the radical side of Islam. The media tend to report stories about *burqa, jihad*, and *Shari'a* from the context of the fear of Islamic radicalism. The other aspects of Islam have been ignored in the public discourse. My paper seeks to fill the gap by examining the development of public theology in Islam. Public theology seeks to provide resources for people to make connections between their faith and the practical issues facing society. Therefore, the question is: how should Islamic theology respond to the real and practical issues facing Muslims?

Islamic teachings are not confined to acts of worship and prayer and to a set of moral counsels. As Islam has dealt with people's relations with God, it has also given the broad lines of human beings' relations with each other. It has, in various forms, dealt with individual rights and obligations, too. That is why the question whether Islamic theology is applicable or not to the ever-changing circumstances is a valid question.

Let me be clear here that my paper will not examine or challenge the five pillars of Islam: (1) the *shahada* (creed), (2) daily prayers (*salat*), (3) fasting during Ramadan (*sawm*), (4) almsgiving (*zakat*), and (5) the pilgrimage to Mecca (*hajj*) at least once in a lifetime. I will also not discuss six pillars of faith: Belief in Allah (God), Belief in Angels, Belief in Scriptures, Belief in the Prophets (Peace be upon them), Belief in Life after Death and Belief in *Qadr* (Divine Decree). Those are the basics elements of Islamic faith and belief (*aqidah*). Islamic theology in my paper consists of *kalam* (discourse) and *falsafa* (philosophy) that seeks the understanding of theology through dialectic. Some Muslim scholars try to separate between of *kalam* and *falsafa*,[1] but for the purpose of my paper, I simply put them into one category: Islamic theology.[2]

My paper will first provide a brief overview of theology in Islamic tradition. Secondly, I will discuss some thoughts and ideas of modern Islamic scholars on theology. And finally I will observe how the relationship between early and modern Islamic discourses on one hand and current social reality of Muslims on the other. I would argue that a new approach of Islamic theology is required to make Islam as a living religion that deals with public issues in the modern world.

Islamic Theology: A Brief Overview

It is not the intention of my paper to cover every aspect of Islamic theology within the history of Islamic tradition. In this section, I will only provide a brief explanation of different schools of thought in Islamic theology to illustrate the dynamic and richness of the discourse. *Ahl al-Sunna wa al-Jama'a (Sunni)* theology consists of the *Ash'ari* and the *Salaf* schools of thought. Although the schools have different opinions on several aspects, Muslim tradition recognises and calls them *Ahl al-Sunna wa al-Jama'a*. It stands in between the *Mu'tazila* (rationalist) and *Jabariya* (non-rationalist) positions.[3] I will focus on those four schools of thought.

The primary topics addressed by all four of these theological schools concern the relationship between God and His attributes (*sifat*) and between God and human agency (*qadar*). Other topics found in theological works include the nature of prophecy, the question as to whether faith increases or decreases according to one's deeds, epistemology, the believers' vision of God in Paradise, and the justice of God.[4]

1. See Tim Winter, 'Introduction', in *The Cambridge Companion to Classical Islamic Theology*, edited by Tim Winter (Cambridge: Cambridge University Press, 2008.
2. See, for instance, *Islamic Philosophical Theology*, edited by Parviz Morewedge (Albany, NY: State University of New York Press, 1979).
3. More information can be found in W Montgomery Watt, *The Formative Period of Islamic Thought* (Edinburgh: Edinburgh University Press, 1973); and Wilfred Madelung, *Religious Schools and Sects in Medieval Islam* (London: Variorum Reprints, 1985).
4. See Ignaz Goldziher, *Introduction to Islamic Theology and Law* (New York, Princeton University Press, 1981)

The Ash'aris distinguished themselves through the affirmation of seven eternal attributes that are 'neither God nor other than God': (1) knowledge, (2) power, (3) life, (4) will, (5) seeing, (6) hearing, and (7) speech. Imam al-Juwayni (d. 1085) and al- Ghazali (d 1111)—both from Ash'arites—reconciled the dogmatic position of the seven eternal attributes above and God's ninety-nine names *(asmaul husna)* by means of the construction of categories of names, such as those names that signify God's essence or the eternal attributes and those names that relate to actions. However, a Salaf scholar Ibn Khuzayma (d 923) affirmed all of the names and attributes by which God describes Himself in the while simultaneously insisting that none of these attributes—including God's hands, eyes, and face—is truly anthropomorphic because of the vast gulf between the natures of temporal humans and the infinite deity. The general Mu'tazila opinions (rejected by most Sunni theologians) about this topic were the denial of essential divine attributes that were 'neither God nor other than God'. Most Ash'ari theologians did not hesitate to apply metaphorical interpretations to Qur'anic verses that mention God's hands, eyes, and face.[5]

The three positions adopted by Sunni theologians concerning human acts could be summarised as: (1) al-Ghazali's views in which God creates the individual's power (*qudra*), will, and the actual act; (2) Fakhr al-Din al-Razi (d 1209): God creates the power and will in a human, who acts as an agent for the divinely created act; and (3) Abu Bakr al-Baqillani (d 1013): God creates the act, but man 'adds specific qualifications' to the act, which are uncreated.[6] Despite these positions, Ash'aris school argued that humans are responsible for their actions through a form of acquisition, which is called *kasb* (acquisition). God, according to the Ash'arites, is the creator *(khaliq)* of human actions and man acts only as the acquisitor *(muktasib)*. Man is free only in making the choice between alternatives and also in intending to do the particular action freely chosen, and in making this choice and intending to do the act, man acquires *(iktisab)* either the merit of appreciation and reward from God if he or she makes the right choice, or the demerit of condemnation and punishment if he or she makes the wrong choice.[7] The Ash'arites, thus, in order to avoid

5. . Scott C Lucas, 'Sunni Theological Schools' in *Medieval Islamic Civilization: An Encyclopedia*, volume 1 edited by Josef W Meri (NY and London: Routledge, 2006), 809.
6. Richard McCarthy, *The Theology of al-Ash'ari* (Beirut: Imprimerie Catholique, 1953).
7. Hasan Qasim Murad, 'Jabr and Qadr in Early Islam: A Reappraisal of their Political and Religious Implications', in *Islamic Studies Presented to Charles J Adams*, edited by

the fatalistic position, introduced the doctrine of acquisition by which, they thought, they could account for man's free-will and lay responsibility upon him.[8]

On the question of free-will or on the ability of man to choose and produce actions, the Jabrites maintained a pure fatalistic view. They held that human actions are-predetermined and predestined by God. Man has no power to produce any action. Everything is from God. God has absolute power over everything including human will and human actions. The Mu'tazilites, on the other hand, held that man has full power to produce an action and has complete freedom in his choice, though the power was created in him by God—this is against Ash'arites' views described above.[9]

The Ash'arites also differ from the Mu'tazilites on the question whether reason or revelation should be the basis or source of truth and reality. Both the schools recognise the necessity of reason to understand the Holy Book, but they have different views whether revelation or reason is more fundamental and, in case of a conflict, which one is to get preference. The Ash'arites held that revelation is more fundamental as reason should only confirm what is given by revelation. The Ash'arites prefer revelation to reason in case of a conflict between the two. By contrast, the Mu'tazilites hold that reason is more fundamental and if there be a conflict between the two, reason is to be preferred and revelation must be so interpreted as to be in conformity with the dictates of reason.[10]

It is worth noting that Imam al-Ghazali made the Ash'arite theology so popular that it became practically the theology of the Muslim community in general and has continued to remain so up to the present time.[11] In this sense, it is important to highlight the 'debate' between al-Ghazali and Ibn Rushd (1126 – 1198) that influenced the progress of Muslim communities. Just fifteen years before Ibn Rushd was born, al-Ghazali (d 1111) had died after striking a blow against Muslim Neoplatonic philosophy, particularly against the work of the philosopher Ibn Sina (Avicenna). From such bleak circumstances emerged the Spanish-Muslim philosopher, Ibn

---

Wael Hallaq and Donald P Little (Leiden: Brill, 1991), 117–132

8. George Makdisi, 'Ash'ari and the Ash'arites in Islamic Religious History', in *Studia Islamica* XVII and XVIII (1962/1963).
9. Further information see Abdullah Saeed, *Islamic Thought: An Introduction* (NY and London: Routledge, 2004), 61–70.
10. M Abdul Hye, 'Ash'arism', available at http://www.muslimphilosophy.com/hmp/14.htm.
11. Ira Lapidus, *A History of Islamic Societies* (New York: Cambridge University Press, 1988).

Rushd, who came to be regarded as the final and most influential Muslim philosopher. He is considered to be one of the greatest interpreters of Aristotle's philosophy, and is largely responsible for introducing Europe to Greek philosophy.

His influential commentaries on Aristotle revived Western scholarly interest in ancient Greek philosophy, whose works for the most part had been neglected since the sixth century. He critically examined the alleged tension between philosophy and religion, and he challenged the anti-philosophical sentiments within the Sunni tradition sparked by al-Ghazali. Al-Ghazali wrote a work entitled *The Incoherence of the Philosophers*; Averroes replies with The Incoherence of the Incoherence—a defence of the philosophers, or rather of Aristotelian philosophy. Ibn Rushd contended that the claim of many Muslim theologians that philosophers were outside the fold of Islam had no base in scripture. Ibn Rushd also challenged Ash'arite conceptions of God's attributes and actions. He strived to demonstrate that without engaging religion critically and philosophically, deeper meanings of the tradition can be lost, ultimately leading to deviant and incorrect understandings of the divine.[12] As interest in philosophy waned in the Muslim world after Ibn Rushd, his writings found new existence and intellectual vigor in the work of Christian and Jewish philosophers who would come to be identified as the 'Averroists'. His works ignited a similar re-examination within the Christian tradition, influencing a line of scholars.[13]

Islamic Theology in Modern Era

The heavy influence of Ghazali's views in the Muslim world has been accused as one of the source of Muslims stagnant, anti-modern and narrow views. In this sense, contemporary Muslim scholars have tried to propose new ideas and approach of Islamic theology. I will briefly discuss some of their ideas here.

The emergence of Western modernity in the nineteenth-century Middle East led to the appearance of a variety of movements that responded to modernity. The military, political and economic dominance of Western powers in the Middle East that resulted in the colonisation or semi-colonisation of many countries of that region illustrated the backwardness

12. M Fakhry, *Ibn Rushd* (Oxford: Oneworld, 2001).
13. R Arnaldez, *Ibn Rushd: A Rationalist in Islam* (Notre Dame, IN: University of Notre Dame Press, 1998).

of Muslim countries which were not prepared for the exposure to Western modernity. Since the beginning of the nineteenth century, Muslims familiarised themselves with Western science, culture, and technology via translations and travels. The main driving force and motivation of the reformists to put an end to the cultural and social stagnation was the following Qur'anic verse: 'God does not change the state of a people until they change themselves' (13:11). They had on their agenda discussion of the causes of—and solutions to—the backwardness of the Muslim world, which was the main theme of the writings of Muhammad Abduh (1849 - 1905).

Muhammad Abduh is widely known as an Islamic rational thinker who placed much effort toward renewal of the classical traditional Islamic thought on the basis of rational thinking.[14] Belief, for Abduh, should be a result of rational thought not an adduced compelling thought from any outside source. In addition, the first duty for any one before being a Muslim is to depend on reason in order to reach the status of believing in God, in order to move forward to believe in his messengers. All this is far-removed from the traditional Ash'arite position. He revived Mu'tazilites teaching that if reason and traditional thought has been in contradiction, then we should follow reason. His best-known writings are a theological treatise, *Risalat al-tawhid* (The Theology of Unity), and an unfinished Qur'anic commentary, *Tafsir al-Manar*, on which he collaborated with his student Rashid Rida.[15]

Like the Mu'tazila, Abduh uses an aesthetic approach. According to the Mu'tazila doctrine, the aesthetic distinction between good and bad (*al-husn wal qubh*) is inherent to human nature. Accordingly, all human beings should agree that there is a basic distinction between both qualities. This aesthetic distinction is transferred to the ethical sphere. Abduh assumes that an intuitive aesthetic competence with an ethical counterpart can distinguish good from bad. In this sense, reason would theoretically be sufficient for the determination of moral values without divine revelation.[16]

Abduh is seen as a representative of Islamic modernism. Abduh's thought influenced Ahmad Dahlan (1868 – 1923), and other scholars like

14. Mark Sedgwick, *Muhammad Abduh* (Oxford: Oneworld, 2009).
15. W Montgomery Watt, *Islamic Philosophy and Theology* (Edinburgh: Edinburgh University Press, 1985).
16. See Richard Martin, Mark Woodward, and Dwi Atmaja, *Defenders of Reason in Islam: Mu'tazilism from Medieval School to Modern Symbol* (Oxford, UK: Oneworld, 1997).

Nurcholish Madjid (1939 – 2005).[17] Madjid took the view that there are no theological reasons why Islam should be in contradiction to human rights, democracy, rule of law, civil society, and pluralism. Given the controversial nature of certain aspects of his political and exegetical thought, it is no surprised that Abduh, Madjid and other reformists became the target of fierce criticism. Conservative quarters and hardliners objected strongly to his liberal religious views and his message of vibrant pluralism within Islam, as well as other religions.

Madjid was also influenced by Fazlur Rahman (1919 – 1988). Rahman was very fond of Ibn Sina, al-Farabi and Ibn Rushd. He read their texts, relished the subtlety of their arguments, found them to be highly skilled and clever, and in the case of Ibn Sina, he wrote a commentary on one of his works. Like the other great Muslim thinkers of his time, the main preoccupation of his intellectual life was: how could Islam as a religious, cultural, political, ethical and economic worldview deal with the rapidly modernising and ever-changing world that we live in today? In Fazlur Rahman's view, neither classical modernism nor neo-revivalism constituted an acceptable alternative to traditional Koran studies. If Abduh's reform ideas were based on modernist rationalism, Rahman introduced a new label: 'neo-modernism Islam'—seen as a synthesis of modern and traditional scholarship.[18] Neo-modernist scholars like Rahman and Madjid promote ideas that might be called 'modern' and they formulate these ideas by consulting not only the Quran and Sunna, but also traditional normative and intellectual sources. They actually accuse the Islamic modernists for neglecting the textual treasury of classical Islam as they themselves find it a valuable instrument in arriving at answers to questions and problems important in the Islamic world of today. They do not treat these classical authors as absolute authorities, but as important efforts of each author to reach solutions to challenges in their respective context.

It is worth noting that both modernist and neo-modernist scholars are still based their ideas on the concept of western modernisation. In other words, their ideas could be considered as modernising Islamic theology vis-à-vis the challenge of modernism. Hassan Hanafi (b 1935), another

17. On Ahmad Dahlan, see Charles Kurzman, *Modernist Islam, 1840-1940: A sourcebook* (Oxford: Oxford University Press, 2022), 344; on Nurcholish Madjid, see *Reformist Voices of Islam: Mediating Islam and Modernity* edited by Shireen T Hunter (Armonk NY: ME Sharpe, 2008), 190–193.
18. Fazlur Rahman, *Islam and Modernity: Transformation of an Intellectual Tradition* (Chicago, IL: University of Chicago Press, 1982).

reformist, challenged this position. Hanafi is Professor of Philosophy at the Cairo University. He received his PhD in philosophy in 1966 from la Sorbonne in Paris. His ideas could be seen as reactions to western hegemony. In the 1980s he began calling for the creation of an 'Islamic Left', a socialist ideology rooted in religion. He also promotes an interpretation of Islam supporting the development of a global ethics. Hanafi has argued that Islam needs to be understood in way that facilitates human freedom and progress.

He explains in his own words that:

> Methodologically, socialist Islam begins with an absolute priority of text over reality and of public welfare over textual arguments. It has its sources in jurisprudence (*fiqh*), Malikism, and the methodology of Jurisprudence (*Usul al-Fiqh*) by al-Shatibi and al-Tufi, and in modern reformism by al-Afghani. It depends on theories of ownership, the public sector, industrialisation, agricultural development, labour as a source of income, banks without interests, and redistribution of wealth—not only through alms (zakat), but also through nationalisation, and even confiscation of exploiting capital. Sometimes it is called radical Islam and is accused of being a disguised form of Marxism by reigning political authorities as well as by traditionalists.[19]

The last modern scholar that I want to mention is Asghar Ali Engineer (b 1939). He proposes to develop 'Islamic Liberation Theology'. While Hassan Hanafi's Islamic Left is inspired by socialist movements, one could suspect that 'Islamic liberation theology' gains insight from liberation theology movement in the Christian world. Accordingly, Liberation Theology originally is a Christian movement in political theology which interprets the teachings of Jesus Christ in terms of a liberation from unjust economic, political, or social conditions. It has been described by proponents as an interpretation of Christian faith through the poor's suffering, their struggle and hope, and a critique of society and the Catholic faith and Christianity through the eyes of the poor.

19. Hassan Hanafi, 'New Directions in Islamic Thought' Brief No 4, Center for International and Regional Studies, Georgetown University School of Foreign Service in Qatar, available at http://www12.georgetown.edu/sfs/qatar/cirs/HassanHanafiBrief.pdf

According to Engineer, the Islamic faith was a force of liberation and has some main concepts within the theory of liberation. They are: social liberation, economic justice and tolerance towards other religions. Since the coming of Islam to Arabia, Islam has not failed to impress upon its followers the idea of liberation. Initially, it was the liberation of faith from all that is false and later the liberation of Arabia from oppressive forces of the pagan Arab aristocracy. The faith of Islam cannot but be a liberating force.[20]

In his evaluation of liberation theology, Engineer shows that from the beginning Islam has sided with the oppressed and the weak. If this Islamic teaching is interpreted from its theological and sociological viewpoints, Engineer argues that Islam promotes justice and equality. He criticised classical Islamic theology that did not imply human liberation as it concerned exclusively in metaphysical sense. Their concern was the hereafter; not the current world. They stayed far away from the real problems of human life. In addition, the rational theology of Abduh and other modern scholars has been criticised by Engineer as merely intellectual exercise for the elite; they do not appeal to grass root levels. In his ideas, Islam should become an instrument of social change when it is formulated as liberation theology.[21]

Islamic Public Theology

So far I have shown how the classic and modern Muslim scholars have examined the issues of theology. While classic scholars only referred to theology as a pure-God-matter, modern scholar have been trying to use theological teachings of Islam as a basis to modernise, reform or liberalise Muslim communities. Nowadays, one of the greatest challenges for Muslim communities across the region is how to retain this Islamic cultural heritage in the age of the industrialisation, globalisation, and digitisation; to embrace the modern world while maintaining the cultures and traditions as anchors of identity. This will make Islam as a living religion that can provide ethical and spiritual considerations in contemporary issues and public debates.

20. See his autobiography *A Living Faith: My Quest for Peace, Harmony and Social Change* (Orient Longman, 2011).
21. See M Agus Nuryatno, Asghar Ali Engineer's views on liberation theology and women's issues in Islam: an analysis, Master Thesis, McGill University, 2000.

For instance, a living religion can discuss issues of family planning in a crowded world, or other religious accommodation to environmental constraints. As Australian cities move to higher level water restrictions, Islamic communities can respond with appropriate *fatwa* on ablutions and recycled water. The traditional interpretation that requires ablutions to be performed three times may not be recommended, and could be reduced into one time only. The definition of clear water for the purpose may include suitably purified recycled water, as in Singapore, where so-called 'newater' is recycled to drinking quality. The issue of water recycling continues to be divisive in Australia, and there is room for religious leadership and socially responsive *fiqh* in a community that places such ritual as well as aesthetic importance on water, and in a place where it has such environmental significance. At a practical level, religious authorities and local communities could even install modern water-saving technology at mosques, making use of sensor taps, for instance. These possible approaches to water as an example of ways in which religion can respond to as well as lead debate in matters of everyday life and social significance.[22]

The global financial crisis shook assumptions about the role of experts, as financial institutions across the world spun out of any of the orbits familiar from the discourse of mainstream economists. Subsequent debate has been dominated by references to 'moral hazard', a curiously old-fashioned term that carries ethical overtones into its dry economic usage. The search for understanding of the phenomenon and ways out of it has seen references to *Shari'a* financial products (banking and insurance, to name a few).[23]

Does theology matter in economic crisis? Islamic economists continually refer to the global economic crisis as a result of interest rates from the great depression to the crisis in the western countries. Huge budgetary imbalances, excessive monetary expansion, large balance of payments deficits, insufficient foreign aid, and inadequate international cooperation can all be related to flaws in the theory of interest, which is also the root of the crisis. On the other hands, without having the interest as in the Western Banks, core principles of Islamic economics system are justice, equity and welfare that seek to establish a broad-based economic well-being with

22. Nadirsyah Hosen and Richard Mohr, 'A Posteriori: The Experience of Religion', in *Law and Religion in Public Life: The Contemporary Debate,* edited by N Hosen and R Mohr (NY and London: Routledge, 2011)
23. See *Handbook Of Islamic Banking,* edited by MK Hassan and Mervyn K Lewis (Edward Elgar Publishing, 2009)

full employment and optimum rate of economic growth to ensure the stability in the value of money to enable the medium of exchange to be a reliable unit of account and a stable store of value.[24]

This new approach of Islamic Public theology requires collaboration between religious leaders and scholars from related disciplines. It is collective *ijtihad* (interpretation). The justification for collective interpretation comes from the Qur'an [3: 159 and 42: 38] which advocates *Shura* (consultation). It also refers to the sayings of the Prophet: 'I ('Ali b Abi Talib) said to the Prophet, 'O, Prophet, [what if] there is a case among us, while neither revelation comes, nor the Sunnah exists.' The Prophet replied, '[you should] have meetings with the scholars—or in another version: the pious servants—and consult with them. Do not make a decision only by a single opinion'.

This collective effort is a viable tool through which a society can adjust itself to internal and external social, political, and economic change. Religious scholars need to recognise that they are not the sole authority to solve all problems. They also need to listen to other views. For instance, when discussing on human cloning, rather than simply stating whether such practice is *haram* (forbidden) or *halal* (permitted), they should consider the views of scientists, medical doctors, lawyers, and so on. Therefore, the advice given on the issue will be more comprehensive.

It is suggested that accordingly theologian and *Shari'a* scholars should reduce their dependence on the classic methodological debate, which was a product of the sociological structure of classical and medieval Muslim societies. For instance, they need to depart from the debate on God's attribute, free-will or the justice of God. That does not mean such debate is useless, but it will take a lot of time to revisit such debate. They should start to offer new concepts or a reformulated methodology to deal with contemporary issues. In other words, they need to develop new interpretations of original sources while studying the interpretations of the past, both to learn from their insights and to understand them as products of their historical environment. I have shown how modern scholars consider the views from western ideas such as modernism, rationalism, socialism and even liberation theology.

---

24. MN Siddiqi, 'Current Financial Crisis and Islamic Economics', in *Radiance Views weekly*, volume XLVI No 38 (2009); see also Abu Umar Faruq Ahmad, *Theory and Practice of Modern Islamic finance: The Case Analysis From Australia* (Boca Raton, Fla: BrownWalker Press, 2010).

The issue of women in Islam is also illustrative. New interpretation on Qur'anic verses focusing on female, veil, polygamy, divorce, and male superiority and disobedience or rebellion (*nushuz)* should be conducted. Equality of men and women is constituted in the essential doctrine of Islam (*tawhid)*, and hence understood not as monotheism but as unity and equality.[25]

The final example is on halal consumption. Halal is a Quranic word meaning lawful or permitted. In reference to food, it is the dietary standard, as prescribed in the Quran the Muslim scripture. The Holy Qur'an regulates Muslims on this matter with such a beautiful phrase *'halalan thayyiban'* (Al-Baqarah: 168). *Halal* means permissible based on Islamic law. *Thayyib* means good, that refers to good quality, healthy, environmentally friendly and respecting of human values. *Halal* & *Thayyib* together build the harmony of life, the balance of universe. Unfortunately, Muslims focus too much on *halal* and neglect about *thayyib,* as illustrated below.

Halal certificate is becoming a global symbol for quality assurance both for Muslims and companies in a global trade. It is no longer a simple matter of *halal–haram* in a traditional sense. The development of new technology in food processing, cosmetics, and medicine, to name a few, along with the potential market of a few trillion dollars creates some challenges for Muslim scholars and leaders. An understanding followed by cooperation amongst Muslim scholars and leaders on one side and scientists, who investigate and audit the products, together with companies and business certifiers including a related government officers on the other side of the spectrums, is a must.

In recent years, the ritual method of slaughter as practiced in Islam (and also Judaism) has been decried as inhumane by some animal welfare organisations in the UK and Australia who have stated that it causes severe suffering to animals. At least 15 abattoirs in Australia servicing the domestic halal and kosher meat market have permission from state governments to slit the throats of fully conscious livestock. The Australian standard provides for and includes provisions for ritual slaughter without pre-stunning. Animal-welfare legislation in Europe requires that abattoirs stun all animals prior to slaughter unless they are being ritually killed according to the practices of a non-Christian religion.

On 15 January 2002, the German Constitutional Court allowed slaughtering without pre-stunning ('Muslim butchers can be granted an

25. See Khaled Abou El Fadl, *Speaking in God's Name: Islamic Law, Authority and Women* (Oxford, England: Oneworld, 2001).

exceptional permission for ritual slaughter').[26] In early 2011, members of the European Parliament, by a vote of 559 to 54, passed Amendment 205 to the food-information regulation, which would require all meat from ritually slaughtered animals to be labelled: Derived from animals that have not been stunned prior to slaughter.[27] In June 2011, after eight days of intense public pressure following the exposure of horrendous cruelty documented by Animals Australia investigators, the Gillard Government announced a suspension on the live cattle trade to Indonesia. But, in July 2011, the government lifted the ban. The live cattle trade between Australia and Indonesia is worth $320 million.[28]

Islamic public theology must consider this development and to work closely with governments, abattoirs, companies, and animal rights activists in order to find win-win solution. This requires new interpretation of what *thayyib* means in the contemporary context. This is another challenge facing Muslim scholars in public issues.

Conclusion

At the outset of this article, I have asked: how should Islamic theology respond to the real and practical issues facing Muslims? I have attempted to provide several answers by looking at historical development of Islamic theology from classic to modern scholars. First, classic scholars focused on the original and pure issues of theology. They had different views and it is impossible to eradicate such diverse views. It seems there was a gap between theological discourse and the real issues facing Muslims at that time. Second, modern scholars have realised the situation facing Muslims vis-à-vis modernity. They are more concerns on how theology could contribute to the development of Muslim societies. They are open to the ideas of revisiting Islamic theology from the 'outside' perspectives such as rationalism, modernism, socialism, and borrowing from liberation theology. Their views can be summarised as attempting to 'maintain that which is old and good, and embrace that which is new and better'. [29]

26. The Court's decision can be read here http://www.bundesverfassungsgericht.de/entscheidungen/rs20020115_1bvr178399en.html
27. Soeren Kern, 'Europe Goes Halal' available at http://www.stonegateinstitute.org/1799/europe-goes-halal
28. Compilation of stories and news on this matter can be accessed here: http://www.smh.com.au/environment/cattletrade
29. See Ann Black and Nadirsyah Hosen, 'Fatwas in the Contemporary Secular Australia', in *Griffith Law Review* 18/2 (2009): 405–427.

Third, Islam as a minority religion in the Western communities should be able to contribute to peace and order. It is worth considering that the civil and social laws of Islam are in conformity with the simple life of the pre-Islamic Arabs, and are mostly based on their customs and usages. In this sense, contemporary Muslim scholars must find a way to determine which Islamic teachings that should be maintained (doctrines and worship), and which ones that should be adjusted through collective *ijtihad*. Flexibility and adjustability to the requirements of time conform to the spirit of Islam and are not against its teachings. *Wa Allahu a'lam bi al-Shawab* (God knowest the truth).

Islamic public theology still faces some challenges in terms of methodology. Collective interpretation not only from religious leaders but also from 'secular' scholars of related disciplines is required. My article provides some real examples of the new challenges facing Muslim communities that demand some answers from Islamic theology viewpoints. Should Islamic theology succeeds in providing options or answers to those real contemporary issues; this will make Islam as a living religion, applicable and adjustable to social needs.

PART B
PUBLIC THEOLOGY AND SOCIAL LIFE

Interface Vol 15 1&2/2012

On the Future of Humanity: Enhancing the Image of God?

Brian Edgar

Professor of Theological Studies
Asbury Theological Seminary
Kentucky and Orlando, USA and Melbourne, Australia

It is neither difficult nor outlandish to suggest that the twenty-first century will bring a transformation of human functioning that will rank, for significance, alongside the industrial revolution of the nineteenth century and the information technology revolution of the twentieth century. It will be a self-directed evolution of human functioning that will modify the nature of the human person in a way that will have a far greater significance than either of these previous revolutions.

The first part of this paper describes the various technologies that will change human nature. The focus is not on any individual technology but on the implications of the convergence of a number of technologies and the significance of the synergy emerging from them. The second part is a biblical examination of the nature of the human species as made both 'from the dust of the earth' and 'in the image of God' and is a theological reflection on the way that an eschatological perspective provides a way for us to embrace, rather than fear, these developments. This can be significant in the development of the human person and our understanding of the *imago dei.*

Part One: From Homo Sapiens to Homo Creator

The twentieth century saw the precursors of this revolution in the various technologies that allow people to be treated and enhanced in a variety of ways. Medical technology is now able to intervene in the reproductive processes at the beginning of life to end, modify and bring about human life in ways that were previously unimaginable. And many who would otherwise have suffered or died are able to live well through the use of surgery, chemicals, hormone-producing implants, prosthetic limbs, organ transplants, xenotransplantion, artificial hearts, pacemakers, bionic ears, and soon the use of electronic technology to restore vision. Nor can these changes simply be considered as peripheral because they not only affect the body but also the character, through gene therapy and medication that can modify emotion, thought, personality, sexual orientation and behaviour.

These technologies have, of course, brought many ethical issues with them. There are inequitable levels of access to medical care (something profoundly influenced by whether you happen to be born in Africa or Australia) and questions about the morality of embryo experimentation, the storage of artificially created embryos and the appropriateness of the use of donors and surrogates. And at the end of life while medical technology has become incredibly efficient at enabling people to live longer, healthier lives it has also sometimes extended the process of dying, which raises serious questions about euthanasia. Gene technology not only enables the re-design of agricultural crops but also of humans. Through the powerful combination of reproductive and genetic technologies the notion of 'designer children' is already, gradually, being realised.[1]

Eventually the cumulative impact will be such that the boundaries of human nature will be challenged and the future form of the human species debated. What, for example, does it mean to be human, as we are now, in comparison with potentially radically enhanced forms of life? To what extent can the species homos sapiens direct its own future evolution? This will involve questions about our relationship with other forms of life. One dimension of this has already been raised in the species-ism debate about the differences between humans and intelligent animals and their relative moral status.[2] But this challenge to the moral differentiation that occurs at

1. It is interesting that during the writing of this paper full page advertisements have been appearing in the 'life-style' section of the weekend newspaper that are aimed directly at prospective parents who might want 'advanced embryo selection' via an overnight process that allows for immediate embryo selection based on a comprehensive pre-implantation gene diagnosis. *The Age Good Weekend*, 30th April, 2011.
2. Speciesism, a term term coined by Richard Ryder and popularised by Peter Singer, is a bias towards the interests of members of one's own species and against those of members of other species. Richard Ryder, *Animal Revolution: Changing Attitudes Towards Speciesism* (Blackwell, 1989).

species boundaries is only one of a forthcoming series of debates because biotechnology is pressing forward in a number of ways that will challenge previously well-established notions of the nature of human being.

The reproductive technologies, for example, give rise to the possibility of human cloning and others are working on creating life from proto-cells, which amounts to creating life from scratch in the laboratory using cells with lifelike properties created from non-living materials.[3] The popular press has declared on a number of occasions that 'life has been artificially created' and although the claims are over-stated dramatic developments have taken place. The J Craig Venter Institute has succeeded in creating the first living organism—a bacterium—with a completely synthetic genome.[4] Perhaps that is not as dramatic as saying 'we have created life', but it is, nonetheless, a great scientific achievement. In stem cell research scientists have been able to work with the fact that an adult human body has more than 200 different types of cells that are all derived from a single fertilised cell that multiplies and differentiates. Stem cells, obtainable from various places including embryos, umbilical cord blood and bone marrow, are able to change into various types of cells and they can be manipulated to change on demand. The cells produced are now being used in bone marrow disease and leukemia and there is the potential for this technology to dramatically impact the treatment of a wide variety of diseases including cancer, spinal cord injury and multiple sclerosis. There are many other technologies in the process of development that may well end up being closely related to stem cell research. They include the research to produce 'organs-on-demand' through bio-printing. This is a process which utilises a modified ink-jet printer (an extremely sophisticated piece of very inexpensive equipment) to spray out cells—instead of ink—onto successive layers of gell—instead of paper—in a computer generated pattern to build up a three dimensional replica of a bodily organ. Cells sprayed in this way can be used to create organs for transplantation or research on the effect of various treatments.[5]

3. Steen Rasmussen and Mark Bedau, *Bridging Nonliving and Living Matter* (MIT Press, 2008).
4. J Craig Venter Institute, 'First Self-replicating Synthetic Bacterial cell' http://www.jcvi.org/cms/research/projects/first-self-replicating-synthetic-bacterial-cell/overview/ Retrieved 2/5/2011
5. Vladimir Mironov, 'Bioprinting', *Medical University of South Carolina Bioprinting research center*, n.d., http://www.musc.edu/bioprinting/html/how_to_.html. Retrieved 2/5/2011.

It would be possible to do more than nominate the representative technologies, but the essential point is the cumulative effect of these technologies. Alone they are important but when significant developments coincide the impact is profound. The reproductive revolution of the late twentieth century came about through the synergy of developments in cell biology with the technological expertise to manipulate single cells and improved surgical techniques, but when combined with gene splicing and nanotechnology the overall technological, and therefore social, effects will be multiplied many times. Nanotechnology[6] promises to bring about some of the most dramatic changes to human life. It is suggested that the effect of nanotechnology on the health, wealth, and lives of people could be at least as significant as the combined influences of microelectronics, medical imaging, computer-aided engineering, and man-made polymers developed in the twentieth century.[7]

Nanotechnology will be influential in the enhancement of human intelligence and the development of artificial intelligence, potentially bringing about changes that could well mark a shift from the present situation of modifying and manipulating existing human nature to developing and enhancing humanity in a way that should be considered evolutionary in scope. The potential for intellectual enhancement, genetic modification and radical increases in life-span mean that the possibility of a move towards self-directed evolution is not unrealistic. The human person of the present is already technologically empowered and enhanced in ways that would have been unimaginable to many of our ancestors. Our inability to define any specific moments of transition does not deny the conviction that homo sapiens evolved from previous forms of hominid and mammalian life and, likewise, the inability to precisely define what biotechnological enhancement would constitute an evolutionary change does not deny the possibility of such a change. The next stage in evolution that takes us beyond the twentieth century's technological modifications of individuals

---

6. Nanotechnology involves manipulating material at the atomic or molecule level in order to achieve certain properties or behaviours. Materials can be made stronger, lighter, more conductive or reactive and molecular sized devices can be created, utilising their natural abilities to manufacture, repair, connect, break down or energise. It can be used in electronics and manufacturing and in human medicine and enhancement. There are already over 800 commercial processes that use nano-scale materials and processes.
7. According to the US government National Science and Technology Council (NSTC). *National Nanotechnology Initiative: The Initiative and its Implementation Plan*. (Washington, DC, 2000). See http://www.nano.gov/you/nanotechnology-benefits.

to a twenty-first century transformation of the species may not occur in the next few years, but it is no longer inconceivable.[8]

Contemporary research into intelligence enhancement and artificial intelligence and their implications for humanity involves a collection of many diverse research programs operating over a variety of levels that examine theory, systems and potential practices. It is a field that is not easily summed up and an area where it is difficult to predict future successes. Research into reasoning, knowledge, communication, perception and other areas is taking place in the expectation that it will be possible to simulate human intelligence and eventually exceed it. Researchers have already implanted computer chips in the brains of people with quadraplegia who have been able to move a cursor around a computer screen solely by thinking about it. Brain signals are associated with specific movements of the cursor and participants are able to write emails without any action other than thought.[9] The boundary between person and machine is diminishing.

Other research involves DNA computing, something that also has obvious implications for human enhancement. Presently, computers store data in strings made up of the numbers 0 and 1. Living things store information on chromosomes of DNA with the human genome found in nothing other than long sequences of four nucleotides represented by the letters G, A, T and C. As long as computers are silicon based they are not 'us' but as they become DNA they can become integrated as part of the human person. The work has a long way to go, but it proceeds with enthusiasm because of the significant advantages with DNA computers[10] and it is possible that, at some point, they will be introduced into the human person. This research into intelligence is, like all scientific research, the application of innate human intelligence and this intelligent investigation of the self is a reflection of that essential characteristic that gave rise to the species name of homo sapiens. But it also leads on to a potential re-invention of the self through another essential human characteristic—that of creativity, whereby *homo sapiens* becomes *homo creator*.

8. Philip Hefner, *The Human Factor: Evolution, Culture, and Religion* (Minneapolis: Fortress Press, 1993); Brian Edgar, 'Biotheology: Theology, Ethics and the New Biotechnologies', in *Evangelical Review of Theology* 29/3 (2005): 219–236.
9. Michael Spezio, 'Brain and Machine: Minding the Transhuman Future', in *Dialog* 44 (2005): 375.
10. It has a cheap source, is non-toxic, can be smaller than current computers, can potentially hold more data and does computing in parallel.

Challenging the Meaning of being Human

Mary Shelley was only eighteen years old when she envisaged the artificial creation of 'human' life in her classic account of 'Frankenstein's Monster', an idea that was so thoroughly bizarre and terrifying that for almost 200 years it was the classic horror story. But artificial intelligence along with genetic and other research involving the creation of life brings science fiction into the realm of the believable, though hopefully with a less dramatic outcome! And the history of film from Hel (the very feminine robot of Fritz Lang's 1927 silent classic 'Metropolis') to Hal (the manipulative computer in '2001: a space odyssey') is replete with examples of robotic, intelligent machines that are uncannily human. The relationship between the human and the non-human machine is one that has been the subject of much speculation and it was in 1960 that Manfred Clynes and Nathan Kline wrote a speculative article about the difficulty of space exploration and the incredibly large amounts of time it would take to get anywhere really interesting.[11] They proposed that the rigors of extended space travel could be alleviated if it was possible to alter the form of the human person so that machines and electronic devices became a part of them. They called such people 'cybernetic organisms' or cyborgs for short.

Cybernetics expert Kevin Warwick of the University of Reading, UK, claims to be the world's first cyborg. Since 1998 he has had various implants that allow him to operate doors, lights, heaters and communicate with computers. He has a neural interface and is connected to the internet so that he can, for example, control a robotic arm on another continent.[12] His wife also had a chip implanted in her and so, via neurally connected chips and the internet, they have experienced the first 'telepathic' communication.[13] This is a radical development but a symbiotic relationship between humanity and machinery actually already exists very widely. That is, many people simply cannot envisage life without immediately available technology 'at their fingertips' (almost as a part of them), whether it be a mobile phone, a personal computer, a car or a coffee machine. There is no doubt that biological machines and controls will become a part of

11. Their idea is the basis of the 1982 movie, 'Blade Runner', in which the enhanced humans, the Cyborgs, are engaged in mining operations in the farther reaches of space. M Clynes and N Kline, 'Cyborgs and Space' 26/7 (September 1960): 75–76.
12. K Warwick *et al*, 'Controlling a mobile robot with a biological brain', in *Defence Science Journal*, 60/1 (2010): 5–14.
13. K Warwick *et al*, 'Thought Communication and Control: A First Step using Radiotelegraphy', in *IEE Proceedings on Communications*, 60/1 (2004): 5–14.

the human person and this will intersect with the rapidly developing field of neuroscience, an interdisciplinary field with great potential involving psychology, the biology of the brain, engineering, computer science and philosophy. Great advances have been made with neuro-imaging and the study of neural networks. The overall task is to explain behaviour in terms of brain activity and while obvious applications include treatments for disorders such as Alzheimer's, Parkinson's and various mental illnesses it also has the potential for extending fundamental capacities of memory and perception and developing our understanding of consciousness, religious experience, free will and morality.

In an earlier era, where human relationships with animals were more significant there was speculation about centaurs—half human and half horse, or the Sphinx—a lion with a human face. Today the focus falls on cyborgs and bridging the gap between humans and biological machines, but basic genetic research is also re-opening the possibility of interaction between humanity and other animal species. All genes are simply made of DNA and from the molecular point of view there is no difference and such thing as 'a human gene', a 'plant gene' or an 'animal gene'. It may be said, however, that 'there are genes that humans have', and genes that animals and plants have, but they are not fundamentally different and they can be moved around. The whole concept of species boundaries comes under question.

These are discussions that must engage the general public in something more than a superficial and populist manner. The conventional wisdom (especially among those closely involved in the development of new technologies of any kind) is that, initially, new technologies inevitably engender a degree of apprehension in the public realm but that with appropriate education and the familiarity that comes with time this resistance tends to move to acceptance. However, the situation is actually more complex than this. The degree of resistance to new technology fluctuates according to the kind of change involved. Genetic engineering, for instance, that involves the modification of people, animals or crops will always produce a degree of initial apprehension in some people but within that general area there are some specific scenarios that produce greater levels of fear that are not necessarily moderated by educational programs. Genetic modifications that involve, for example, higher levels of cross-species transfer produce a greater level of distaste and moral unease, a view expressed in the title of the Australian Federal Government Senate report into genetic engineering, '*Fish Don't Lay Tomatoes Do They?*' This reflects the general concern the study detected concerning 'un-natural' modifications to the perceived structure of the natural world. The greatest level of anxiety, however, occurs when the historically inviolable boundary of *human* being is challenged.[14] The idea of introducing human neural cells into monkeys or fertilising a human ovum with the sperm of an animal is simply morally abhorrent to many people. It produces a reaction that goes beyond the commonly experienced resistance to new technological endeavours, and sometimes, education and familiarity actually produce higher levels, and more sophisticated forms of resistance.[15] The higher level of reaction to genetic engineering that involves trans-species (or trans-kingdom) gene transfer points to a concern that there are natural boundaries, including that of 'species', that should be respected.

At the same time the question of the extent of the human life-span is being investigated. It is obvious that many people in advanced western societies are living longer, healthier lives but the overall maximum life expectation has not really changed from the biblical 'three-score and ten'. Many more people are achieving that age, and some even more, but the present reality is that people of a good age who are cured of one disease or disorder inevitably die of another! But there are people working on changing the upper expectation. It is a serious possibility that telomere therapy will, in this century, be available for radically extending human life span. The technology involved goes beyond attempting to establish optimum standards of good health in order to achieve greater longevity, and well beyond attempts to eliminate individual diseases. Telomere

14. Anxiety about maintaining the animal–human boundary was not only a major source of opposition to Darwin's theory of evolution but the same anxiety was evident in the 1890s in the debate over cowpox vaccination, when Edward Jenner's discovery was opposed because it introduced something from a cow into people — despite its potential to save millions of lives. Similarly, there is currently some opposition to xenotransplantation (transplanting a foreign tissue into another species), as well as to patenting life forms. It is notable that the preface to the Senate report 'A Cautionary Tale: Fish Don't Lay Tomatoes, Do They?' states, 'One major area of concern was the gene crossover, sometimes described as transgenic, from one species to another. There was much less concern about wheat genes being used in wheat than bacterial genes being used in wheat, for example . . . While there may be genetic exchange between species occurring in nature, genes from fish do not get into tomatoes under normal circumstances.', *A Cautionary tale: Fish Don't Lay Tomatoes, Do They?*, (Canberra: Commonwealth of Australia, November 2000), xii.
15. Celia Deane-Drumond, B Szersynski, and R Grove-White, 'Genetically modified theology: the religious dimensions of public concern about agricultural biotechnology', in *Studies in Christian Ethics* 14/2 (2001): 23–41.

therapy is aimed at investigating and manipulating the most fundamental aging mechanisms of the human body so that there can be an almost unlimited extension of human life.[16] Several studies have shown that human cells which were made telomerase positive exhibited delayed senescence, exceeding their normal life span by at least twenty doublings, thus indicating that telomere loss may be the intrinsic timing mechanism in human cells.[17] This is a significant step forward in the treatment of a number of disorders and although it may turn out to be only part of the whole story of aging, but if it does itself not produce a radical change in life-span the research will simply continue to the next stage. As a therapy it has the potential to help in atrophy of the skin, muscular degeneration and atherosclerosis.[18] Down's syndrome and failed bone marrow transplants could also benefit from telomerase treatment and it may be an answer for those with Hutchinson-Gilford syndrome (juvenile progeria) who have an average life-span of around thirteen years.

However, beyond the therapeutic lies enhancement. One of the simplest ways for anyone to gauge the social significance of such a discovery is to ask happily married people what they think it would be like to be married 'till death us do part' if both partners are going to live for two

---

16. Brian Edgar, 'A New Immortality? Reflections on Genetics, Human Aging and the Possibility of Unlimited Lifespan', in *Evangelical Review of Theology: Journal of the World Evangelical Fellowship* 23/4 (1999): 363–382; M Fossel, *Reversing Human Aging* (New York: William Morrow and Co, 1996).
17. The various component organs of the body have different cells that reproduce at different rates. The life of the whole organism is longer than that of any of the individual cells of the body but the life span of the organism as a whole is restricted if the various organs are not able to reproduce cells. Telomeres are structures found at the ends of eukaryotic linear chromosomes and consist of thousands of tandem repeats of the DNA sequence TTAGGG. Every time a cell divides the chromosome is duplicated and its telomeres get shorter. It is likely that the telomeres are the molecular clock that triggers replicative senescence. Once a threshold number of TTAGGG repeats is reached cells become unable to divide. Some cells, however, produce an enzyme called telomerase that rebuilds and maintains the telomeres and thus extends their replicative life. It is significant that there are very high levels of telomerase in cancer cells that are virtually 'immortal' (the problem of cancer is that some cells keep on replicating themselves for too long, the problem of longevity is that other cells stop replicating too soon). Optimism concerning these processes is reflected in the awarding of the 2009 Nobel Prize in Physiology or Medicine to Elizabeth H Blackburn, Carol W Greider and Jack W Szostak for their work on telomerase. The Nobel Foundation, http://nobelprize.org/nobel_prizes/medicine/laureates/2009
18. A Bodnar, 'Extension of Life-span by Introduction of Telomerase into Normal Human Cells', in *Science* (January 16, 1998): 349ff.

hundred years! There are enough significant implications for career and work patterns, global population, marriage and family structures and social relationships to guarantee a large-scale social transformation.

Of course, no one particular aspect of any of this research is guaranteed to produce the expected results (although unexpected developments are likely to match the failures), but that is not the primary point of this review. More important is the recognition of the overall scenario, the overwhelming number of potentialities and, especially, the synergy that is achieved through the interaction of these various sciences. While the timing and direction cannot be precisely defined there is absolutely no doubt that developments are taking place that will challenge the common understanding not only of the human person but of the nature of the human species as a whole, for no longer will we be dealing with non-heritable treatments for isolated individuals but with radical and inheritable changes. There is an unverifiable but useful principle[19] which asserts that there is a human tendency to exaggerate the speed at which new developments will take place, and to underestimate their significance when they do actually occur.

Conclusion to Part One

Resistance to these potential changes sometimes emerges because they are sometimes associated with other ideas that are more speculative or metaphysical. But these can be left aside. Firstly, one does not have to accept the idea that there will necessarily be an intermediate 'trans-human' state[20] that will inevitably lead to a fully 'post-human' state in order to understand the significance of the possible changes. One may argue about the terminology without dismissing the possibility of the human person with radically extended capacities. Secondly, it is possible to avoid adopting the various philosophical, religious and quasi-religious aspects of transhumanism. The fundamental idea is simply that human nature is not necessarily static and that species boundaries will be challenged.[21] Nor is it

19. This puts it in the same category as Ockham's Razor—that, all else being equal, the simplest solution is likely to be the right one. These are widely accepted but essentially un-provable theorems.
20. A term that goes back to Pierre Tielhard de Chardin, *The Future of Mankind* (New York: Harper and Row, 1959), 239.
21. Nick Bostrom, 'A History of Transhumanist Thought', in *Journal of Evolution and Technology* 14/1 (April 2005); Donna Haraway, 'A Cyborg Manifesto: Science, Technology, and Socialist-Feminism in the Late Twentieth Century', in *Simians, Cyborgs*

necessary to adopt the notion that there will be a 'singularity' involving an 'intelligence revolution'.[22] Changes may be revolutionary or evolutionary, although the convergence of disciplines means that self-directed evolutionary changes will inevitably be fast by comparison with natural selection. Fourthly, it is possible to avoid the emotional extremes of dystopian nightmares (technology as fundamentally evil) and messianic expectation (technology as salvation).

Despite these various qualifications the question of what it means to be a human being remains one of the most religiously and philosophically significant questions of life, ranking alongside other fundamental questions about God and the universe. Answers to this question influence the way life is lived but, up until now, the question has always been asked in the knowledge that there haven't been any viable alternatives to the form of life that we know at present. The question has really been about the manner and meaning of human life as we know it, but now it is necessary to look at the possibilities and questions involved in humanity as it might be one day. The question is one of human *becoming* and not only human *being* and it seeks clarity about the limits and responsibilities of the creative, self-directing nature of human life. These are questions that will demand more and more philosophical, religious, ethical and legislative attention and in between the extravagant speculations of science fiction and the unfortunate delusion that everything will stay fundamentally the same there is the possibility, and even the moral necessity, of a rational and theological assessment of our likely common future.

Significant changes are, in fact, already taking place. Humanity is considerably enhanced from previous eras. The merging of people and machines has, in a social sense, already begun. Modern western people are now completely reliant on machines and they are gradually being integrated into us in the form of devices such as pacemakers and the symbiotic relationship between human and bio-machine will inevitably continue to develop. The concepts of 'human', 'animal', 'plant' and 'machine' are all

---

and Women: The Reinvention of Nature (New York: Routledge, 1991), 149–181; Ray Kurzweil, *The Age of Spiritual Machines* (New York: Viking, 1999).

22. The term is used analogously with the concept in physics where prediction becomes impossible at the singularity where the laws of physics change (prior to the Big Bang or in a black hole). Ray Kurzweil, 'Reinventing Humanity: the Future of Machine-Human Intelligence', *The Futurist* (April 2006), http://www.kurzweilai.net/reinventing-humanity-the-future-of-human-machine-intelligence.

concepts that will evolve and, in some respects merge together. Clearly, the limits of human-ness will be tested.

Part Two: The Significance of Species and the *imago dei*

As a result of this the concept of species, always an important biological concept, becomes an important part of a wide range of theological and ethical discussions of life. Unfortunately, it is one of those terms which one knows what it means until one attempts to explain it. It appears to be endlessly flexible. In an attempt at comprehensiveness RL Mayden listed twenty-two definitions of 'species'[23] but subsequent commentators simply added more.[24] Although greater precision is ultimately needed it is possible to utilise the concept by recognising that however it is finally defined the notion of species involves the recognition of the importance of *definition* and *differentiation*. Ambiguity about the overall definition of what is involved in the idea of 'species' has been present at least since the time of Charles Darwin's *On the Origin of Species,* in which he said, 'No one definition [of 'species'] has as yet satisfied all naturalists; yet every naturalist knows vaguely what he means when he speaks of a species'.[25] A vague idea of what was involved was all that was required for him to be able to discuss the origin and the fluidity of species (in radical opposition to the existing belief in the fixity of species) and, despite continual refinements in scientific understanding, the presence of no less than 22 definitions of species indicates that the situation has not really changed: no one definition has as yet satisfied all naturalists.

The concept of species and the differentiation of life-forms is deeply involved in a range of theological and ethical implications issues. Some are listed here and most arise as a result of the emerging technologies described above, but others are included in anticipation of further developments. There are five categories dealing with species in general; the human species; animal species; plant species; and alien species. The first category asks about *the theological and moral function of the concept of species*

23. RL Mayden, 'A Hierarchy of Species Concepts: The Denouement in the Saga of the Species Problem', in *Species: The Units of Biodiversity*, edited by MF Claridge, HA Dawah, and MR (London: Chapman and Hall, 1997).
24. Jason Scott Robert and Francois Baylis, 'Crossing Species Boundaries', in *The American Journal of Bioethics*, 3/3 (Summer 2003).
25. Charles Darwin, *On the Origin of Species by the Means of Natural Selection*, first edition (London: John Murray, 1859), 44.

in general? This includes questions about the fixity or fluidity of species, the dignity of specific forms of life and the value of all related orders (such as species, genus, family, order, class, phylum, kingdom and domain). To what extent are these differences to be preserved? When is it appropriate to merge species or dismiss the concepts as morally or theologically irrelevant? More specifically, this raises questions about the ethical and theological appropriateness of the production of chimeras[26] or inter-species forms of life (as through trans kingdom or trans-species gene transfer).

The second category deals with *specific questions about the human species*. For instance, can the moral and theological uniqueness of the human species be retained in the light of evolutionary development and the emergence of the human species from pre-human forms? And is there any theological validity in seeking to modify human nature to produce 'designer children' or cyborgs ('cybernetic organisms' or human-machine hybrids) or trans-human forms of life (the radical enhancement of the human form and psyche to produce a form of humanity which extends beyond current capacities)? Issues in the third category relate to *the relative moral status of other animal species* (including competing claims about 'species-ism') and also about the treatment of animals in farming and other contexts while the fourth category relates to questions about *the moral status of plant species* and thus about the ethics of the conservation of species and the maintenance of biodiversity. Finally, there are questions about attitudes towards *possible but currently unknown extra-terrestrial life* (especially, but not only, of intelligent forms).

Questions about species are 'boundary issues' which have traditionally been found difficult by many people because they challenge deeply held

---

26. This can involve, for example, the creation of a human-to-animal embryonic chimera through the addition of human cellular material (such as pluripotent or restricted stem cells) to a nonhuman blastocyst or embryo; the insertion of human neural stem cells into the brain of a monkey to assess stem cell function; the creation of a mouse with a significant proportion of human stem cells in its brain. Robert Streiffer, 'Human/Non-Human Chimeras', *The Stanford Encyclopaedia of Philosophy*, Spring 2011, http://plato.stanford.edu/archives/spr2011/entries/chimeras.

religious, cultural and social values[27] about the nature of things.[28]This is exemplified most clearly in the debate about evolutionary theory. Those who refuse to accept this concept do so primarily because by blurring the boundary between species it threatens the uniqueness of humanity. Although objections to the theory usually includes resistance to any species change it is unlikely that opposition would be sustained if evolutionary theory did not include humanity. The present debate about changes to the various forms of life is intimately connected with the debate about evolutionary theory and so it will prove helpful to review some aspects of the historical situation before turning to an examination of relevant scriptural material and undertaking a theological assessment of the situation.

Changing Concepts

Prior to Darwin the fixity of species was generally assumed. One of the first to suggest a formal arrangement of species was the seventeenth century English naturalist John Ray (1627–1705) for whom species were groups of populations with inherited differences. Carolus Linnaeus (1707–1778) developed a naming system for species. He too believed the species were unchanging. Categorisation was made on the basis of similar morphology, but it was not long before the problems with this, especially the somewhat arbitrary nature of classification, was recognised, a problem which continues even though the methods of classification have changed along the way.

Darwin began with the existing notion of species, 'I look at the term species', he wrote, 'as one arbitrarily given for the sake of convenience to a set of individuals closely resembling each other.'[29] It was, he admitted, a difficult but a necessary process. In the *Origin of the Species* he described the cause of this similarity of individuals within a population in tradi-

27. It is not only Christians who question boundary issues but also Muslim, Jewish, Hindu and Buddhist. In Aoteraoa New Zealand Maori cultural concerns about the natural world and the connection of Maori identity with it is also well documented. Similar concerns could well exist with Australian indigenous communities. Brian Edgar *et al*, 'The Ethics of Trans-Kingdom Gene Transfer' (Office of Gene Technology Regulator, December 2006), http://www.ogtr.gov.au/committee/gtec.htm.
28. Research on attitudes to gene technology shows that 'public concerns relate not only to the physical risk and health matters associated with gene technology, but also exist at an existential level concerning ontology (the nature of things), including the meaning of human nature and the presence of some fundamental order in the natural world', Edgar *et al*, 'The Ethics of Trans-Kingdom Gene Transfer'.
29. Darwin, *On the Origin of Species by the Means of Natural Selection*, 52.

tional terms as being the result of 'a distinct act of creation' by God. 'No one definition has as yet satisfied all naturalists; yet every naturalist knows vaguely what he means when he speaks of a species. *Generally the term includes the unknown element of a distinct act of creation*.'[30] Naturally, this fitted with a literal interpretation of the Genesis account of creation. But later, in *The Descent of Man*, he realised that he needed to change his view, 'It is a hopeless endeavour to decide this point on sound grounds, until some definition of the term 'species' is generally accepted; and the *definition must not include an element which cannot possibly be ascertained, such as an act of creation*.'[31] That is, it had be more scientific and measurable. It did, indeed, become more precise with the focus shifting from similar characteristics to common descent (which produce those similar characteristics).

Darwinian theory required both the recognition of a degree of *fluidity between species* because species produce other species, and also the recognition of *variability within species* (which is the basis of natural selection for changes in species as a whole). There is inevitably a tension between fluidity and fixity. The fluidity of species is limited in the natural world by time (even a quick changes take a long time by human standards) and by the limitations on breeding. Species are not fixed, but they nonetheless remain observable and a useful, albeit debated, form of categorisation.

Taxonomic classifications utilise observable characteristics, ability to inter-breed, variations in cell type, levels of organisation and other factors to identify five (Animalia, Plantae, Monera, Protista and Fungi), six (Bacteria, Chromista, Plantae, Animalia, Fungi and Protozoa) or some other number of kingdoms. The changes reflect fluxations in scientific opinion. The more recent shift towards using similarity in structural DNA in parts of the genome in order to establish patterns of descent and to form families and indicate the closeness or distance of different populations is ostensibly a more precise form of differentiation, using, as it does specific percentage figures. Levels of similarity expressed in terms of percentages are popularly used as when, for example, it is said that humans have 99.4% similarity of DNA with gorillas, and 82.9% similarity with cattle, 54.2% with frogs, 14.4% with lampreys (jawless fish), 13.1% with sea slugs and

30. Darwin, *On the Origin of Species by the Means of Natural Selection*, 44 The emphasis is mine.

31. Charles Darwin, *The Descent of Man, and Selection in Relation to Sex*, volume 1 (London: John Murray, 1871), 228 The emphasis is mine.

15.1% with soybean.[32] If DNA is used as the sole discriminator then it is inevitable that species boundaries are going to be blurred or made redundant because, despite the differences, the sole determinant, DNA, is the same in individuals no matter how distantly related.

This kind of change in the scientific definition of species has the potential to alter responses to all of the ethical and theological questions relating to species that were noted earlier. It has the potential to change the assessment of the moral status of the great apes, influence considerations of the value of species biodiversity, challenge the unique moral status of humanity and influence any consensus regarding the appropriateness of genetic engineering that transfers genes from one species or kingdom to another. This kind of concern has ethical significance even though there is a conflict between popular and scientific perceptions of what constitutes a species or a kingdom. That is, for example, people tend to see poriferans (sponges), pigs and people as belonging to different kingdoms, but scientifically they all belong to the same kingdom, *animalia*. Therefore what the general public considers to be gene transfer between two different kingdoms may actually be gene transfer within the same kingdom.

The significance of this change in taxonomic methodology can be overstated, however, if one fails to observe the reductionist shift of meaning that occurs when scientific thinking that sees gene structure as fundamental to an entity's phenotype assumes that it is also fundamental in philosophical, ethical or theological terms. Not only is it the case that the level of similarity in structural DNA is not a good indicator of differences between species where there is a large difference in phenotypic expression, (for example, humans and great apes; humans and cattle) but a view of life which operates from a molecular perspective is not the only, or necessarily the best, perspective from which to make decisions which affect the form and relationships of whole organisms and societies of plants, animals, people, societies and ecosystems.

This kind of reflection on the implications of our understanding of species could be repeated in an examination of all the other ethical and theological questions that were mentioned previously. Each will involve a different range of issues but common to them all is the concept of species and the continuity and differentiation it suggests. It is an illustration of the way that scientific, ethical and theological thinking are connected. It is

32. Edgar *et al*, 'The Ethics of Trans-Kingdom Gene Transfer'.

important to avoid both a theology that is scientifically uninformed and a science that believes it alone can interpret all of life.

Scripture on Species

In seeking to relate scientific, ethical and theological dimensions of our understanding of life the question must now be asked about the relationship, if any, between the concept of species and scripture as the foundation of theological reflection. The history of the relationship between scripture and evolutionary theory has, of course, been controversial and has involved very different relationships between science and scripture with the role of modern science in interpreting the biblical narrative often being over-stressed. At one end of the interpretive spectrum scripture is read *literally* and understood as a fundamentally eye-witness account of creation, a form of science that excludes any scientific observation that contradicts the literal reading of the text. This over-reading of scripture as modern science is unsympathetic towards scientific evolutionary theory because of a fundamental conflict regarding the age of the universe. It also inevitably interprets the different 'kinds' of plants and animals described in the text in terms of scientific categorisations and so, again, conflict is inevitable. Alternatively, scripture can be read in an historical, contextual, *literarial* manner that takes into account literary genre and the cultural and historical context, a process that is preferable from a theological and hermeneutical point of view, let alone from the point of view of contemporary science. This hermeneutic can also, however, over-stress the role of modern science in interpreting scripture, albeit in a different manner – through an over-application of science to the text itself. Twentieth century hermeneutics stressed the application of scientific technique to the text through grammatico-historic exegesis where the meaning of scripture is seen as being located in its history (with source, history, tradition and redaction criticism) and 'what it meant then'. This hermeneutic was uneasy with more traditional non-scientific aspects of biblical interpretation and moved towards the elimination of the non-scientific concepts such as miracle, the dual nature of Christ and physical resurrection. It adopted a form of scientism in which alternative explanations of reality were subjected to the dictates of science and it meant the evacuation of much of the ultimate meaning of faith. In short, a recognition of the literalist error (that the biblical narrative is not written as modern scientific text) has to be balanced with a recognition of the literary error (that the text itself cannot be interrogated and interpreted solely in terms of reductive scientific rationalism), rather there has to be a recognition of the cultural and literary context, the changing nature of science itself and of the ecclesiastical tradition that calls for a reading in terms of broader theological and canonical issues[33]

So what, if anything does scripture say about species? As part of the six days work of creation, with all things done in order, the creation narrative in Genesis speaks of the vegetation, sea creatures, birds and then animals being created according to their own 'kind' (Hebrew: *miyn*):

> The earth brought forth vegetation: plants yielding seed of every kind, and trees of every kind bearing fruit with the seed in it. And God saw that it was good.[34]
>
> So God created the great sea monsters and every living creature that moves, of every kind, with which the waters swarm, and every winged bird of every kind. And God saw that it was good.[35]
>
> And God said, 'Let the earth bring forth living creatures of every kind: cattle and creeping things and wild animals of the earth of every kind.' And it was so. God made the wild animals of the earth of every kind, and the cattle of every kind, and everything that creeps upon the ground of every kind. And God saw that it was good.[36]

This is followed in the story of Noah with the animals entering the ark 'two of every kind'.

> Of the birds according to their kinds, and of the animals according to their kinds, of every creeping thing of the ground according to its kind, two of every kind shall come in to you, to keep them alive.[37]

---

33. See, for example, Joel B Green and Max Turner, *Between Two Horizons: Spanning New Testament Studies and Systematic Theology* (Grand Rapids: Eerdmans, 1999).
34. Genesis 1:12.
35. Genesis 1:21.
36. Genesis 1:24–25.
37. Genesis 6:20

> On the very same day Noah with his sons, Shem and Ham and Japheth, and Noah's wife and the three wives of his sons entered the ark, they and every wild animal of every kind, and all domestic animals of every kind, and every creeping thing that creeps on the earth, and every bird of every kind—every bird, every winged creature. [38]

The notion of 'kind' is associated with *distinction*, *comprehensiveness* and *order*. That is, the point of the concept is to distinguish different categories of animals as part of the overall categorisation according to days of creation and types of animals that were taken onto the ark. There is also a stress on the comprehensiveness of what is taking place in both creation narrative (the repeated emphasis on 'every kind') indicating that God is the Creator of all, and in the account of the ark (every domestic animal, every creeping thing, every bird) the fact that all were saved. And it is all done with a sense of order, according to days, kinds and pairs. C Westermann says of the term 'kind' that 'Its meaning is precisely the same as that of the word used today in the natural sciences, namely species or genus'. Unfortunately, this overstresses the precision involved because 'species' and 'genus' have different meanings, and nothing can be *precisely* the same as both. But the general point is valid when he goes on to say that, 'The function of the classification of the plants and animals lies in its significance for people'.[39] That is, it is not intended as a form of scientific categorisation, but as a means of classifying life forms for social, especially religious and theological purposes. The comprehensiveness of the creation of every kind in the creation narrative stresses the complete control and lordship of God. And subsequently the category 'kind' has use for religious purposes in defining clean and unclean animals—again, not a scientific taxonomy.

> Everything in the waters that does not have fins and scales is detestable to you. These you shall regard as detestable among the birds. They shall not be eaten; they are an abomination: the eagle, the vulture, the osprey, the buzzard, the kite of any kind; every raven of any kind; the ostrich, the nighthawk, the sea gull, the hawk of any kind.[40]

---

38. Genesis 7:13–14.
39. Claus Westermann, *Genesis 1-11*, first edition (Fortress Publishers, 1994), 126.
40. Leviticus 11:13–16.

> Of them you may eat: the locust according to its kind, the bald locust according to its kind, the cricket according to its kind, and the grasshopper according to its kind. But all other winged insects that have four feet are detestable to you.[41] These are unclean for you among the creatures that swarm upon the earth: the weasel, the mouse, the great lizard according to its kind, the gecko, the land crocodile, the lizard, the sand lizard, and the chameleon.[42]

Some see an underlying, ontological issue that has moral implications that go beyond those that arise from cultic requirements. D Kidner suggests that creation according to kind shows that while God has bound together all creatures in a common dependence each has been given a distinctive character and 'one implication of this is that it is part of godliness to respect the limitations within which we live as natural creatures, as from him.'[43] G Wenham also argues that the presence of species bears testimony to God's creative plan: 'The implication, though not stated is clear: what God has distinguished and created distinct, man ought not to confuse . . . Modern readers tend to be preoccupied with scientific and historical questions about the origin of the world, whereas the OT . . . is suggesting a moral stance to be adopted towards the natural world. Things are the way they are because God made it so, and men and women should accept this decree.'[44] It should be noted that this view of the moral need to preserve existing forms of life and maintain species distinctions is not diminished, but perhaps supported, by the fact that the term 'kind' is not used with reference to human beings who stand apart, distinct from the world of species.

This interpretation of the scriptural material is supportive of views that are influenced by a strong theology of creation—emphasising the goodness and the appropriateness of the structures, processes and order of the world—and consistent with moral approaches that build upon principles of natural law which argue that human reason can rightly discern in the natural world the way things ought to be and should seek to maintain

41. Leviticus 11:22.
42. Leviticus11: 29–30.
43. Derek Kidner, *Genesis: an Introduction and Commentary* (Golders Green: IVP Academic, 2008), 48.
44. Gordon J Wenham, *Word Biblical Commentary, Volume 1: Genesis 1-15* (Waco: Word, 1987), 21.

or restore these original and divinely sanctioned natural processes and structures. This, overall, is conducive to a generally conservative attitude towards the deliberate manipulation of the natural world, to the effect that things ought to remain as they are. Consequently, for example, this general approach thinks that medical interventions should preferably be limited to restoring diseased or damaged parts of the person, approves of genetic engineering that is used to overcome particular limitations that disadvantage people but has reservations about radical enhancements and trans-species gene transfer.

But, counter to this is the view that the scriptural material concerning 'kind' is not provided as scientific data intended to guide moral distinctions but rather that it is intended to show, firstly, for theological purposes, the comprehensiveness of God's creative activity and, secondly, for cultic purposes, those animals that are edible and those that are not. These are not statements about he complete detestability of certain species (they are, after all described as 'good' in the creation narrative) but they are simply not suitable for eating or sacrifice. It also seems, from the context, that the instructions about not mixing species in breeding, sowing crops or making clothes[45] are the result of cultic factors rather than from concerns about any underlying ontological issue.

This approach is supported by the observation that although humanity is described in terms of being made in the image of God, and thus as special and unique, it is wrong to ignore the other description of humanity as being 'made of the dust of the earth'[46] a description that connects humanity very closely with the rest of the created order. While the description of humanity as made in the image of God focuses upon the *uniqueness* of humanity the description of humanity as made from the dust of the earth points very clearly to the *continuity* of humanity with the natural world. It places humanity on the side of the animals and plants that are given for food.[47] Humanity is not fundamentally separate from the natural world, indeed, the most obvious observation is that through eating the inanimate becomes a very real part of us. All this points towards an approach that does not demand either a rigid demarcation between humanity and other forms of life or a view of creation as fixed and unchanging in its various expressions of life. This is particularly so if there is a greater recognition of

45. Leviticus 19:19.
46. Genesis 2:7.
47. Genesis 2:18.

the value of an eschatological approach that looks forward to redemption rather than back to creation for moral guidance.

There can, of course, be no fundamental division between creational and redemptive approaches for the future of the creation is always new creation. Creation is the framework for redemption and without it redemption is not possible. The Redeemer is none other than the Creator. Yet there can be differing emphases, one stressing the goodness and the appropriateness of the existing structures, processes and order of the world, and the other stressing the way in which God is seeking a new creation that is transformed and different to the present order of things. A theology of redemption is not based on the way things were created but how they are to be at the end.

Moral principles concerning the manipulation of human, plant and animal species that are drawn solely from creational theology (without explicit reference to an eschatological dimension) will inevitably tend towards supporting a conservative, 'don't play God', approach that is reluctant to approve anything that is not simply a restoration of the situation at creation (and it therefore has a tendency to assume a very static view of creation, one that can be opposed to evolutionary science). The tension between this approach and those that are more focused upon the formation of a new creation (with the attendant possibility of humanity actively working to bring this about through) is an implicit dimension of any number of ethical discussions. Those who lean towards a creational approach tend towards views based on order, conservatism and the maintenance of existing forms of natural, personal and social life. Consequently, the various technologies that are available should do no more than restore diseased or non-functioning parts of the created order back to the way that God intended them to be. On the other hand those who lean towards an eschatological approach tend toward a more idealistic approach that sees in the various technologies the possibility of going further and improving and enhancing human life in order to achieve the over-arching goal of the present life—the love of God and neighbour.[48]

God and the Fixity and Fluidity of Species

What is to be concluded about all this? Firstly, It is clear that God loves diversity. It would be wrong to see no value in the differentiation of spe-

48. Matthew 22:37–40.

cies of animal and plant life. God appreciates them all, they are 'good', not only the popular koalas, polar bears, roses, apples and butterflies but also the less glamorous worms, parasites and bacteria. It makes little theological difference whether the number of species is reckoned, as various estimates say, to be seven or one hundred million, it is clear that God has created a wonderful diversity of life. The fundamental nature of the physical universe is not to be discovered in discerning some configuration of sub-atomic particles—important though such research is for understanding life—but in the more obvious fact of the constant, universal presence of relationships. The diversity of life speaks of the essential and on-going nature of the interactions that constantly take place between the many, various, diverse forms of life. The universe is built upon mutual dependency, in systems of all kinds or, we might say, in communion.

Secondly, it is equally clear that the multitudinous species—the various 'kinds' of scripture—are not absolute in value. Theologically speaking, any interpretation of Genesis that allows for evolution is really committed to the ideas that species and different kinds are not absolute in value, and to the idea that species boundaries can be crossed, because that is the way that new species come into being. Creation occurs, theologically, both *ex nihilo* and *ex materia*. The connectedness of the whole creation points towards all species having independent, intrinsic value, but they also have value as an ecological part of the whole, in contributing to the overall life dynamic of the whole creation. This can mean the loss of individual life or the loss of or species as part of the on-going evolution of life. There seems to be a value to extinction. While biodiversity has increased (when one starts with few and simple forms of life there is only one way to go) there has always also been an associated loss of species. At times this has almost been catastrophic but this should not necessarily be seen as entirely negative. Large-scale fluctuations are vital to the dynamics of large systems and can actually promote the development of new and more robust species. God produces new, creative forms of life not just despite, but sometimes through the loss of other species. This principle of sacrifice extends throughout creation for life would not continue without death for food. Consequently, neither individual death nor species loss should be seen as intrinsically inappropriate from a theological point of view. The notion that death is always, intrinsically evil and that there could have been no death prior to an historic fall is both unnecessary and unhelpful.

Thirdly, there is both fluidity and fixity in specific species. Part of the conflict between evolutionary theory and Christian faith has come about because science has tended to stress the fluidity of species while theology has tended to stress their fixity. Indeed, evolutionary theory has sometimes been interpreted as necessarily implying the complete denial of any essential nature for specific species. That is, evolution has been perceived as simply involving a perpetually changing succession of individual entities with no on-going, underlying, essential nature.[49] This fluidity stands in contrast to pre-Darwinian scientific convictions about the fixity of species and also to Christian support for that concept, typically based on interpretations of 'kind', that stress a divine given-ness to all species and, even more importantly, on the concept of the image of God—a biblical notion expressing the unique, immutable, essential nature of persons.

However, this conflict between scientific fluidity and theological fixity can be resolved because not only does evolutionary theory also have room for a *stability* of essential nature but theology has room for a degree of *fluidity* in the understanding of the human person. Despite Darwin's ambivalence about their precise formulation, evolutionary theory recognises the existence and stability of species, and the fluidity that allows for change from one species to another does not destroy this. Human beings, for instance, exhibit both fluidity and stability of nature. The emergence of homo sapiens from other hominid forms of life points to fluidity and change within species but there is also a degree of stability: there is evidence that the human species now has essentially the same brain, that enables rational and abstract thinking, language, art, religion and moral intent, as people had in the stone age. There is no evidence of any significant, species-modifying change to humanity for 35, 50 or even 100 thousand years.[50]

It is this stability that is usually affirmed by theology relying, as it does, on the on-going presence of the *imago dei* as a fixed *something* that defines and distinguishes humanity, providing a unique moral status, free will, certain capacities and future potential. But can this understanding of the *imago dei* cope with the possibility of a changing form of human

49. This is, incidentally, a view that aligns with a post-modern, social constructivist view of the person for whom the human person is constituted entirely by social and cultural factors. Michel Foucault wrote that 'nothing in man, not even his body, is sufficiently stable to serve as a basis for understanding other men'. Michel Foucault, *Language, Counter-Memory, Practice: Selected Essays and Interviews* (Ithaca: Cornell, 1977), 153.

50. Even though recent research reveals apparently increasingly rapid changes to the structure of the human genome. Peter Ward, 'The Future of Man—How Will Evolution Change Humans?', in *Scientific American* (January 2009).

nature? The potential problem of past evolutionary changes and the presence of the *imago dei* can be avoided by claiming that the *imago dei* was not present until the emergence of homo sapiens, but what of potential, future, self-directed changes to human nature? Is the essential form of homo sapiens as bearer of the *imago dei* now fixed and would any change to homo sapiens necessarily involve a diminishment of God's intentions for humanity? One common approach is to allow the therapeutic use of genetic and other biotechnologies but to be more reserved about enhancements, as in the statement of CB Mitchell, ED Pellegrino, *et al*,

> It is too early to attempt to define specific boundaries for the use of biotechnology, especially enhancements . . . when enhancement is the sole intention of the use of biotechnology, when there is no disease present but only the desire to pursue perfection, immortality, super performance, a competitive edge, and so forth there seems little justification for physician participation and good reason for morally excluding it.[51]

But are all proposed enhancements necessarily negative? Or is it possible that some might actually *enhance* the image of God either through beneficially extending the physical form of the person or their capacities, or by enabling an improvement in their relational life? Could human life be enhanced without this having implications for our understanding of the *imago dei*? It might be possible to avoid these difficult questions by suggesting that the changes proposed are simply physical enhancements that have nothing to do with the more intangible dimensions of humanity represented by the *imago dei*. This may seem to be an easier solution, but it may not be the only direction in which one can move.

Understanding the *imago dei*

The problem with the concept of the *imago dei* is that, despite its apparent importance, it is difficult to know exactly what it means.

> 26 Then God said, 'Let us make mankind in our image, in our likeness, so that they may rule over the fish in the sea and the

51. C Ben Mitchell *et al*, *Biotechnology and the Human Good* (Washington DC: Georgetown University Press, 2007), 135.

> birds in the sky, over the livestock and all the wild animals,[a] and over all the creatures that move along the ground.' 27 So God created mankind in his own image, in the image of God he created them; male and female he created them.

Generally speaking there have been three broad streams of interpretation of the concept. Strictly speaking they are not alternatives because they can build on each other in order to provide a coherent theological understanding of the concept. It seems appropriate to use visual images to help define the concept of the image of God and so the first two streams correspond roughly to the two different kinds of 'images' that one can picture. The first is the kind of substantial image that can be inscribed upon an object, such as the image of a sovereign on a coin. The other is the more intangible kind of dynamic image one sees in a mirror. The first of them holds that *the imago dei is imprinted on the person in the way that an image is impressed on a coin*. The image is thus some intrinsic characteristic that reflects the way that God has made humanity. The only issue to be resolved is whether it is personality, creativity, rationality, spirituality or something else. But whatever conclusion one comes to in that regard it is generally related to a strong theology of creation, with the implication that this is the way that God has made humanity and, therefore, it ought not to be changed. It is therefore generally interpreted in terms of a limitation on anything like cloning, human trans-genics, cybernetics or any attempt to modify the human form that might be construed as trans-humanism.[52]

The second interpretation views *the image as being more like the dynamic and relational image in a mirror* that can change and be sharper, or less clear, depending upon the conditions and the relationship between the mirror and the object. This view takes Genesis 1:26 to be typical, Hebrew, poetic parallelism with two differently phrased statements that humanity is created in the image of God ('so God created mankind in his own image' and 'in the image of God he created them') with a third statement ('male and female he created them') as an intentional parallel that extends the meaning into the realm of relationships. *The third approach is closely related to this but views the image in more teleological terms* so that the image is not so much a given but a possibility that only begins to be actualised in this present life and which is ultimately realised in the future

52. This is an example of the problem of the validity of the meta-ethical shift from the descriptive ('the image is like this . . .') to the prescriptive ('it ought to stay that way . . .').

through a life of conformity to Christ Jesus who is the true image of God.[53] This more relational and dynamic view of the image is more grounded in a theology of redemption than in creation alone and it suggests that the reason that there is a difficulty in determining which human characteristic is *the* defining aspect of the image of God in us is precisely because it is *not* something to be defined in terms of any one aspect of us. The image is not a *past* tense but a *future* element and it is formed in us in our being human in being all that we are. There is no one specific characteristic that makes us human, rather, God is found in us in the whole of life. The *imago dei* is a destiny, a direction, a destination rather than a statement about our origin. Ultimately, the meaning of being made in the image of God is found in conformity with Christ. This redemptive focus opens the way to a more creative and transformative view of the person. God is not going to return humanity to the original created form but is engaged in the transformation of human nature. The question then is whether, and in what way, humanity can participate in this creative work of personal transformation. Interpretations of the *imago dei* that stress the created nature of the person will inevitably seek to maintain and preserve that status, but more redemptive approaches are likely to be willing to go beyond eliminating disorders and support the attempt to develop and enhance the human person in a way that the more conservative, creational theology would typically allow.

The alternative, as noted earlier, is to conclude that the changes that can be made all relate solely to the physical aspect of the person and that this has nothing to do with the *imago dei* that is found in the soul, rationality, original righteousness, dominion of the natural world or in existential relationships. Even though the precise location is disputed the tradition that the image of God can only be found in the incorporeal nature of the person is strong. It was influenced by the work of the most important theologian of the second century, Irenaeus of Lyons (c130–c200). It is significant though, that Irenaeus himself did not ignore the role of the body. He said that the person who is 'of an animal nature' possesses the image 'in his formation (*in plasmate*)'. But his use of the parallelisms 'image' (the soul's natural endowment of reason and free will which took place *in plasmate*) and 'likeness' (a super-natural endowment of the soul by the action of the Spirit) led to a tradition of interpretation whereby the image of God was seen in

53. Romans 8:29; Colossians 1:15; 2 Corinthians 4:4; Hebrews 1:3.

the soul or the faculties of the soul.[54] For Irenaeus the focus fell on rationality but for others the image was primarily expressed in self-consciousness, self-determination, immortality, personality, or the rule and dominion of creation. The role of the body was not completely eliminated though. Subsequently, John Calvin said:

> There is no doubt that the proper seat of his image is in the soul. I do not deny, indeed, that our outward form, in so far as it distinguishes and separates us from brute animals, at the same time more closely joins us to God. And if anyone wishes to include under 'the image of God' the fact that 'while all other living beings being bent over look earthward, man has been given a face uplifted, bidden to gaze heavenward and to raise his countenance to the stars' (Ovid), I shall not contend too strongly—provided it be regarded as a settled principle that the image of God, which is seen or glows in these outward marks, is spiritual.[55]

Just as in the ancient church Irenaeus' interpretation of the image as a spiritual mark expressed as part of the physical form of the person was followed by a tradition that overwhelmingly focused on the non-physical so too Calvin's refusal to exclude the body from participating in the image was followed by views of the image that had little room for the physical. This was accentuated by the trend towards a dualist anthropology with body and soul understood as two substances able to exist independently. The natural tendency was to split body and soul and to treat the soul as the real person with the body as non-essential and of lesser value. But the most recent trend in biblical theology has been to return to a more holistic anthropology with the person as an integrated unity of body and soul together, rather than as two, distinguishable, separable, independently existing parts and this has implications for the understanding of the *imago dei*. The exclusion of the physical form from the concept of being in the image of God may, in part, be aimed at avoiding trite interpretations which, for example, see the image as being present simply in the upright posture

54. Irenaeus, 'Adversus Haeresies', in *The Ante-Nicene Father: The Writings of the Fathers Down to AD 325*, edited by A Roberts and J Donaldson (Grand Rapids: Eerdmans, 1978), V 6.1.
55. John Calvin, *Institutes of the Christian Religion* (London: Westminster Press, 1961), 1.15.3.

of the human species but this must not be allowed to control the concept. Gerhard von Rad makes the point very strongly that interpretations 'which proceed from an anthropology strange to the Old Testament and one-sidedly limit God's image to man's spiritual nature' are to be rejected. 'The marvel of man's bodily appearance is not at all to be excepted from the realm of God's image'.[56]

The *imago dei* should be understood holistically, as relating to the whole person. Scripture speaks of the possibility of a complete transformation of the person that is conformity to the image of Christ. This involves, variously, the renewal of mind, will, emotions, desires and the moral life,[57] but we know that God is also concerned about the body because, firstly, physical healing is important and, secondly, there is no way that the transformation of the person can be considered to be complete without a transformation of the body. The resurrection of Christ is a confirmation of the way that the whole person is to be re-made in the image of God.

The ultimate transformation of the person takes place, of course, in the resurrection but humanity is also called to actively participate in this process of change in the present age. These present changes to our life today also affect who we shall be in God's eternal future because God takes and transforms the real, actual person and not some abstract concept. The transformation of personal, social and physical life always involves what might be described as 'enhancement' as well as 'therapy'. That is, personal changes include growth in holiness and the development of a new way of thinking as well as repentance for sin and the elimination of vice, while the social changes include the formation of a new community as well as the restoration of broken relationships and the elimination of war. Similarly, the transformation of the physical dimension of humanity not only involves therapy—healing disease, restoring deformed limbs and eliminating neurologically influenced mental disorders, behaviours and addictions—but also enhancement through the creation of a new physical body.

56. Gerhard von Rad, *Genesis: A Commentary*, third edition, Old Testament Library (London: SCM Press, 1972), 58 Note that the context indicates that 'excepted' is to be preferred to 'expected'. Also see W Eichrodt, Theology of the Old Testament, (2 volumes, translated by JA Baker, London: SCM Press, 1960) Vol.2, 122-125. A physical interpretation of the general concept of image is to be found in Genesis 5:3 in which Seth is described as being born in the image and likeness of his father. It would seem that the reference is to there being a physical resemblance.

57. Romans 12:2; Ephesians 4:23; Colossians 3:10; Galatians 5:1; Philippians 3:12–14; Colossians 3:5; Galatians 5:24; 1 Thessalonians. 4:3, 7; 1 Corintians 1:2.

The missiological validity of ministries focusing upon therapy is well established and there is no reason for not viewing positively at least some of the aims of biotechnology in regard to enhancement. Indeed, not only is a complete distinction between therapy and enhancement difficult in practice, but it is also difficult to argue that the biblical narrative only ever implies therapy and not the creation of that which is new. The biblical imagery of redemption 'begins with the tale of a garden and ends with a city of gold'. There is never a thought that humanity should simply return to the form of life of the garden of Eden: God is a creative God who takes the world on to new things. Humanity is not merely to be 'restored' to the image of God but is to be, more actively, 'formed' or 'conformed' to the image of Christ, and this is not so only individually but also socially and, we might say, as a species that is changed as a part of the transformation of all things.

Conclusion: Continuing the Human Journey

Human participation in this creative activity means reflecting, or imaging, the nature of God and the creativity of Christ. In it the image of God is clarified and expressed. The central issue is ensuring that this creativity is expressed in ways that promotes the common good and the values of the kingdom of God. It is possible to avoid the extremes of optimism and pessimism concerning new technology that produce either messianic expectation or a dystopian nightmare. It is certainly possible that new technologies will impact humanity negatively. Frail and sinful humanity can certainly find new ways of damaging society, engaging in war, mistreating others and making tremendously damaging mistakes, but equally obviously, this frailty and sinfulness will not be eliminated, nor human life automatically enhanced, by refusing to even consider new biotechnologies. Moreover, although human sinfulness is exceedingly great, it is possible, theologically, to trust in the providence of God and, practically, to note that there are some limitations on the kind of scenarios that are sometimes envisaged. Firstly, there are limits of logic with regard to what can happen. For example, there is no doubt that various medical treatments are already changing people's personalities through the use, of antidepressants, anti-psychotics and other treatments, but it should not be assumed that by a process of simple extrapolation that it will ultimately be possible to modify personality characteristics so that people are more or less loving, kind, generous, peaceful, angry, evil, selfish or depressed. To attempt to eliminate attitudes such as 'hate' or 'anger' which cause fighting, strife and war from the human character is to attempt the impossible. Such attitudes are too context specific for that. Hate and anger can be good and proper attitudes in certain circumstances: one may be angry when someone suffers because one loves God and seeks justice. In short, to eliminate anger is to eliminate love. Any genetic process that eliminates anger has effectively 'killed' the person—even if their body is still functioning. It is, indeed, possible that technology will find new ways of killing people, but there is nothing new in that.

Another limitation to the modification of human nature is the intrinsic difficulty involved in envisaging changes that are not merely extensions of existing capacities. One could consider the radical extension of, say memory or the introduction of 'telepathy' (as per the Kevin Warwick experiment) as a trans-human capacity, but there is also a sense in which they are both extensions of the existing capacities of memory and interpersonal communication. It is actually extremely hard to envisage genuinely new capacities because of the limitations of our present capacities. Some things cannot be imagined, as physicists have observed about the problem of envisaging what happens beyond the reach of the known laws of physics ('before' the Big Bang or in a Black Hole). No animal could have envisaged the development of rationality or altruism. To be able to envisage the human you have to be one.

Three sets of questions emerge that will need to be answered. Firstly, *to what extent is it possible to imagine beyond humanity?* And where might we look for new characteristics: our own imaginations? animals? God? Secondly, *what kind of new capacity or level of functioning would constitute a new form of humanity?* Would the ability to fly or breath underwater constitute such a change (bearing in mind that we do such things now, albeit in planes and with diving equipment)? Or is it more important to look towards enhanced mental or moral attributes for genuine enhancement? But love, grace and patience do not seem to be the kind of capacity that one could engineer in any way—although hate, aggression and impatience can appear to be influenced by one's neurobiology. While divine omniscience is not attainable does the extent of knowledge that is immediately available from the internet change us if it is accessible through a brain implant (as distinct from coming through a computer at one's fingertips)? Thirdly, *what change to the human person, whether and enhancement of through the loss of attributes, would constitute a form of de-humanisation?* In this regard it is interesting to reflect on our assessments of those who have seriously diminished capacities as the result of infirmity or accident. These questions are not easily resolvable, but they cannot be taken as negating the possibilities described above. Radically new developments do indeed take place. There has been a whole process of evolutionary change including radical modifications that have involved the development of consciousness, rationality, altruism, love, morality, creativity and spirituality. The real issue is to ensure that changes enhance, and do not detract, from human life and flourishing.

Achieving this will not be easy, but that is the way life is. Specific answers to particular possibilities cannot be advanced ahead of time but it can be said that a faithful journey into the future will need to be plotted within the area covered by four sets of tensions. The first relates to *the tension between the physical and the spiritual.* Positively, there is a sense in which the conscious appropriation of biotechnology strengthens our awareness of our connection with the whole created order. Much modern thought and social behaviour has tended to distance humanity from creation and it may well that we become more human (and humane) through the recognition of our connectedness. Obviously I do not think that we should decline to participate in this part of the human journey[58] that has, so far, brought us from pre-human through hominid to homo sapiens and which, we know by faith, will one day lead to New Creation, but in doing so it is important that we understand our true calling, which is not to technological achievement and physical perfection but to maturity in faith and the perfection of holiness.[59] But this ordering of priorities, which places the spiritual ahead of the physical, ought not to be construed as denying the importance of the physical. The opposite of 'spiritual' is not 'physical' but 'un-spiritual' (or 'flesh' or 'carnal'). The spiritual involves both the immaterial/non-physical and the physical as well. A priority to the spiritual involves the transformation of the whole of life and it is important that we continue to recognise the spiritual role of the physical form of the person.

The second tension exists *between that which is biologically given and that which is technologically possible.* The possible is, of course, not always

58. Jacqui Stewart argues that 'because humans themselves are evolved creatures within the natural world, technology and the advent of the cyborg is itself natural, is part of the journey of exploration of the species that is described in Genesis as being in the image and likeness of God', Jacqui Stewart, 'Technology and Christianity', in *God, Humanity and Cosmos*, edited by Christoper Southgate (New York: T&T Clark, 2005), 357.

59. James 1:4; 1 Thessalonians 3:13; 1 John 4:17; 1 Corinthains 2:6; Ephesians 4;13; Philippians 3:15.

beneficial and there is certainly both a scientific and a moral prudentiality in not acting quickly in crossing species or undertaking species-altering procedures, not least because any science that ignores society's values and wishes is behaving unethically. Developments need to be guided not simply by what is technologically possible, but by that which is morally preferable and consistent with the common good. The fundamental aim has to be to improve human life and living in order to enhance the love of God and neighbour.

The third tension is *that which exists between homo sapiens as one species among many (fashioned, in biblical terms, 'from the dust of the earth') and, on the other hand, as persons called to bear the image of God.* Because humanity is part of creation it is important not to set up un-necessary barriers between humanity and the rest of the world or to reject, for example, the possibility of the use of genes from non-human sources. Yet humans are not merely animals, but moral, spiritual creatures able to reflect God's creativity. It has been argued that human beings are now 'co-creators' with God, and that our purpose is to be part of bringing about the future. The merit of this approach is that it recognises the responsibility that we have as God's unique creation, and it calls for responsible decisions about the future of the world. But the weakness is that the term allows too great a level of responsibility and freedom and ignores the danger inherent in human sinfulness. I prefer the traditional term 'pro-creators', although I use it in a somewhat different way to the traditional usage (which simply refers to bearing children). But the point is that humans are procreators[60] who, under God, have always had the power to create life. Today, however, that power is not merely through sexual relationships but through technology and it is not a capacity to be denied, but rather utilised carefully and appropriately. It is connected with the notion that we are called to be 'administrators',[61] called to care for the world and to be responsible for it. This view does not give a definitive answer to any particular position but it recognises the way humanity is called to share with God in the care of the world. It stresses human creativity and freedom and is very open to new forms of human life.

Finally, there is *the over-arching theological tension between the creational and the eschatological.* The point has been made that humanity is not so much called to restore the *imago dei* as much as to become it,

60. In the sense of standing in for, or representing someone else, as a proconsul or pro-vice-chancellor.

61. Genesis 1:28.

through conformity to the life of Christ. It is a destiny rather than just a statement about origins, and when viewed in this way it encourages us to participate in God's ministry of transformation and to consider positively the possibilities inherent in the new biotechnologies. They are not to be rejected outright not adopted unthinkingly, but to be measured according the possibility of enhancing the common good.

It should be clear, from all of these tensions, that rather than there being a distinct and clearly defined biblical path to follow into the future there are, instead, scriptural boundary markers which define a rather broader territory which humanity must inhabit as we look not only at the potential of human *being*, but also at the possibilities inherent in human *becoming.*

Interface Vol 15 1&2/2012

Is there a Theology of Values Education?

Brian V Hill

Emeritus Professor of Education,
Murdoch University, Western Australia

Over the centuries, many theologians have paused in their system-building to reflect on the nature of Christian involvement in education. But the development in the last 200 years of state schools operating in the public domain, and the growing religious pluralisation of society in the present day, oblige us to revisit some of our basic assumptions in this area. Most contemporary Christian commentators, however, are committed in advance to the Christian school solution, a pre-emptive assumption which also needs to be re-examined, particularly in the light of the growing debate about 'values education' in democratic societies like our own.

This article seeks to foreshadow a form of discourse which could enable Christian educators to communicate across denominational and other divides about such issues. It then identifies some central theological concerns which bear directly on how, whichever sector we work in, we may conceptualise and work together on values education.

The Need for Mutual Theorising

The matter is urgent. Currently, education is big business, and the dominant paradigm is the schooling/instructional model. But this model is also a focus of great controversy; for example, as to whether schools for the rising generation should be public or private, religious or secular, intellectual or vocational. Just in Christian circles alone, there is heated diversity of opinion. Some abhor the idea of sending their children to allegedly 'godless' state schools, others view Christian schools as foxholes which fail to prepare their graduates for effective witness in the public domain. Catholic and Reformed educators view each other with suspicion, while many other Christians deplore the degree to which both have put all their educational eggs in the schooling basket.

Such divisions mirror an even greater cultural fragmentation. Christendom is behind us. Agreement in the public domain as to what constitutes the Common Good is tenuous. Since the 1960s, the democratic value consensus in Australian society has been steadily eroding, and by default, in order to maintain social cohesion, laws have proliferated spelling out in increasing detail what constitutes correct behaviour. But it is a fallacy to suppose that legal enforcements can ever supersede moral agreements as sustainers of the Common Good, for so much depends on voluntary endorsement of agreed common values, which no amount of behavioural compulsion can ever by itself ensure.

Ironically, this very state of affairs has opened a potential door for communal dialogue. Whereas, in recent memory, public discussion of shared values and visions was marginalised by an attenuated Liberal ideal of the right to live as you please, provided only that you didn't infringe the rights of other individuals to do the same, the current hiatus has provoked calls for more effective values education and the identification of publicly agreed 'values'—both procedural and teleological.

But in recent years Australia has seen a significant flight of many Christian parents and teachers from the public sector. The proportion of Christian schools to state schools has increased nationally from around one in four in the 1980s to one in three in 2010.[1] Meanwhile over the same period there has been a rising tide of concern in the state school sector about values education, resulting in several state departments conducting values audits of their curricula.[2] In addition, the Commonwealth Government has in the last decade allocated significant funding to a National Values Education Project resourcing pilot programs for the teaching of values in both public and private schools.

My own sometime involvement in the public debate and on government committees has obliged me to reflect constantly on the biblical-

1. 'Since 2000 the number of students in private schools has increased by 21% compared with an [*sic*] only 1% increase in students attending government schools. Since 2000 the proportion of students in private schools has increased to 34%, or more than 1 in 3, up 4% over this period.' (ABS statistics - 4221. 0 - *Schools, Australia*, 2010).

2. Summarised in Brian V Hill, 'An Education of Value: Towards a Value Framework for the School Curriculum', in *Report of the Review of the Queensland School Curriculum 1994: Shaping the Future* (Brisbane: Queensland Government, 1994), 233–276.

theological perspectives which should inform my participation, and this essay seeks to share some of this reflection.

Some Definitions

At the outset we must guard against pre-emptively equating the term 'education' with 'schooling' (in all its manifestations from 'preschool' to university and vocational training), meanwhile consigning other sites of learning to the periphery of our enquiry as comparatively incidental. Even Christians fall into this trap when, for example, they remit the primary responsibility for faith education to the 'Sunday school' or allow the 'home schooling' model to compromise their ways of relating interpersonally with their children.

Such relapses are incongruous, given that neither the terms 'school' and 'education', nor the schooling model as such, feature in the biblical record.[3] Rather, the text highlights other avenues of education such as informal parental dialogue, prophetic admonitions, mentoring relationships, and voluntary discipleship groups.[4]

One consequence of privileging the schooling model is that, if you believe you have discovered the truth, there is a strong temptation to use the powers of compulsion inherent in this model to indoctrinate rather than educate, thereby inhibiting the learner's ability to make truly personal and adequately informed life-choices, especially regarding the divine offer of reconciliation with God.

These observations suggest that discussion about education in Christian circles is bedevilled by competing sub-discourses. The present article

---

3. I have argued elsewhere, for example in Brian V Hill, *The Greening of Christian Education* (Sydney: Lancer Books, 1985), 22–25, 30–32 that the few instances where older translations employed the word 'school', have been clarified in later translations, given that the original Hebrew/Greek did not carry the connotations associated with that term today, and other teaching contexts were implied. As regards the concept of education, WE Andersen, in 'A Biblical View of Education' *Journal of Christian Education, Papers 77* (July 1983) 19 suggests that the closest equivalent might be the Greek *paideia,* sometimes translated 'edification', but its biblical application is specifically to the nurture of believers in the understanding of their faith—what I will here call 'Christian education. '
4. See also Alan G Harkness, 'Intergenerational Christian Education: an Imperative for Effective Education in Local Churches', *Journal of Christian Education*, Part 1, 41/2 (1998) 5–14; Part 2, 42/1 (1999) 37–50; and Sylvia Collinson, *Making Disciples: The Significance of Jesus' Educational Methods for Today's Church* (Carlisle: Paternoster, 2004).

is in part a prologemena to the substantive dialogue on these matters that needs to occur between Christians in different camps. Essential to such a dialogue will be a glossary which as far as possible avoids programmatic sub-text. Here is a beginning:

Theology refers to enquiries into (i) the reality and nature of God; and (ii) God's relation to the created order and particularly to human persons. It also requires (iii) evaluation of the sources of our beliefs in this domain. For Christian theology, the primary epistemological source and validator is biblical revelation.

Learning refers to those modifications of human perception and behaviour which result from (i) experiences which are initially subconscious, including cultural osmosis and conditioning; and (ii) conscious (cognitive and aesthetic) processing of our experience, skills practice, and the exercise of agency in the external world.

Education refers (i) descriptively, to interventions in the learning of persons by other persons such as parents, mentors, professional teachers, and public authorities; (ii) prescriptively, to such interventions as are deemed to be in the learner's best interests. **Miseducation** refers to interventions which are detrimental to the learner's best interests. **Self-education** identifies efforts by individuals to consciously take control of their own learning through such initiatives as book study, net browsing, travel, and voluntary dialogue with potential resource persons—particularly, in the present case, persons in the Christian faith community.

Christian education refers to (i) that part of a person's education which is particularly concerned with teaching beliefs and values derived from God's self-revelation, in the hope that students will sense what the Spirit of God is saying to them personally; and (ii) interpretation of other areas of learning in the light of the Christian worldview, in the hope that this will season the learner's witness in the wider world.

Evangelism in the Christian sense is the attempt, in the context of voluntary association, to persuade other people to consider the claims of God in Christ on their lives through both verbal testimony and quality of life.

Indoctrination refers to teaching interventions which pre-empt the right of maturing persons to choose what they shall believe and value, typically at the emotional level by the application of group pressure, and at the cognitive level by restricting access to information about opinions and worldviews which contest the belief system of the teacher or the school.

Formal education is the institutionalisation of learning through the employment of professional teachers, using planned curriculum processes which include assessment of success in facilitating learning.

Schooling is a particular mode of formal education, usually reliant on large group learning directed by professional teachers and administrators who are thereby in a position to exercise degrees of compulsion with respect to (i) student selection, attendance, and behaviour; and (ii) what is learnt, how it is assessed, and to whom it is reported.

Values are the priorities which individuals and societies attach to certain beliefs, objects and experiences when deciding how they shall live and what they shall treasure.[5]

Understanding the Human Learner

Since education deals with human persons, theology must clarify the nature of persons. The Bible teaches that human beings are an animal species into which God has breathed something of his own nature. Many have sought to identify the implications of being made not only in the form of an animal, but also in 'the image of God'.[6] It is generally agreed that this implies, at the least, a 'self'-consciousness which enables rational thought, moral responsibility, and creative agency in the external world. These are spiritual traits, and they have given rise to a unique historical deposit of ideas, social institutions and material artefacts.

While habitual behaviour may be modified by conditioning and motor-skill training, in humans as with other animals, an account of teaching which focusses primarily on such methods as these short-changes the human learner. But equally problematic is the privileging of rationality at the expense of other spiritual powers. Thus Kierkegaard objected, albeit with

5. Hill 'An Education of Value', 233–276.
6. Genesis 1: 26–27; 2: 7.

typical hyperbole, to Descartes' famous summation: 'I think, therefore I am', by substituting, in effect, 'I choose, therefore I am'.[7]

The power of spiritual agency invokes not only rationality but the domain of good and evil—a category opaque to scientific discourse and inapplicable to other animals.[8] This adds force to the unpopular biblical teaching that self-will is the seat of that rebellion against God which has contaminated the human story, a fact which must also be factored into any account of the scope and limits of education. Additionally, it suggests that the primary thrust of the notion of the *imago dei* is not the derivative spiritual traits just identified, but the relationship they enable us to have with God, if we so choose.

It is then the more to be regretted that, as a result of our alienation from God, all our spiritual functions have been impaired. This includes the power of reason, on which secular world-views place such hope. Without the spiritual power of reason, we would not be able to exercise spiritual agency, or even interpret the biblical revelation.[9] But where reason should have been the servant of relationships, it has become a tool in the hands of the alienated self. New Atheists laud the objectivity and neutrality of reason, while concealing the presuppositions, embraced by rebellious will, which for them determine its use. As Alasdair McGrath has pointed out:

> Instead of speaking of human 'rationality', we must speak of 'rationalities'. The Enlightenment turns out to be a rational multiverse, with competing and diverging accounts of the nature and scope of human reason . . . public reason is not neutral: it is shaped by a theory of the good.[10]

---

7. Kierkegaard cogently argues that Descartes' argument was circular, since *cogito* equals not 'thought' but 'I think', hence, he says, Descartes' dictum becomes 'I am thinking, *ergo* I am; but if I *am* thinking, what wonder that I *am*'. Søren Kierkegaard, *The Concept of Dread*, translated Walter Lowrie (London: Oxford University Press, 1946), 77–80. The gloss of Kierkegaard's position as 'I choose, therefore I am' was by George F Kneller, *Existentialism and Education* (New York: Philosophical Library, 1958, 67). Perhaps he would have done better at representing Kierkegaard's point with 'I am, therefore I choose'!
8. Try imputing promiscuity to a lion or eco-vandalism to a beaver damming a river. See also Romans 1: 18–20.
9. Which even so still requires the intervention of the Holy Spirit to mitigate our captivity to false reasoning and guide us into truth (John 14: 16–17).
10. In support of his contention, McGrath, in *Surprised by Meaning: Science, Faith, and How We Make Sense of Things* (Louisville, Kentucky: Westminster/John Knox Press,

Another key theological insight concerning the nature of persons is that the primacy of conscious relationship with God extends to our relationship with other persons, since they also are made in his image. The gospel is too often reduced to an individualistic focus on **my** relationship with God, with little concern for how this flows on to our communion with other beings and our stewardship of the created order. The writings of NT Wright[11] have done much to reclaim the 'big picture' narrative of Scripture, with regard to both the corruption of the Old Creation and the incursion of the New into the world's post-Easter history through the Spirit-engendered community of believers.

This puts a premium on the idea of 'learning together', which relies at least as much on relationships as reasoning. This is not to denigrate private study and meditation, as one attempts to re-cognise the world, and one's place in it, in the light of the salvation story. But it is to celebrate the fact that learning in community is a necessary complement to self-education, since so much of what we need to learn concerns relationships: with God, with fellow-believers, with those who still walk in darkness, and with the natural order.

What Knowledge is of Most Worth?

If this analysis of human personhood holds good, then, where education is concerned, what knowledge is of most worth? Herbert Spencer[12], a leading nineteenth century philosopher, sought to answer this precise question. Inspired by reading Darwin's *Origin of Species*, he embraced the ideas of naturalistic evolution, and coined the phrase 'survival of the fittest', equating it with ineluctable progress and the élitist views of the Eugenics lobby. Marrying these with his Utilitarian sympathies, he saw education as the acquisition of such knowledge as was conducive to the individual pursuit of happiness and posed the question: 'What knowledge is of most worth?' His emphatic answer was: 'Science!'

While Spencer may have thought that these conclusions were validated by neutral rationality and the scientific method, his judgments ultimately rested on underlying assumptions which predetermined how he would view the facts available. We understand this more clearly, a century and

---

2011), 105 cites Alasdair MacIntyre's *Whose Justice? Which Rationality?* and Michael Sandel's *Liberalism and the Limits of Justice.*

11. For example, Tom Wright, *Surprised by Hope* (London: SPCK 2007) part 3.
12. Herbert Spencer, *Educational Essays*, 1859, reprinted (London: Everyman, 1949).

a half later, as a result of many analyses demonstrating the philosophical circularity of his survival maxim and the inability of scientific method *per se* to validate ultimate beliefs and values. In particular, where human goals and moral responsibility are concerned, we all ultimately live by faith in our respective world-views. Though not provable, these may be judged more or less reasonable. Spencer's value judgments were not unreasonable—given his ideological starting point—but nor were they incontestable.

They certainly had a notable effect on what he thought an educational curriculum should look like. In commenting on each area of the curriculum, he began with studies relevant to 'self-preservation', gaining a livelihood, and rearing offspring, through to 'leisure tastes and feelings'. In every case, the pedagogic key was seen to be scientific method. Thus the 'science of life' grew out of biology and the 'science of society' out of economics. In regard to moral education, he considered the notion of an 'ideal humanity' illusory, and relied on the discipline of natural consequences to produce a self-governing individual. Cultural evolution would take care of the rest.

While we may be disposed to consign Spencer to the Victorian Age of Optimism, there are uncomfortable resonances with his thought in much modern educational theory and policy. In particular, Economic Rationalism's commitment to promoting endless growth through the free play of market forces is turning human beings into statistics, important only for their roles either in the production or the consumption of material goods. *Homo economicus* lives only to produce, consume, and reproduce. Marginson has observed that:

> The education system is expected to absorb youth unemployment and play a key role in the modernisation of the economy . . . The notion of education as being important for its own sake and a key to equality in society seems to have been set aside, and economics now dominates debate on education policy.[13]

Some Christian educators in Australia have been to the fore in the public arena in deploring these trends and arguing for a more magnanimous vision of the Common Good. Others have reacted strongly by focussing

13. Simon Marginson, *Education and Public Policy in Australia* (1993) cited at: <www.cambridge.org/aus/catalogue/catalogue.asp?isbn=9780521439633>

on the development of more Christian schools. But this has not meant that the latter have necessarily escaped the net of Economic Rationalism. This net has been strengthened by strong expectations in the older church schools that curricula will promote social mobility, and by the obligation of all schools to meet government benchmarks which prioritise the knowledge and skills considered most marketable in an industrial economy. In the circumstances, prioritising Christian values in either school sector is an uphill battle.

Some Attempts to Nominate Values

At this point, it is appropriate to ask: 'Where do our values come from?' The relevance of the question is underlined by the tendency in modern discussion to appeal to lists of values supposedly hanging somewhere in neutral space. I have discussed elsewhere[14] some of the lists which may be found on the web, underlying packaged approaches to values education. Many schools have fallen back on these in lieu of developing their own considered approaches.

The packages currently attracting the most attention in the state sector vary significantly in the values they list. One such is called *Living Values Education.* It lists twelve values and is now widely promoted by UNESCO. It did not take much detective work to establish that it has come from Brahma Kumaris, a Hindu society[15]. Another package, listing fifty-two values, is called *The Virtues Project.* It is being vigorously promoted by Relationships Australia. It took somewhat more detective work to establish that though *The Virtues Project* claims to be a secular approach, it actually comes from a Bahá'í source[16].

A third package, widely used in public schools in the USA, is *Tribes Learning Communities.* It was originally developed in California from a behavioural base of research in group psychology, and purports to be an impartial investment in 'character education.'

---

14. For example Brian Hill, 'Does It Matter How Schools Teach Values?' *Proceedings of Australian Christian Lobby National Conference* (Canberra, October 2005).<www.acl.org.au/pdfs/load_pdf_public.pdf?pdf_id=424&from=NATIONAL>
15. See <www.interfaithstudies.org/ethics/valueseducation.html>
16. See Popov, Linda Kavelin, *et al, The Family Virtues Guide* (Toronto: Penguin Canada, 1997). For a reliable investigative Christian critique, see <http://www.ccgm.org.au/articles/Articles/ARTICLE-0056.htm>

> It is the repeated practice of working with and connecting supportively to others that moves a young person from an isolated focus on 'me' to an altruistic concern for others and society . . . The list of character values so desperately needed now within young people are the human values of honorable and caring civilisations.[17]

A fourth example, recently endorsed by the New South Wales Government for use in public schools, is *Teaching Ethics in Schools*[18] which aims to nurture ethical discourse in the classroom, working from a primary commitment to the power of impartial rationality. In all these cases, a comparison of what they say about persons and values with our earlier theological observations shows that none of these approaches can be described as value-neutral. Discussion of implicit world-views is unavoidable, if it is education we are aiming at, and not indoctrination.

The awkward fact is that no values education approach is ideology-free. Even the National Values Education Project. The Federal Minister's Department promulgated nine core values derived from a survey of the sixty-nine schools involved in the 2002 pilot stage of the national project. At least these nine values were coming out of the Australian experience, and purported to reflect the values of our multicultural democracy. But they were philosophically random and did not take us far into the socio-political philosophy which supposedly underlay them, let alone implicit views of human personhood and community.

Sourcing values

From whence then do we source our values? Once again, though the words 'beliefs' and 'values' are often run together, our glossary needs for the sake of logical clarity to distinguish between them. Values, on the definition supplied earlier, are detected in actions which reveal the priorities we accord to certain beliefs above others. By their fruits you shall know

17. Gibbs, Jeanne (2007). 'Tribes TLC and Character Education: Internalizing Character Education Values By Living and Learning Within A Caring School Community.' Available at <www.tribes.com/about/ tribes-tlc-and-character-education>
18. Sue Knight, *NSW Ethics Course Trial: Final Report* (Sydney: NSW Department of Education and Training, 2010). Available at <www.det.new.edu.au/detresources/Ethics_Evaluation_Final_Report _11112010_HQssrhmwpK.pdf>

which beliefs really matter to the individual. Diagram 1[19] implies several different modalities in the process of moving from belief to acting in accordance with that belief. It has significant implications for teaching.

Acquiring a Belief

One is that the progression of modalities from understanding to action is not seamless. Personal choices come into play at each step. First, the teacher seeks to bring a truth claim in some domain of knowledge to the student's notice, aiming at understanding. Second, if the teacher is a true educator, the student is encouraged to weigh up the available evidence for and against this claim. The teacher's hope is that this will foster a disposition to base one's 'knowledge' on the beliefs which are most probably true.[20] But at this point, a person may be held back from

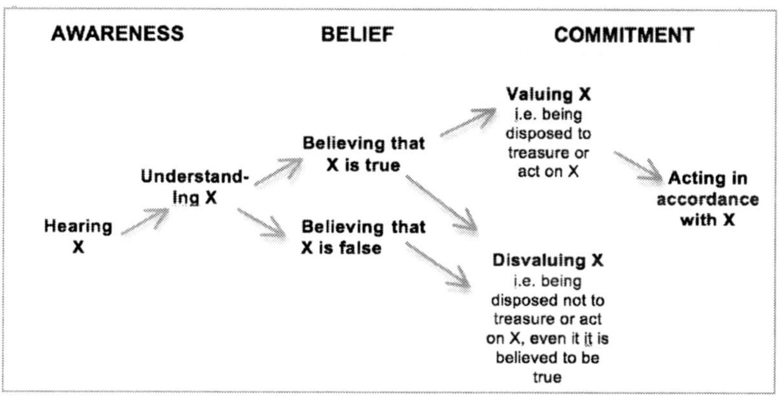

Diagram 1: From Hearing to Commitment

19. Brian V Hill, 'The Schooling of Ethics' *Educational Philosophy and Theory*, forthcoming.
20. This may sound pedantic, compared to the more familiar philosophical rubric defining knowledge as 'justified, true belief'. But in most domains of knowledge, particularly at the level of initial presuppositions, certain proof is unavailable in this world order. Even in science, as Thomas Kuhn showed, in *The Structure of Scientific Revolutions* (Chicago: University of Chicago Press, 1967), experiment is not random but proceeds from guesses (hypotheses) generated within a paradigm of enquiry based on certain assumptions about reality which prescribe what shall count as verification, but which are themselves therefore beyond this kind of verification. At a wider level, it is argued below that all constructive thought proceeds from what I call 'Reasonable Initial Bets' which underlie one's framework of rationality—in morality and religion as in science.

accepting the evidence by a prior commitment to a world-view which does not accommodate the possibility of the belief in question being true.

It can happen to a religious fundamentalist; it can also happen, as Kuhn demonstrated, to a research scientist. More often than not the response of scientists, when their basic model of explanation is challenged by an apparently discrepant fact, is to look for 'auxiliary hypotheses' as Lakatos has called them[21], that is, ways of explaining the apparent anomaly which are consistent with the core paradigm, thereby shielding it from refutation. The alternative is to accept that the paradigm (or world-view) to which you were previously wedded is not correct. What may then occur is an intellectual conversion. In the case of the classroom teacher, one can only hope that by encouraging students to examine critically the belief claims which are brought to their notice, we will enable them to purge their own evolving reality framework of serious discrepancies.

Embracing a Value

But knowing is not necessarily doing. There then comes the move from acquiring a belief to according it priority in deciding how to live and what to treasure. Logically speaking, it should follow that we would act on our beliefs. Are we not rational beings? But sometimes, though we might ordinarily be disposed to express our values in appropriate actions, we don't. And the reason for this might be that in this particular case we give higher priority to certain other beliefs.[22] But what Rationalists are reluctant to allow is that what may have happened is that an exercise of defiant will overrode our reason, and we made a choice that we knew was wrong or likely to cause harm—even to ourselves. In regard to moral choices, the Apostle Paul's description of the pathology in Romans 7 cannot be bettered.

This suggests that in the teaching of values we must not suppose that indoctrination, or even a supposedly impartial and rational 'community of discourse', will ensure that students embrace the values we are commending to them. In the first instance, to attempt to pre-empt their choices by trading on the school's capacity to compel or bias would be to encroach on

---

21. As he once rather overstated: 'no experimental result can ever kill a theory: any theory can be saved from counter-instances either by some auxiliary hypothesis or by a suitable reinterpretation of its terms' (I Lakatos, and A Musgrave, editors, *Criticism and the Growth of Knowledge: Proceedings of the International Colloquium in the Philosophy of Science* (Cambridge: Cambridge University Press, 1970), 4.
22. See Hill, 'The Schooling of Ethics' (2011).

their rights as God-breathed persons. In the second, to rely on the capacity of rationality to guarantee the acquisition of right values would be to ignore their fallen natures.

Our best hope lies in teaching for understanding, complemented by authentic personal modelling and participation in voluntary community life. The best example of the latter should be the form of life generated by Christian parents and faith communities. God forgive the church's frequent lapses at this point. In any event, the result will be out of our hands; ultimately, in God's hands.

The Study of World-Views

Noted earlier was the tendency to generate lists of values, resting on the apparently pragmatic claim that they seemed to be generally endorsed and the lists could therefore be regarded as impartial. But such lists vary in length and coherence. More importantly, they do not of themselves provide logical means of resolving conflict between the values. Those philosophers who defend the autonomy of ethics, or claim universality for Rationalist ethics, are at first glance more able to suggest guidelines for the resolution of moral dilemmas, but thanks to intractable human willfulness, the problem of motivation remains.

Again, then, we must go back to our theological analysis of personhood, noting particularly the spiritual traits which enable moral responsibility. These do not rely exclusively on stages of cognitive development, as postulated by Piaget.[23] From birth, a human being is, in Charles Taylor's words, 'an embodied agent, engaged with or at grips with the world'.[24] There is increasing evidence of this, such as the fact that, within days of being born, babies can register that other persons and objects are external to themselves, and they can recognise their primary carers.[25] Hence,

> The perceived reality each individual inhabits is unique and, from birth, constantly under construction. It is the source of

---

23. Jean Piaget, *The Moral Judgment of the Child*, translated by M Gabain (London: Routledge and Kegan Paul, 1968).
24. Charles Taylor, *Philosophical Arguments* (Cambridge, Mass: Harvard University Press,1995), 11.
25. See, for example, <www.sciencedaily.com/releases/2009/05/ 090506154245.htm> and <www.techeye.net/science/babies-brains-more-advanced-than-previously-thought>.

> personal meaning, identity, and purpose. And yes, elements of cultural tradition, encounters in the external world, and internal reflections all contribute to the development of one's perceived habitat or world-view.[26]

Clearly, though, as we mature and try to make sense of it all, we begin to make reasonable, albeit contestable, assumptions about what is behind it all. We develop a reality framework which becomes the conceptual habitat of our 'self'. Though it may be heavily indebted to borrowed ideas, it is a world-view unique to this individual. Though ultimate beliefs don't necessarily come into mind every time we make a choice, they are our ultimate court of appeal, and supply the motivation to value this over that.

The moral of this part of our story is that values education is a 'headless chook'[27] without there being somewhere in the curriculum an organised study of world-views, pitched at a level appropriate to the respective age levels of students, which enables them to interrogate their own cultural conditioning and confront the challenge of diverse reality frameworks competing to answer their questions of meaning, purpose, and redemption. Traditionally this was the office of 'religious education' so-called, but as with conceptions of Christian Education, definition of this area is in disarray.

Viewed in the past as the vehicle for the promotion of one world-view—the Christian—but even then cocooned in denominational subsets which reduced its perceived worth as an educational activity, RE has been marginalised almost to the point of extinction in the public curriculum. One of the ironies is that opponents coming from Secularist stables deny that religious studies have a place in the public curriculum, yet advocate approaches to values education which are clearly indebted to alternative, mostly Rationalist world-views.

In a recent book[28] I attempted to rehabilitate the area traditionally referred to as 'religious education', repositioning it in the larger across-the-curriculum project of values education, and requiring that it include the development of an understanding of some of the major world-views competing for our allegiance in today's society, along with facility in employing

26. Hill, 'The Schooling of Ethics'.
27. Brian V Hill, 'Is Values Education a Headless Chook?', in *Religious Education Journal of Australia* 22/2 (2006): 14–17.
28. Brian V Hill, *Exploring Religion in School: A National Priority* (Adelaide: OpenBook Publishers, 2004).

tools of critical analysis and self-examination. Given also the significant part played in the development of Australian democracy by the Christian heritage[29] I argued that to underplay this in the public curriculum, in the name of some mythical neutrality, would be to distort the social reality and its representation in many other areas of the school curriculum, from the Arts to the Sciences, and deprive students of the knowledge of how the Bible views human personhood and the path of redemption.

This is not a call for indoctrination, but education. And part of my project was to suggest that the argument for world-view studies of this kind was, for that reason, no less applicable to the Christian school. It has direct relevance to both the justification and motivation of values.

Assessment of Values Education

Finally, space permits only a brief mention of assessment in values education, on which I have written at length elsewhere.[30] The basic problem is ethical. What is it legitimate for us to attempt in the assessment of values education, having regard to the theological obligation to respect the individual's right and responsibility, before God, to choose what they will value?

We have noted that the student needs to acquire a knowledge base, relating to what values are, how we acquire them, and how the main world-views impacting on the student's community view them. There is also a need to develop the student's skills of critical analysis and evaluation of values, and of the truth-claims (beliefs) by which people seek to justify them. Equally, we need to provide settings in which students can develop greater empathetic understanding[31] of why other persons embrace the

---

29. See Stuart Piggin, *Spirit of a Nation: The Story of Australia's Christian Heritage* (Sydney: Strand Publications, 2004); and Kevin Rudd, 'Christianity, the Australian Labor Party and Current Challenges in Australian Politics', paper delivered at the first National Forum of the Australian Christian Heritage Forum, Canberra. Go to: <http://www.achf.com.au/resources/papers.html > - and follow the links.

30. For example, Brian V Hill, (1989) 'Is Assessment Compatible With Agape?', in *Journal of Christian Education, Papers 96*, (December 1989), 5–21; and Brian V Hill, 'Evaluation and Assessment: The Tail That Wags the Dog?' in *An Agenda for Educational Change*, edited by Trevor Cooling and John Short (Leicester: Apollos, 1997), 132–147.

31. Yet another glossary problem. 'Empathy' and 'sympathy' are frequently confused with each other. Literally, 'empathy' means 'feeling into'—a capacity to interpret the feel-

values they do. Typically, this is facilitated by learning in groups and being involved in community service. Ultimately, success will be gauged by the extent to which students choose to live by values which their mentors deem to be healthy and worthy.

So how many of these learning tasks and teacher expectations may we formally assess and report on? The brief answer is that we may test capacities, but not commitments. We may hope for ultimate success in the sense just mentioned, but when operating within the schooling paradigm we may not make a student's pass or fail mark depend on whether they have decided to embrace the values of teacher or school. As a case in point, would a religious school be entitled to fail a student who passed all its formal exams but rejected the value system it stood for? No. While social control may be exercised over behaviour at school, personal commitment is beyond the school's jurisdiction. Would writing a character reference about that student then be also out of bounds? No, provided the student had requested it confidentially, and retained discretion as to where or when to use it.

Conclusion

I have tried to fashion a discourse that could minimise situations where Christians of differing persuasions talk past each other when discussing values education. Drawing on a theological perspective, I have also sought to develop a rationale for values education that would be serviceable in curriculum theorising in both Christian and state schooling. But I have also termed this essay a prologemena, because I am not aware that much effort has been made to cross this divide[32] let alone to speak with power in the public domain, where God has bidden us to bear witness to Kingdom values. May there be others who are willing to take this discourse further.

---

ings of another, whereas 'sympathy' means 'feeling with'—a commitment or supportive attitude towards the other. I commend this usage for clarificatory purposes.

32. Hill, Brian V 'Bridging the Divides: A Christian Brief for Values Education in Schools', in *Journal of Religious Education*, 51/3 (2003): 34–43.

Interface Vol 15 1&2/2012

Biblical Ethical Principle and Its Critics

Clive Beed and Cara Beed

Honorary Fellows, Australian Catholic University and
Centre for Applied Christian Ethics, Ridley Theological College
University of Melbourne.

Introduction

This paper has three aims. One is to demonstrate how contemporary Christians have deduced normative ethical principles from the Bible to apply to social and economic issues (as practiced by such as Hay, and Tiemstra *et al*).[1] An overview of the principle approach in general is presented in this section, and then a recent instance of its application to a socio-economic issue is canvassed. This review leads into a second more encompassing objective that in Section 2 is to evaluate criticism that has been directed to the principle approach as such. If this methodology is found to be defective, it cannot reliably be related to any issue, socio-economic or otherwise. Four recent critics of the principle approach to biblical ethics are assessed, but their criticism is found not to be compelling. The third aim, explored in section 3, is to argue that the principle formula has been relatively neglected in the areas of evangelical theology and theological ethics, in which it should form a constituent element. This assertion is demonstrated only for socio-economic matters.

The underlying rationale for the principle approach applied to any area of human existence is that the Bible's 'message is relevant for later genera-

1. Donald Hay, *Economics Today: A Christian Critique* (Leicester: Apollos, 1989); John Tiemstra, Fred Graham, George Monsma, Carl Sinke, and Alan Storkey, *Reforming Economics* (Lewiston: Edwin Mellen, 1990).

tions, not just its original readers'.[2] However, it does not involve trying to reduce this message or normative teaching to rules and commands; no implication arises that everything in the Bible can be reduced to principles. Indeed, derivers/users of principles have to be on guard that they do not come to love the principles more than the Bible itself.[3] Rather, the methodology conforms to Marshall's proposal that '*we must inquire into the underlying theological and ethical principles*' expressed in a biblical exhortation. The next step in Marshall's exercise is 'to work out how to translate those principles into appropriate exhortations for today'. Marshall has promoted this proposal into the present, seeing 'Scripture as instantiating general principles of universal validity by expressing them in specific ways that may be tied to particular situations or cultural expressions'.[4] What is sought are normative principles, postulates, guidelines, norms, precepts, intentions, trajectories, bases for action, themes and paradigms that underlie a biblical text and that are then reflected in the Bible as a whole. For the purpose of the principle approach, each of the aforesaid terms is regarded as expressing or implying the same idea, sufficiently similar in meaning to be used interchangeably.

According to Klein *et al*, 'recent evangelical analysis has come to a consensus that the key to legitimate application involves what many writers call "principalising"', the 'attempt to discover in a narrative [that is, a text] the spiritual, moral, or theological principles that have relevance for the contemporary believer'.[5] Advocated by such as Kaiser Jr and Silva, and Virkler and Ayayo, the search for theological principle continues to be an orthodox mode of biblical interpretation.[6] It has been supported from Goldingay to Duvall and Hays who express it that 'many texts in the Bible are specific, concrete, revelatory expressions of broader, universal realities or theological principles', where the principle is 'applicable to all of God's

2. William Klein, Craig Blomberg, and Robert Hubbard Jr, *Introduction to Biblical Interpretation* (Nashville: Thomas Nelson, 2004), 478.
3. David Clark, *To Know and Love God* (Wheaton: Crossway Books, 2003), 96.
4. I Howard Marshall, 'Using the Bible in Ethics', in *Essays in Evangelical Social Ethics*, edited by David Wright (Exeter: The Paternoster Press, 1978), 39–55, at 50; original emphasis; Marshall, *Beyond the Bible: Moving from Scripture to Theology* (Grand Rapids: Baker Academic, 2004), 34.
5. Klein *et al*, *Introduction to Biblical Interpretation*, 483.
6. Walter Kaiser Jr and Moises Silva, *Introduction to Biblical Hermeneutics* Rev. ed. (Grand Rapids: Zondervan, 2007), 92, 325; Henry Virkler and Karelynne Ayayo, *Hermeneutics: Principles and Processes of Biblical Interpretation* (Grand Rapids: Baker Academic, 2007), 194–209.

people at all times'.[7] 'Principle' in the formulation here means a fundamental truth or primary normative element traversing the biblical text, from which a code of right conduct can be determined. This exercise can legitimately be regarded as part of theological ethics that, according to Geisler, is concerned with what is right and wrong on the basis of scriptural understanding.[8] 'Right' may be understood as conforming to God's nature and to His will expressed in scripture, and is to be prescriptive.

Practitioners of the principle methodology do not suppose it to be hermeneutically straightforward. Klein *et al*, and Virkler and Ayayo outline issues in its application, and one of its socio-economic exponents, Hay, discusses problems involved, such that it is too simplistic and naive.[9] Only brief treatment can be given here. For instance, although trans-contextual and trans-historical principles are sought, this does not mean that their derivation is made acontextually or ahistorically. Nevertheless, principles derived from one context are still applicable to others. The underlying purpose is that historical studies of the Bible should be related 'to contemporary needs' for an 'important aspect of the historicity of Scripture [is] its ability to speak to people of different times and places, and to relate to their particular situation'.[10] Hermeneutical issues, some of which may never be resolved, are held not to defeat this enterprise, for if it were so, every part of the Bible would be condemned to the same judgement. No meaning of any part of the Bible could be extracted to relate to modern life. This view contradicts a usual understanding of Judeo-Christian faith and thought. Nevertheless, since the principle methodology relies on interpreting the biblical text, hermeneutical difficulties remain. Even so distinguished an analyst of biblical hermeneutics, as Thiselton, shows there is no one, definitive answer to the question of how hermeneutics should be practiced.[11]

---

7. John Goldingay, *Models for Interpretation of Scripture* (Grand Rapids: Eerdmans, 1995); J Scott Duvall and J Daniel Hays, *Grasping God's Word*, second edition (Grand Rapids: Zondervan, 2005), 21.
8. Norman Geisler, *Christian Ethics*, second edition (Grand Rapids: Baker Academic, 2010), 15.
9. Klein *et al*, *Introduction to Biblical Interpretation*, 477–503; Virkler and Ayayo, *Hermeneutics*, 194–209; Donald Hay, *Economics Today: A Christian Critique* (Leicester: Apollos, 1989), 309–313.
10. Gerald Bray, *Biblical Interpretation Past and Present* (Downers Grove: InterVarsity Press, 1996), 586.
11. Anthony Thiselton, *Hermeneutics: An Introduction* (Grand Rapids: Eerdmans, 2009).

Further, even if principles can be deduced, no direct relation occurs between scripture and contemporary socio-economic life. Therefore, an additional interpretative problem is to work out how the principles might relate to modern life. This is in light of the widely accepted Christian view that God's self-revelation in the Bible is meant not only to be read and studied, but also applied to the world. The two stages of the deriving and of the relating the principles to contexts other than those in which they were formulated assumes that scripture is the timeless word of God, that 'God has revealed himself and his purposes in a written text'.[12] While the Bible and its underlying normative principles are meant to speak to different cultures, the task for the peoples of those cultures is to ascertain what those principles mean in their particular context, and how they might be applied.

An example is outlined below of how principalising has been used to derive socio-economic ethics. The principle in question is the assertion that normative biblical teaching advocates greater equality than existed in biblical times, and than exists today, even though the term, 'equality' is not mentioned in the Bible. Equality is a multi-dimensional term, applying to relations between the sexes, to forms of hierarchy within organisations, and to distributions of wealth and income. Two evangelical theologians who have pursued these issues are Forrester (2001) and Bauckham (2002). Focusing on hierarchical dimensions of equality, Bauckham argued that 'the overall direction of biblical thought . . . is egalitarian', that 'running through biblical traditions is a strongly egalitarian *direction* of thought'. Similarly, Forrester maintained that 'the Judaeo-Christian tradition . . . is the major . . . source of the modern worldwide emphasis on equality', that 'the Bible suggests that equality is the original, the final, and the proper condition for human beings'.[13] Both Forrester and Bauckham systematically progress through the Bible, considering the meaning of relevant texts as they occur. Each author explains the pertinent texts, and the case is developed throughout scripture that the texts possess an internal consistency to accumulate and support each other toward a normative egalitarian orientation. Their approach is like lawyers building up evidence to support a case. Neither author employs a hard and fast definition of equality, for none exists, but normative principles relating to equality emerge

12. Bray, *Biblical Interpretation*, 14.
13. Richard Bauckham, *God and the Crisis of Freedom* (Louisville: Westminster John Knox, 2002), 118; original emphasis; Duncan Forrester, *On Human Worth: A Christian Vindication of Equality* (London: SCM, 2001), 79, 82.

from their analysis, such as disfavour of hierarchical relationships and structures. Various practical proposals emerge from their analysis, such as 'the church is to be understood as showing in its life, fellowship and worship an egalitarian alternative to the "way of the world".' This is in line with Hauerwas' ideas, quoted approvingly by Forrester, that 'the task of the church [is] to pioneer those institutions and practices that the wider society has not learned as forms of justice'.[14]

Further inferences can be drawn from this mode of biblical analysis to the contemporary world. For example, in premonarchical Israel the economic unit was the extended family household, and measures were in place in the Mosaic Law to ensure relatively egalitarian distributions of wealth between these families. Today, the economic unit can be extended from the family to the firm, but there is no reason to suppose that the principles underlying the Mosaic Law have been superseded, given Jesus' advocacy and interpretation of their essence. Bauckham argues that that 'since power and privilege come from the accumulation of wealth, real equality must have an economic base'.[15] Therefore, a challenge for contemporary Christians is to encourage forms of economic units (firms) that have low degrees of hierarchical control within them, and that through their productive activities generate relatively egalitarian distributions of wealth and income for their workforces and for society as a whole. Worker cooperatives, self-employment and partnerships are more likely to achieve these ends than joint stock companies. It might seem a big leap from the Mosaic Law principles, and from Jesus' interpretation of them, to reach these conclusions for the modern world. But if Bauckham and Forrester are correct than an egalitarian trajectory or principle runs throughout the Bible, a legitimate hermeneutical deduction trends in the directions above.

A helpful supplementary test of the veracity of normative egalitarianism in the Bible is the extent to which it is supported by theologians who arrive at their conclusions via other routes than explicitly searching for biblical principles. That this occurs lends confidence to the nomination of egalitarian conclusions. Thus, Hicks expounds characteristics of 'the Christian ethical commitment to equality and solidarity' from examining the work of Richard Niebuhr and Gustavo Gutierrez.[16] Aspects of the egalitarian biblical orientation have been maintained by such as Grasssi who

14. Forrester, *On Human Worth*, 105, 211.
15. Bauckham, *God and the Crisis*, 120.
16. Douglas Hicks, *Inequality and Christian Ethics* (Cambridge: Cambridge University Press, 2000), 232.

argued that land 'was meant to be equally distributed' in the Old Testament, while '*equal sharing*' in the New Testament is to be given a practical dimension.[17] Theologians, such as Berman (2008), Wright (2004), Hoppe (2004), Mott and Sider (1999, 27), Pilgrim (1981), and Gottwald (1979) stress what they see as the normative egalitarian bias in the Old and New Testaments. The egalitarian theme is also accepted by other theologians, although not discussing it directly. Thus, Bray suggests that the egalitarian inference contained in the Mosaic Law 'may be more difficult to counter'.[18] That this normative egalitarian tendency is rejected by theological ethicists, such as Hays,[19] underlines that the principle approach is not yet held in high favour.

Criticism of the Principle Approach to Formulating Biblical Ethics

The principle approach has been criticised on diverse grounds. It was assessed by Hays[20] in his influential treatment of New Testament ethics, concluding that discerning principles does not have pride of place in constructing biblical ethics. Hays asserted that theologians may appeal to scripture as a source of four constructs in formulating New Testament ethics—rules, principles, paradigms, and symbolic worlds. All these are held to play a part in deriving New Testament ethics. Principles are to be given no privileged place in this construction. The argument below is that the four categories all resolve to principles as defined in section 1, so that it is the principles that are of prime importance. The implication in Hays that these four derivations are distinct from each other is not tenable. Hays' use of the 'principle' term is analogous, but not identical, with that adopted in this paper—a principle is a guide to requirements for right

17. Joseph Grassi, *Informing the Future: Social Justice in the New Testament* (New York: Paulist Press, 2003), 1, 207; original empasis.
18. Joshua Berman, *Created Equal* (Oxford: Oxford University Press, 2008); Christopher Wright, *Old Testament Ethics for the People of God* (Leicester: Inter Varsity Press, 2004); Leslie Hoppe, *There Shall Be No Poor Among You* (Nashville: Abingdon, 2004); Stephen Mott and Ronald Sider, 'Economic Justice: A Biblical Paradigm', in *Toward a Just and Caring Society*, edited by D Gushee (Grand Rapids: Baker, 1999), 15–45; Walter Pilgrim, *Good News to the Poor* (Minneaplois: Augsburg Publishing House, 1981); Norman Gottwald, *The Tribes of Yahweh* (London: SCM, 1979); Bray, *Biblical Interpretation*, 516.
19. Richard Hays, *The Moral Vision of the New Testament* (San Francisco: Harper, 1996), 467.
20. Hays, *The Moral Vision*, 209.

conduct. For Hays, principles are 'general frameworks of moral considerations by which particular decisions about action are to be governed'. It is unusual for a principle to be identified as a framework. In line with usual meaning of the term, we use principle not in the sense of a framework, but as a fundamental truth or primary normative element traversing the biblical text, from which a code of right conduct can be determined.

Hays distinguishes his conception of principles from rules that are 'direct commandments or prohibitions of specific behaviors'. However, direct commandments fit into the process of constructing principles, both in terms of Hays' definitions and ours. Thus, Jesus' prohibition of divorce (a 'rule') is better understood as contributing to a principle or guide for the requirement of right conduct in marriage. Indeed, trying to interpret a text in itself may not yield a clear principle. Instead, normative principles can be discerned via identification of commandments or prohibitions from different texts (together with Jesus' other teachings) that accumulate to become a principle for behaviour. Undertaking this type of search is important, for Jesus did not emphasise the articulation of explicit principles. They are revealed in His parables, stories, commands, conversation and behavior.

Paradigm is used in this paper as a set of interrelated principles constituting a pattern and coherent whole, intended to guide moral behavior. An example might be the socio-economic provisions of the Mosaic Law that, if followed, would have assisted in the formation of a particular type of pre-monarchical Israelite society. Paradigm in this manner is the 'unified picture' notion mentioned above, seeking to relate to given questions of conduct. Hays uses paradigms in a different and more restricted way, as 'stories or summary accounts of characters who model exemplary conduct' (or reprehensible conduct). Jesus' parable of the Good Samaritan is cited as an example of this meaning of paradigm. However, once again, inferences to principles can be drawn from the parable, and exegetes usually interpret it this way. Thus, to Lucie-Smith the story 'is about the universal nature of the call to be a good neighbour to strangers' with no upper limit—a trans-cultural moral value. Similarly, Bock holds the normative essence of the parable to be that 'all people . . . are to be loved and treated fairly.'[21] The inferential principles contained within the parable are those Jesus what getting at, the parable being a hard-hitting, exciting

21. Alexander Lucie-Smith, *Narrative Theology and Moral Theology* (Aldershot: Ashgate Publishing, 2007), 206; Darrell Bock, *Baker Exegetical Commentary on the New Testament: Luke 9:51–24:53* (Grand Rapids: Baker Books, 1996), 1028–1029.

story designed to challenge hearers to search their minds for its underlying meaning. With this interpretation, Hays' notion of paradigm is made up of underlying normative principles.

Finally, Hay's fourth category is 'a symbolic world that creates perceptual categories through which we interpret reality'.[22] Symbolic worlds are listed because they provide a context in which moral considerations may be determined. How relevant is this to Hays' three other forms of normative appeal in scripture? Two objections may be offered against symbolic worlds being on a par with Hays' three previous items. Symbolic worlds are taken to offer 'perceptual categories through which we interpret reality,' they provide 'a context for moral discernment.' However we seek moral discernment, reality has to be interpreted. Symbolic world is just an abbreviated term stressing that we have interpreted reality (rules, principles, paradigms) in some contextual manner. Symbolic worlds do not serve as an independent variable by which we make moral judgments. They cannot be placed on an equal footing with rules etc.

A second objection is that Hays offers two illustrations of the operation of symbolic worlds, in which, supposedly, no moral directives or principles are proposed. If this were the case, it substantiates the first objection above; symbolic worlds only provide a context in which moral choices can be exercised. However, the texts cited turn out not to be of this nature. One text is Romans 1:19–32. These texts are taken to offer 'a diagnosis of the fallen *human condition* without explicitly articulating any moral directives'. It is arguable that Paul's moral directives are revealed in his implicit comparison between the ways people do behave and the ways they should behave. Thus, Bowen *et al* hold verses 20 and 21 to mean that 'people should . . . honour and serve the Supreme God as he deserves', echoed by Keener that people need to recognise God's power and character, His benevolence in providing creation, and worship Him as such.[23] Even a 'plain sense' reading of the texts suggests that Paul's whole tenor is normative. He is more than merely describing the sinful human state. He is pretty clearly condemning those who do not honor God, the converse of which might be viewed as a normative principle. Hays' idea that Paul's exhortation offers no more than a diagnosis of the fallen human condition is not plausible.

22. Hays, *The Moral Vision*, 209.

23. Roger Bowen, Samuel Escobar, and Sang-Ehil Han, *A Guide to Romans*, third edition (London: SPCK, 2009), 23; Craig Keener, *New Covenant Commentary Series: Romans* (Eugene, OR: Cascade Books, 2009), 32.

The second illustration of symbolic worlds is held to be Jesus' teaching at Matthew 5: 43–48. The emphasis in these texts is taken to proffer a characterisation of God who makes His sun rise on the evil and the good. No moral directives supposedly occur in these texts. Again, most exegetes do not interpret these texts as stopping short at illustrating God's common grace or His general revelation. For example, Keener argues that 'Jesus' teaching here develops a principle already present in the law: one should not allow personal animosity to prevent acts of kindness or justice'.[24] Again, a 'plain sense' reading suggests that Jesus enumerates the normative principles of loving enemies and praying for those who persecute you, and of being perfect as your heavenly Father is perfect. Much more than a mere description of a symbolic world is offered in these verses.

It is rare for Jesus to offer description without warrant. Equally, one can recognise that all Jesus' teaching occurs in the context of symbolic worlds that serve as contexts for His moral discernment. It can be agreed with Hays that symbolic worlds create 'the perceptual categories through which we interpret reality'. But so does every framework or worldview through which we apprehend reality. Whatever the interpretation of reality, Jesus' teaching involves revealing moral principles. No argument need be made that discourse within the New Testament can be interpreted via Hays' four categories (although we have argued that symbolic world is not on a par with the three previous items). What is at stake is whether the four modes are separate from each other, or whether they can be reduced to searching for underlying normative principles, as has been argued above. The hermeneutical task is to extract such ethical norms from the various 'modes of Scripture's speech.'[25]

Another critic recognises that 'a common approach to ethics is to seek the basic moral principles that lie behind all the rules, laws and instructions of the Bible'. But Adeney raises the question, 'are biblical principles the heart of Christian ethics?', and answers that 'they should not be elevated to become the central source' of ethics. Part of the reason for this conclusion is that Adeney has a conception of principles as 'abstractions that live primarily in the world of thought and words'.[26] He equates them with the broadest of generalities, such as that Christians should practice justice,

---

24. Craig Keener, *A Commentary on the Gospel of Matthew* (Grand Rapids: Eerdmans, 1999), 202.
25. Hays, *The Moral Vision*, 209.
26. Bernard Adeney, *Strange Virtues: Ethics in a Multicultural World* (Leicester: Apollos,1995), 92, 88, 93.

mercy and faith. At this level of generality, the door is left wide open for their diverse interpretation, even for sorting them into hierarchies. This need not be the case, for the more precisely principles are defined, the less likely is ambiguity.

Practitioners of the principle methodology specify their principles as finely as they are able, and relate them to concrete situations in which some trade-offs in their application may be required. In the socio-economic context, for example, Hay specifies a biblical principle to be that 'in his work man should have access to resources and control over them'.[27] He demonstrates that particular types of work organisation (such as cooperatives) attain this principle more than others (such as the joint stock company). Therefore, principles need not remain at the level of abstractions. Contra Adeney, the specificity of principles is sought by relating them to 'cultural reality', for it is certainly true that 'the real meaning of a principle can be understood only as it touches reality'.[28] Nor is there any question that principles somehow can usurp the message of the Bible. God and Jesus reveal what they want for humankind through a rich variety of means in the Bible. The parables, for instance, are gripping stories intended to convey certain messages to people. Each parable is far richer than any principle that can be derived from it. But if the messages of the parable are to be related to other situations, the essence, meaning and principles embodied in the parable have to be extracted. A story cannot be related to another situation, but its message or didactic principles can.

Another line of criticism is that the principle approach is not helpful for formulating applicable biblical ethics. Adeney, for example, argued that far more than acting from a set of beliefs or principles, 'people usually act in relation to their interpretation of the way the world really is'.[29] This is to overlook the purpose of normative biblical teaching to provide a set of beliefs (or principles) that might be pitted against how 'the world really is'. The beliefs both serve as the filter through which the world may be interpreted, and as the ideal to which God calls the believer to pursue in the fallen state of reality. Interpreting 'the way the world really is' presupposes some set of beliefs by which this might be done, and the biblical worldview aims to provide just these. Indeed, Adeney concedes this position,

27. Hay, *Economics Today*, 74.
28. Adeney, *Strange Virtues*, 93.
29. Adeney, *Strange Virtues*, 86.

that Christians must 'see the world from the perspective of God's work in history'[30]

Contrary to Adeney, it may not be unreasonable to regard the biblical prohibition of theft as a 'timeless ethical principle that we must translate into different cultural idioms'. At the same time, such a translation can acknowledge that 'the meaning of theft may differ from culture to culture with varying definitions of property rights'. To say that Christians today are 'bound to follow the *meaning* of the [Old Testament] law', implies that underlying that meaning are principles expressing God's timeless truths. As Adeney points out, these are far more profound than merely obeying the letter of the law, and Jesus gives such an example in Matthew 5: 27–28. Adeney cannot escape his understanding of rules as basic to biblical conviction, and therefore, analogous to how principle is used in this paper. Thus, from the Mosaic Law are sought, 'concrete applicable rules that are as relevant today as when they were first given by God.' Indeed, he concedes that 'principles are tools to help us reincarnate moral practices from one context to another'.[31]

A further concern for critics of the principle approach is the 'question of how one derives the principle', 'which principles or themes should be adopted, and how we derive them from the text.' The hermeneutical problem raised is that evangelical ethics in the past has interpreted 'Jesus' words . . . in a naïve or uncritical manner'.[32] Burridge gives no examples of an author interpreting Jesus' words like this, although certain books as a whole are criticised for so doing. It can scarcely be claimed that the ways in which Forrester and Bauckham interpret scripture are 'naïve or uncritical'. Nevertheless, this type of criticism persists. Consider Burridge again, who gives an example from the South African church where 'the same method of looking for a principle applied to the same text produced two contrasting principles'.[33] What Burridge does not explain, however, is how exegetes interpreted the text in question. Instead, he confines his attention to conclusions drawn by one theologian, and by one institutional church. But the nature of the exegesis by either party is not stated. We have no way of knowing from Burridge whether either interpretation was simplistic or naïve.

30. Adeney, *Strange Virtues*, 95.
31. Adeney, *Strange Virtues*, 92, 94.
32. Richard Burridge, *Imitating Jesus: An Inclusive Approach to New Testament Ethics* (Grand Rapids: Eerdmans, 2007), 369, 11.
33. Burridge, *Imitating Jesus*, 371.

A final sympathetic evangelical critic of principalising is Clark who worries about the difficulty of drawing principles from individual texts, for which he gives two examples. However, as the cases of Forrester and Bauckham showed, this is not how principalising should be done. The issue is to examine every text in which the given principle seems to arise, and then to establish a trajectory underlying normative biblical teaching as a whole. Clark is also worried about the misuse of principalising, that it can lead to valuing principles more than the Bible. However, the two are not to be regarded separately, each is dependent on the other. Abstract propositions have no meaning unless they are related to the biblical text. Clark is not totally negative toward principalising for he believes that 'drawing out principles from the total teachings of scripture is one of the important tasks of theology'.[34] He is concerned that it should be done with principles taking account of the culturally-nuanced environment in which the biblical text was formulated. Derivers/users of biblical principles usually acknowledge this requirement.

The Principle Methodology, Theology, and Theological Ethics

The argument of this section is that the principle formula is a legitimate component of evangelical theology, given its compass of theology, and of theological ethics, but has been relatively neglected in both areas. This contention is demonstrated only for the case of socio-economic ethics. It is argued below that theological ethics is deficient in how it derives and applies its ethics to socio-economic matters. The principle approach seeks to overcome this problem. The principle method can be regarded as having affinities with other forms of theological analysis, such as Catholic Social Thought (CST), usually regarded as an orthodox sub-set of the theological enterprise. CST also seeks to pose normative principles applicable to contemporary socio-economic life. Thus, the president of the Pontifical Academy of Social Sciences holds that 'the Gospel and the social doctrine of the Roman Catholic church . . . contain those essential principles . . . which no economy, if it wants to be a good economy, can forget.'[35] 'Official' CST principles show a fair degree of overlap with the Protestant principle approaches and outcomes.

---

34. David Clark, *To Know and Love God* (Wheaton: Crossway Books, 2003), 92, 93, 94.
35. Marcelo Sorondo, 'For a Catholic Vision of the Economy', in *Journal of Markets and Morality* 6/1 (2003), 7–31.

Another affinity is with liberation theology, particularly with how it performs its analysis. For instance, its 'concept of salvation' is 'closely linked with the socioeconomic situation of the region' in which it was formulated and applied. The normative principle or concept of salvation is interpreted from the biblical text, and then applied to contemporary life. Both the principle technique, liberation theology and CST emphasise the social applicability of their approaches, offering 'models for transformative action'. They seek changes in socio-structures to accord more with their given principles.[36]

Arguing that the principle approach constitutes a legitimate component of theology depends on what is meant by theology. Extant definitions cover a wide compass, no uniform definition is proposed, definitions are debated. Consider, for example, how theology is viewed in survey texts by two evangelical theologians. Starting with an historical interpretation of the meaning of theology, Clement of Alexandria in the second century is cited approvingly by McGrath that theology referred to 'Christian truth claims about God'. However, these claims need to be attested to by scripture, and a second barrier arises in that 'Christian theology is obliged to wrestle with the [biblical] text which transmits knowledge' of God and Christ. Accordingly, 'Christian theology is intimately linked with the science of biblical criticism and interpretation'.[37] Indeed, explicitly evangelical 'theology must be nourished and governed at all points by Holy Scripture'. If biblical theology is an effort to bring 'together the basic ideas of Scripture into an orderly presentation', the principle method comports with this orientation.[38] Another widely-used evangelical theology text maintains the same dependence of theology on scripture. Erickson defines theology as the discipline 'that seeks to understand the God in the Bible and to provide a Christian understanding of reality', it aims 'to give a coherent statement of the doctrines of the Christian faith, based primarily on the Scriptures'.[39] Both McGrath's and Erickson's definitions of theology fit with the principle methodology that seeks to understand God's dealings with humanity, and to determine from scripture how His dealings are

36. Alister McGrath, *Christian Theology: An Introduction,* fourth edition (Malden, MA: Blackwell Publishing, 2007), 108, 109.
37. McGrath, *Christian Theology*, 103, 106.
38. Alister McGrath, *Scientific Theology Volume 1: Nature* (Edinburgh: T&T Clark, 2001), xix; McGrath, *Christian Theology*, 51.
39. Millard Erickson, *Christian Theology,* second edition (Grand Rapids: Baker Books, 1998), 17, 23.

meant to apply both in the times the biblical texts were formulated and in the contemporary world.

Even if the principle method were to be regarded as a legitimate component of evangelical theology, a further problem arises. Neither McGrath nor Erickson, for instance, progress from their analyses to assess how theological truth-claims might apply to contemporary social life. This tendency prevails in most theological books and journals. Erickson, for instance, has a chapter on the social dimension of sin, but gives little empirical detail how social sin might be recognised in the contemporary world, provides few instances of its occurrence, or how it should be tackled. Thus, users of the principle approach face a hiatus on two counts. One, they can gain little guidance from theology as to whether normative biblical socio-economic principles actually exist. Two, therefore, theology does not allow them to show how its truth-claims or principles might apply in the socio-economic world of biblical times or today. The problem may be more severe than this, for 'more recently, theology has become increasingly dissociated from the Bible and has looked for its systematic principle within a philosophical framework'.[40] If this is the case, it underlines why discernment of allegedly biblically-based principles is not emphasised in theology. Thus, one complaint is that the normative theme of egalitarianism in the Bible 'has suffered quite extraordinary neglect at the hands of theologians'.[41] Even for evangelical theology, a general complaint is that 'few evangelical scholars have focused on' the topic of scriptural application.[42]

These gaps discussed above are claimed also to be reflected in evangelical theological ethics. Allegedly, this has not shown how it applies to real life, that 'there is still little in them about what actual content New Testament ethics might bring to today's moral issues'. In Burridge's view, 'it is only more recently that a few [evangelical] scholars . . . have really attempted to bridge the gap between the New Testament ethical material and the multiple nature of moral issues today'. Even for New Testament ethics as a whole, 'any attempt to relate it to today… [has] little by way of actual content or application'.[43] Illustrations of this tendency are *The Blackwell Companion to Religious Ethics* (2008) that has no author among its sixty discussing how any tendency in religious ethics might relate to

40. Bray, *Biblical Interpretation*, 42.
41. Forrester, *On Human Worth*, 80.
42. Klein *et al*, *Introduction to Biblical Interpretation*, 479.
43. Burridge, *Imitating Jesus*, 12, 16, 31.

contemporary life. *The Blackwell Companion to Christian Ethics* (2004) has slightly more relation to today,[44] but still falls within Burridge's complaint that none of its thirty-six contributors demonstrate in any depth how their specific ethical issue proceeds from scriptural warrant. Looking at the subject of moral theology does not fill in the gaps, for this is characterised by a similar weak relation to scripture and to deriving norms that might be related to contemporary life. Just one case is Mattison III who proposed that his 'text boldly seeks to present all important topics in the field of moral theology'.[45] However, no discussion of socio-economic matters is provided.

On the other hand, it is possible to cite theological ethics' studies relating biblically-based ethics to contemporary life. Examples are Hays, Grassi, Stassen and Gushee, Pregeant, Cunningham, Rae, and Geisler.[46] Their main relations to the real world are in topics such as marriage and divorce, sexuality, abortion, euthanasia, embryonic cell research, reproductive technologies, cloning, and capital punishment. Most books on Christian ethics do not discuss socio-economic matters. The conclusion we draw from examining their work below is that they appear to be unaware that a biblical principle approach to formulating socio-economic ethics exists or could be constructed.

This is surprising given the opinion of two theologians (Stassen and Gushee), that 'few issues in Christian ethics have generated a literature as massive or polemical'.[47] Yet, from four recent Christian ethics books below, their attempts to derive biblical principle are minor, and efforts to relate their ethics to the real socio-economic world are cursory. Among this literature might be included Pregeant who devotes five pages to economic questions, mainly a critique of laissez-faire capitalism. However, less than a page is given to biblical texts—only from the Old Testament—and it is

44. William Schweiker, editor *The Blackwell Companion to Religious Ethics* (Malden, MA: Blackwell, 2008); Stanley Hauerwas and Samuel Wells, editors, *The Blackwell Companion to Christian Ethics* (Malden, MA: Blackwell, 2004).

45. William Mattison III, *Introducing Moral Theology: True Happiness and the Virtues*(Grand Rapids: Brazos, 2008), 13.

46. Hays, *The Moral Vision*; Grassi, *Informing the Future*; Glen Stassen and David Gushee, *Kingdom Ethics: Following Jesus in Contemporary Context* (Downers Grove: InterVarsity Press, 2003); Russell Pregeant, *Knowing Truth, Doing Good: Engaging New Testament Ethics* (Minneapolis: Fortress Press, 2008); David Cunningham, *Christian Ethics: The End of the Law* (Abingdon: Routledge, 2008); Scott Rae, *Moral Choices: An Introduction to Ethics* (Grand Rapids: Zondervan, 2009); Geisler, *Christian Ethics.*

47. Stassen and Gushee, *Kingdom and Ethics*, 409.

not shown what principles might be extracted from these texts to relate to the modern socio-economic world. Nor does Pregeant consider how capitalism might be changed for the better via the operation of a battery of biblical ethical principles. No sense of a pattern of normative biblical socio-economic ethics emerges from Pregeant's analysis.[48]

Another exception is Cunningham's twenty-six page treatment of work that canvasses questions such as what is work, how work relates to the economic order, why work is important to the Christian, justice in the economic order, and self-control. Work seems to be of great interest to Christians today, such as evidenced in the Boston-based Theology of Work Project. However, in Cunningham, little relation is made to scripture (with only four biblical citations overall), so that no sense emerges of how contemporary work life accords with normative scriptural principles, nor how work life might need to be changed to accord more with such principles.[49] Stassen and Gushee also have a chapter on economics. They start with a four and a half page discussion of the Sermon on the Mount, then offer a selection of Jesus' teachings on wealth, greed, and the 'Great Reversal'. They discuss property rights, reject normative notions of a 'rough equality of outcome,' and review the (now largely obsolete) economic systems debate. In finishing the chapter with business ethics, no concrete proposals are offered how they might apply. Again, few normative ethical principles emerge from Stassen and Gushee that are applied in any detail to the contemporary world.[50]

Rae has a whole chapter discussing how economic ethics might relate to contemporary life. The canvass includes questions of affluence, consumerism, work, care for the poor, globalisation, sweatshops, child labour, corporate social responsibility, international business ethics, the environment, accounting and finance. With such a range in thirty-three pages, each issue cannot be treated in depth, and one is left wondering how each relates to Rae's given normative biblical principles, of which he enumerates eleven. There are two problems with this approach. First, each listed principle is so general as to be capable of diverse interpretation and application. For instance, principle six is that '*work is inherently good, though marred by sin*'. The problems caused by sin are cited as 'alienation, dissatisfaction with work, exploitation of workers and quandaries in the workplace'. No discussion is offered how these four problems might be miti-

48. Pregeant, *Knowing Truth*, 356-360.
49. Cunningham, *Christian Ethics*.
50. Stassen and Gushee, *Kingdom Ethics*, 421.

gated in the workplace through application of biblical principles, although mention is made of secular principles, such as corporate social responsibility, employees' rights of conscience, and sexual harassment. Admirable as these are, it is possible to progress much further in relating biblical principles to work. This would require more fine-grained distinctions between Rae's principles, involving the expression of further principles. Perhaps this does not occur with Rae because none of the biblical references cited to support the eleven principles are interpreted, but are assumed to be self-evident. This tendency prevails throughout the chapter, in which twenty-six citations are made to Old Testament texts, four to Jesus' words, and eleven to the Apostles'.[51] Because of the approaches some of the above ethicists make toward evaluating the macro-economies, some of their conclusions diverge from each other. Thus, Pregeant has a .low view of capitalism and Rae, a high view.

A particular sub-set of theological ethics is business ethics, such as Rae and Wong, and Hill.[52] Yet, these too, bear the stamp of a low reliance of its ethics on biblical teaching. For instance, no systematic analysis of the Bible is made to derive the ethics discussed. Where biblical texts are cited, their meaning is taken to be self-evident. Christian sources for ethical principles are mainly from secondary sources, such as Niebuhr (1951), the Oxford Declaration on Christian Faith and Economics (1991), and Mott and Sider (1999). Some actual business case studies are discussed, all from secular journals, with others hypothetical. Instead of letting the Bible set the agenda, the ethics proposed are slanted to secular business orientation, covering issues such as honesty, employee loyalty, corporate social responsibility, marketing and advertising, technology, moral leadership in business. This leads to a particular view of business ethics that ignores certain topics. For instance, no analysis is made of how the poor are to be assisted to gain work. In the Third World, bribery and sweatshops are regarded as acceptable because they provide people with employment who might otherwise have none. These views ignore that Christian ethical principles for socio-economic life could provide hospitable work for presently employed sweatshop employees and for the unemployed. No sense emerges of what an overall picture of biblically-based ethics related to so-

51. Rae, *Moral Choices*, 329–361, 337, 347–348, 351; original emphasis.

52. Scott Rae and Kenman Wong, *Beyond Integrity: A Judeo-Christian Approach to Business Ethics,* second edition (Grand Rapids: Zondervan, 2004); Alexander Hill, *Just Business: Christian Ethics for the Marketplace,* second edition (Downers Grove: Inter-Varsity Press, 2008).

cio-economic matters might be, how it might relate to the contemporary world, or how it might be applied to transform non-God-based practices.

Conclusion

The case of this paper is that the principle methodology or principalising is an important part of theology and theological ethics. It endeavours to reveal the relevance of the Bible to the modern world, while conceding that the Bible does not speak directly to the burning issues of today. Two steps are involved. First, interpretation has to be made of its text to derive the normative principles. Second, the principles are related to life today in the context of given socio-economic conditions. Unless the Bible is used in this way, its full impact will not be revealed. The risk is heightened, for 'the modern world has little patience with antiquity for its own sake'. The principle approach is just part of the project of demonstrating the continuing relevance of Judeo-Christian thought to the modern world. Allegedly, this task is becoming more important today, for 'theologians and biblical scholars in the western world are now far more likely to be challenged to think through the practical implications of their ideas than at any time in the past 300 years'. This requirement is not to overlook the prime importance in Christian life of believers maintaining a personal relationship with God.[53]

53. Bray, *Biblical Interpretation*, 587, 508.

Interface Vol 15 1&2/2012

Professions, Business and MacIntyre—Fellow Travellers?

Chris White and Gordon Preece

Chris White
Former Managing Director, UK and Regional Manager, Europe,
Towers Perrin (Human Resources & Actuarial Consultants)

Gordon Preece
Director,
Ethos: EA Centre for Christianity and Society

Melbourne
Victoria

Introduction

Substantial attempts have been made to apply to business, Alasdair MacIntyre's framework of virtues and practices, most explicitly set out in Chapter 14 of *After Virtue* (hereafter AV).[1] But are these attempts ultimately futile, given MacIntyre's broad-based antipathy to capitalism and much of the institutions of business? His development of the Aristotelian notion of practices seems more immediately applicable to professions. But in many respects professions and businesses are becoming more alike. In this article we attempt to answer three questions:

- Is professional practice anything more than a business?
- And can business management be a profession?

1. MacIntyre, A *After Virtue*, second edition (London: Duckworth, 1985).

- Do MacIntyre's concepts of virtues and practices illuminate these questions?

But before turning specifically to these questions, it is appropriate that we review in some detail some of the developments in both business and professions and their interrelationship in recent decades. Aspects of these developments raise important further questions which we can only touch on in this article, but which are relevant background to our consideration of our core questions.

Professions—Origins, Developments, and Questions

The origins of professions lie in the concept of vocation—a calling to which the professional committed him or herself, to serve the needs of the community beyond personal (including economic) advantage. The religious roots of the call to service, as well as to priesthood and other forms of religious life, are deep, and embedded in the origins of the three great professions of church, medicine and law. The disciplined lifestyle and commitment to learning that characterised the development of these original professions have led to significant community respect and, in time, the ability of professional bodies to codify their activity and in particular limit who may practice the profession and how they do so.[2] In more modern times this recognition of professions, and the resultant power accorded to them, has led those in other areas of activity and with other bodies of knowledge to aspire to recognition as professions also.

An important area where professional groupings have exercised influence or control over those practicing in the particular discipline has been the ethics with which those practitioners conduct themselves. For example, in the medical profession, issues of patient confidentiality, the extent to which the practitioner explains the options and risks to the patient, and who makes the choice of treatment, are all the subject of professional codes of ethical practice.[3] These influences or controls typically focus on

2. M Stackhouse, 'Introduction', in M Stackhouse, *et al*, editors, *On Moral Business: Classical and Contemporary Resources for Ethics in Economic Life* (Grand Rapids: Eerdmans, 1995), 15f.
3. See, for example, the American Medical Association's website statement on patient confidentiality; http://www.ama-assn.org/ama/pub/physician-resources/legal-topics/patient-physician-relationship-topics/patient-confidentiality.page. Accessed 21 March 2012.

protecting the interests of the client or patient, but also on the interests of the profession, and sometimes the public interest (however defined).

Particularly as business has globalised, professions serving it directly (such as accounting, law, and the growing array of management consulting services) have increasingly functioned more like businesses than traditional professional practices.[4] And as more professional services (particularly in health-related areas) are funded—and increasingly managed, or at least circumscribed—by government, the nature of the traditional relationship between professional and patient or client has changed. Factors illustrating these and other changes in the ways in which professions have increasingly functioned in recent decades include:

- Employment of professionals, particularly when funded directly by government, versus the traditional self-employment;
- Ownership of professional service firms by other entities;
- Increased commercialisation and competition of professions, and other more business-like elements, versus the traditional cooperation between professionals;
- The growth of multi-disciplinary practice, particularly in professions serving business.

These developments suggest that in a number of areas of practice and in various respects, professions have become, or are in the process of becoming, businesses. If so, does it matter? But is there anything more than snobbery separating professions and businesses? In an increasingly corporatised professional world, are there aspects of traditional professions which are worth preserving? Without considering these questions rigorously, we argue that there are differences between professions and business which should be preserved, whilst agreeing that professions can learn from business as regards such aspects as efficient management and organisational structures. While a detailed discussion of these wider matters would provide important background to our core questions, we do not have space to address them here in detail.

---

4. For a discussion and index to articles on the difficulties of traditional professional partnership structure and the greater clarity of management, professional and ownership roles provided by corporate structure, in the context of larger Australian legal practices, see the blog of J Belshaw (accessed 21 March 2012): http://professionalservicesmanagement.blogspot.com.au/2007/05/corporatisation-corporate-structures.html.

Business—Confidence, Challenges, and Questions

Mention of business ethics often evokes the response –'That's an oxymoron!', or more thoughtfully, 'Ethics in business has never been needed more than now'. The truth is that ethics in business is needed all the time (but particularly when it has the lowest priority, during a boom), and not just when it's most talked about (for example, during crises, especially when ethical failure is most evident). Business cannot function satisfactorily without ethics.

Appropriate legal, regulatory and property ownership structures are essential, but for business to thrive there also needs to be an underlying ethical framework, a core of accepted ethical behaviour. If there is insufficient trust between parties to a potential transaction, it is very difficult for it to be agreed and successfully concluded. (For example in constructed 'nations' made up of rival tribal groups, a truly national business environment can be almost impossible). Even in countries where structures are broadly appropriate to an effective business environment, unethical behaviour, particularly if there is collusion or corruption by significant commercial, political and/or regulatory entities (for example, the devastating impact of Enron's collapse, which while primarily due to disgraceful behaviour by the executives and board, also involved collusion by the auditor, and inadequate exercise of—admittedly inadequate—regulatory powers).[5]

Encouraging or enforcing agreed ethical business behaviour is made more difficult as business has globalised. The impact of legal, regulatory and property ownership structures, still largely specified at a national level, are weakened considerably in their application to transnational businesses and transactions. (It is true that globally, and in some regions—Europe especially—there are transnational agreements and regulations impacting business, but these developments remain a minority.) And the rise of the internet, particularly in retail businesses, has exacerbated the difficulty of regulation (but has also enabled consumers to bypass inefficient retailing structures).

There is widespread scepticism of the morality of business, and while there is plenty of evidence of bad business conduct (corrupt and otherwise), it is not clear that business leaders as a group are greedier or otherwise less ethical than people generally. Suspicions about business morality, or rather the lack of it, are aggravated by the disruptive nature of

5. Stackhouse, *op cit*, 16f.

business, especially in its constant need for innovation, as new approaches are sought and tried in the never-ending search for new markets or preservation of old ones, and aptly described as 'creative destruction'.[6]

Business management and/or governance have traditionally not been seen as professions in quite the same way as law or accounting, albeit similar skill levels may be required in employees or directors specialising in say IT, marketing, or business strategy.[7] But these distinctions are breaking down, and so the corresponding questions to those raised above in relation to professions are: Is there any aspect of the older notion of the profession which could usefully be imported into business management and governance? Or does the creative destruction inherent in business put it in a fundamentally different space to professions? Again, we can only address these questions in a limited way, focusing on our core questions.

Specific Factors Blurring Distinctions Between Professional and Business Environments

As well as the background principles and particular developments in professions and business reviewed above, there are three factors where analogous (and in some cases, related) changes have been occurring in both professions and business which, while impacting each in differing ways, in our view are having the overall effect of blurring many of the former distinctions between business and professions. Given that it is now over thirty years since MacIntyre first wrote *After Virtue*, and a decade or two since much of the discussion on the applicability or otherwise of MacIntyre's framework to business (contrasted with the albeit largely unstated assumption that the framework was more relevant to professions), it is worth examining these three factors before turning to our specific discussion of MacIntyre's applicability.

---

6. A term coined and popularised in J Schumpeter *Capitalism, Socialism and Democracy* (New York: Harper, 1975), 82–85. Schumpeter saw creative destruction as 'the essential fact about Capitalism'.
7. This discussion has taken on renewed life since the GFC of 2007/08, with questions being raised about the necessary skills and responsibilities of business managers, and hence whether they are members of a profession. See, for example, R Barker (2010) *The Big Idea: No, Management Is Not a Profession*, Boston: Harvard Business Review, accessed 21 March 2012 at http://hbr.org/2010/07/the-big-idea-no-management-is-not-a-profession/ar/1.

Service/product and advice packaging, employment & remuneration

Whilst high-skill/low-supply professionals have always charged substantial fees (often related to such factors as degree of difficulty, capacity to pay, or size of transaction), in recent years business-related professional firms have started structuring fees with a substantial 'performance-related' component (such as a 'success fee' in advice on a takeover bid, or a 'no-win-no-fee' basis, now often used in class actions). Further, provision of these professional services in conjunction with other (often financial) services or products, in some cases involving complete 'package' arrangements, with rewards to the professionals involved extending well beyond the specific professional services provided and in some cases including ownership positions in the client activity, means professional services in some areas are increasingly part of larger business arrangements. The professionals involved are often in actual or potential conflict of interest situations (for example working for the deal not the client, or constrained as to services or products to recommend).

These conflicts and constraints on professional advice extend beyond business-related professions. For example, advice and services provided by medical and related health professionals are often constrained by limitations of government funding (for example of the Pharmaceutical Benefits Scheme), and in some cases by the terms of employment of the practitioner (for example in a hospital, whether public or private). Sometimes the conflicts and constraints are more implicit than overt, for example, in the case of medical practitioner/researchers whose work is funded by pharmaceutical companies.

The traditional professional, self-employed or in partnership with similar professionals, charging a fee for service, carrying or insuring professional liability risk, and with no other associations leading to actual or potential conflicts of interest vis-à-vis the client, arguably provides the most transparent relationship. The scope for compromised advice and abuses is greatly increased where this transparency is compromised. Many of the worst examples arise in relation to fees and remuneration, which if not transparent and related directly to the service provided can lead to bad advice, or inappropriate services and products being sold. A contemporary example is individual financial planning, which aspires to professional status, but which has a history of commission-based remuneration (paid by the successful product provider, and often undisclosed to the client or prospect), and resultant selling of expensive or otherwise unsuitable products. Counter to the development outlined in the prior two paragraphs, this 'industry' is now moving to fee for service, with no commissions, prodded by greater public exposure and government pressure, but also due to its aspiration to be regarded as a profession.

Turning now to business management and governance, a significant difference from the practice of earlier decades, emerging relatively recently, is the vastly increased willingness of companies apparently to pay whatever it takes to hire CEOs and other senior executives who promise 'outperformance'—and even to negotiate remuneration arrangements which reward well when performance is anything but exceptional (or even poor), probably in the expectation (or hope) that such circumstances are unlikely to arise. Whereas directors or senior employees of a business were once paid a fixed fee or salary, very frequently they now effectively have substantial 'equity' interests in the business, often with 'downside protection', interests which arguably transcend the equity interests of shareholders.[8]

Particularly when these corporate remuneration arrangements are badly aligned with the frequently long term interests of other stakeholders in the business (which can arise when significant short term incentives are provided to executives), the scope for conflicts of interest in the management of the business is obvious.

The overall point here is that lack of transparency and misalignment of product/service and/or remuneration structures with stated or implied stakeholder goals, have often served to blur the former distinctions between business and professions. They have also led to reduced public confidence, and have often been a major cause of increased regulation, which has not always been either effective or efficient.

The agency problem

Whether an individual in professional practice, or an employee or owner of a business, people in professions and business are frequently confronted with the clash of their own ethical principles (or lack of them!) with those of their client or employer. In some situations, a third party can also impact upon issues with an ethical dimension (for example, medical practitioners using the facilities of an Australian Roman Catholic hospital,

8. For a very substantial body of material on executive pay issues by a vastly experienced US commentator, see http://www.graefcrystal.com/articles.html; specifically on the growth of CEO pay relative to average worker pay, see http://www.graefcrystal.com/images/ceo_worker_pay_ratios_web_7_1_08.pdf (Accessed 21 March 2012).

where government and regulatory policy can bear upon the provision of abortions).

Whose interests do employees or professionals serve and whose ethical principles are they to follow when they act as agents of another?

The minimum requirement is (usually) what is legally required in the situation—whether of the employee or professional on the one hand, or the employer or client on the other. This might be expressed in statute or common law, contract (for example employment or service contract), or professional code of conduct. But even here, there can be contentious areas where the law, contract or code is not clear, or where new circumstances raise doubt as to how it applies.

The difficulties arise more broadly when we consider the conscience or ethical reflections of either party to the relationship, suggesting or requiring conduct which goes beyond the 'legal'. Legal theory accepts that law will not always go as far as society's generally accepted ethical norms might suggest, not least on the grounds of effective enforceability, but also recognising the diversity of public opinion and the desirability of personal freedom (subject to protecting the rights and interests of others). Thus the question arises as to how far individual conscience and ethical values, beyond the requirements of law, can determine conduct in employment or professional relationships.

While most of the discussion and case studies on the agency problem deal with examples where the employee or professional has ethical concerns about what the employer or client is requesting or requiring of them, the reverse can also occur (for example, where an employer has ethical concerns about how a salesman is meeting his targets, or where a family has concerns about the treatment being provided to a terminally ill parent).

Christian ethical discussion of the agency issue deals with scriptural and other ethical principles, and recognises the ambiguity involved. For example, in dealing with agency ethical dilemmas for employees, Hill distinguishes two approaches—the submissive (in which the employee complies with any legal demand of the employer), and the purist (in which the employee is unilaterally guided in acceptable actions by his or her own conscience): Hill has more criticisms of the first than the second.[9] However in discussing the resolution of ethical situations involving ambiguity he recommends that employees

9. A Hill, *Just Business: Christian Ethics for the Market Place* (Carlisle: Paternoster, 1998), 90–104.

- accommodate their employers as neighbours (*inter alia* citing Paul's recommendation to the Roman church that they avoid eating meat offered to idols, not because it was wrong, but because it might offend others (Rom 14:1–4));
- are tolerant in morally ambiguous situations (*inter alia* citing group charitable giving which is mostly used in ways ethically acceptable to the employee, but where a small percentage is used to advocate, but not perform, abortions);
- are not paternalistic (relying on scriptural depiction of God as valuing free will so highly that sinful behaviour is tolerated);
- facilitate positive solutions to ethical dilemmas (prioritising ethical issues, maintaining open and constructive dialogue, etc).[10]

These principles seem sound, and mitigate against taking extremist or single-issue ethical positions, to which some Christians can be prone. Conscientious application of Hill's recommended approach will not always resolve the issue, however, and resignation by the employee or professional, or termination of the contract by the employer or client, may sometimes be the least undesirable outcome.

But it is also true that, in the public mind (no doubt influenced by more aggressive media reporting and commentary on high profile cases), agency problems and the responses to them of the parties involved are evidence of ethical failures in both business and, increasingly, professions.[11] While it is no doubt true that business has always exhibited cases of failure to deal adequately with agency problems, it does seem that the appar-

---

10. *Op cit*, 99–102.
11. As an example, in the case of the failure of HIH Insurance, senior employees of the company (whether company officers with obligations under corporations and insurance law, or employed professionals, for example, actuaries, who are additionally subject to their profession's code of conduct) failed to distinguish their legal and ethical responsibilities from the frequently illegitimate requirements of HIH top management. The performance of the external auditors was also less than optimal, possibly due to agency pressures. See the report of the Owen Royal Commission: N Owen (2003) *The Failure of HIH Insurance*, (3 volumes) (Canberra: Commonwealth of Australia, 2003), especially chapters 15 & 21. In another example, the James Hardie case, external professionals advising the company (both lawyers and actuaries) failed in their professional duties in various ways, under pressure from senior management of their client. See D Jackson *Report of the Special Commission of Inquiry into the Medical Research and Compensation Foundation* (Sydney: Parliament of New South Wales, 2004).

ent incidence of such failures involving professionals have increased over time, perhaps due primarily to the impact of increased reporting. Whether or not the underlying level of such failures involving professionals has increased in fact, the impression that it has increased has been created, and hence a further area of distinction between business and professions has been blurred, at least in the public mind.

Knowledge and/or power differential

An employment or professional/client relationship usually involves disparities of knowledge and/or power; these have changed noticeably in recent decades.

In the case of employment, the last few decades have witnessed the decline of the coverage and power of unions, and with it the decline of centralised determination of wages and conditions (witness the Howard government's Work Choices, in Australia, which modified by Labor to Fair Work, but still a long way from the situation under the former Arbitration Commission). Consequent on these changes have been the increasing use of alternatives by employers such as contractors rather than employees, and other forms of outsourcing (often to cheaper or otherwise preferred arrangements overseas). Businesses in high wage economies such as Australia are increasingly moving out of lower skilled industries, or are outsourcing lower skilled work segments, and hence are concentrating increasingly on service rather than manufacturing industries. It is not our purpose to assess the rights and wrongs of these changes, but rather to point out that the power balance has generally shifted in favour of business, and arguably also in favour of the more highly skilled and mobile employee, particularly if he or she has technical knowledge which is in high demand. In such cases the differential is more one of knowledge than power, but the two are intimately related.

In many situations the professional/client relationship has also changed concerning the differential between the parties, primarily as regards knowledge. Increases in the level of education in business and community generally, and particularly the internet's impact, have meant that many users (or in some cases, former users) of professional services are now much better informed about the subjects on which they are seeking (or previously sought) professional advice. For example, the formerly terrified, intimidated and ignorant patient recently diagnosed with cancer will often now have acquired much internet information about their condition and treatment options. While it may be true that 'a little knowledge is a dangerous thing', the patient is at least much better equipped than previously to ask intelligent questions of the professional, and to probe what were once described as 'doctor's orders'. Particularly in medical and related professions, the impact of professional liability claims and the requirements of insurers has also made it essential for practitioners to explain alternatives and risks in reasonable detail, leaving the decision to the patient/client (albeit the practitioner will usually make a recommendation, which in many cases will prevail).

As well as greater levels of public, or at least client, education reducing the differential between the parties, scandals have led to a reduction in professional esteem, and have increased the willingness of clients to question professional advice, especially if it is packaged (as mentioned above) or if there are other suggestions of conflict of interest.

Thus changes in the relative knowledge and/or power differentials in both business and professions have further blurred the former distinctions between both, especially in the broader public perception.

Our overall conclusion from the foregoing discussion of separate influences on business and professions, and of the three specific factors outlined above (which, we argue, have often influenced both business and professions in related ways) is that the former, more distinct differences between the two areas of activity have become more blurred, at least in the wider public perception. In broad terms, the reputation of professions has been 'dragged down', nearer to that of business.

We now turn to the relevance of MacIntyre's framework of virtues and practices to business and professions, in the context of attempts to apply it to business (despite his general antipathy to business), contrasted with the generally assumed relevance of his framework to professions, and in the light of our foregoing argument that the distinction between the two areas of activity has blurred and lessened in recent years.

MacIntyre's Framework of Virtues and Practices vis-à-vis Business and Professions

MacIntyre's Framework in Outline In his seminal work rehabilitating the Aristotelian and Christian virtue traditions, *After Virtue* (AV), Alasdair MacIntyre argues that there is a core concept of *virtue*, despite the diversity of approaches of thinkers through the ages and their implicit claims to universality. Given the tension between the roots of professions, and also arguably of significant areas of business, in the ethics of principles, and the widespread utilitarianism of much contemporary economic and public life, his approach is particularly significant for our core questions, which go to the fundamental character of both professions and business.

In identifying this core concept of virtue, MacIntyre argues it is essential to recognise a specific type of *practice* in which the virtues can be developed (as well as in other ways); he defines practice as follows:

> any coherent and complex form of socially established cooperative human activity through which goods internal to that form of activity are realised in the course of trying to achieve those standards of excellence which are appropriate to, and partially definitive of, that form of activity, with the result that human powers to achieve excellence, and human conceptions of the ends and goods involved, are systematically extended. (AV, 187)

Practices are complex, such that, for example, architecture is a practice, but bricklaying is not.[12] There are standards of excellence, or *virtues*, relevant to and in part definitive of such a practice, which aims to attain these standards, and in so doing goods internal to the practice are achieved.[13]

---

12. The use of the craft of bricklaying as an example by MacIntyre is developed by Stanley Hauerwas, to uncover and display the logical form of becoming a Christian in the light of MacIntyre's theoretical work (in an essay entitled 'The Politics of the Church: How We Lay Bricks and Make Disciples', in S Hauerwas, *After Christendom? How the Church is to Behave if Freedom, Justice, and a Christian Nation are Bad Ideas* (Nashville: Abingdon, 1991). To quote Woodill:

> MacIntyre has employed readily recognizable skills as analogies to bridge the epistemological gap and to indicate how becoming moral is like being apprenticed to a craft. Hauerwas suggests that an everyday practice [sic] like bricklaying might help Christians to think about what it means to be church. Learning to be a mason involves entering a tradition of skillfulness in a particular way, because no one learns bricklaying as if it were newly minted from the private world of the apprentice. Rather, one learns crafts—and by implication, becomes virtuous – by being guided into the present state of a history or tradition of ends, goods, ways, and mentors.

J Woodill, *Virtue Ethics and Orthodox Christianity* (Washington: Georgetown University Press, 1998), 5f

13. Some argue that virtues are equivalent to internal goods, which may be due to a confusion of MacIntyre's understanding (AV, 191) with that of Aristotle. For a discussion of the understanding of courage in Aristotle and MacIntyre in the context of nursing practice, see L Day, 'Courage as a Virtue Necessary to Good Nursing Practice', in *American Journal of Critical Care* 16 (2007): 613–616.

MacIntyre uses the example of motivating an intelligent but disinterested child in the practice of playing chess by offering sweets for playing and bonus sweets for winning. The *external goods* from playing chess from the child's point of view constitute the sweets, and from that of the interested adults, prestige, status, etc. Playing chess is not the only way these external goods can be achieved. On the other hand there are *internal goods* which can only be achieved by playing chess or some similar game (eg particular kinds of analytical skill, strategic imagination and competitive intensity). (AV, 188f)

In MacIntyre's schema, practices are of necessity housed within and dependent upon an institutional or organisational context, with which they have a potentially fraught relationship:

> Indeed so intimate is the relationship of practices to institutions—and consequently of the goods external to the goods internal to the practices in question—that the institutions and practices characteristically form a single causal order in which the ideals and the creativity of the practice are always vulnerable to the acquisitiveness of the institution, in which the cooperative care for the common goods of the practice is always vulnerable to the competitiveness of the institution. In this context the essential feature of the virtues is clear. Without them, without justice, courage and truthfulness, practices could not resist the corrupting power of institutions. (AV, 194).

The goods internal to those practices are thus critically dependent on the underlying virtues, which in turn are necessary to the institution. In Macintyre's view, the internal goods and associated virtues (such as honesty, diligence and accuracy) are characteristically a 'positive sum game', in that achievement of them by one participant does not limit the potential for achievement by another, but external goods (such as profit, power and status) are characteristically a 'zero sum game', in that achievement by one participant is at the expense of another. (AV, 190f). In his view, this distinction provides the environment for competition, and the corruption of internal goods that the institutional setting of the practice frequently enables.

The institution must hold both the internal and external goods, the goods of both excellence and effectiveness of the practices, in an appropriate balance if they, and we would argue the institution itself, are to flourish. So it is in this necessary institutional setting that, MacIntyre argues, the problem for the maintenance and flourishing of practices derives. The ethics of any practice can be seen in terms of the internal goods or virtues it generates, and the necessity for, but tension with, its institutional context, which tends to focus on external goods such as outputs, profits and status. It is the classic interplay between ends and means, and the extent to which the ethics of one is compromised or sacrificed in the interests of the other.

Can the framework be applied to business?

MacIntyre's attitude to business, as a former Marxist, but more recently an Aristotelian and then Thomist, is generally negative. He argues that '. . . the tradition of the virtues is at variance with central features of the modern economic order and more especially its individualism, its acquisitiveness and its elevation of the values of the market to a central social place' (AV, 254). His opposition to business, and the capitalism within which it is located and which business apologists endorse or at least accept as the least bad option, is set out most clearly in the 1995 Preface to his 1953 work *Marxism and Christianity*[14], where he draws on two central arguments:

> Firstly that institutionally capitalism cannot but fail to adhere to any substantive notion of justice as rewards are distributed without reference to desert and secondly that capitalism miseducates individuals to subordinate desert to desire in their purposes. The drive to have more and more is transformed from a classical vice to a modern virtue.[15]

Despite this negativity on MacIntyre's part towards capitalism and business, interestingly (or paradoxically) there has been considerable effort expended, particularly in business management and ethics journals, in trying to apply the structures developed in AV to produce a virtue-based business ethics, within a capitalist framework, rather than as part of a critique of it. A relatively rigorous attempt has been made by Moore, in a

14. A MacIntyre, *Marxism and Christianity* (London: Duckworth, 1995), xiii, first published in 1953 as *Marxism: An Interpretation*, SCM Press.
15. R Beadle, 'The Misappropriation of MacIntyre', in *Reason in Practice*, 2/2 (2002): 49.

series of articles in *Business Ethics Quarterly*, where he has sought to show that

- business is a practice in Macintyre's sense of the term,
- as with other practices, business can be undermined by institutions, and
- the special function of management is to protect the practice of management from the corporatist and capitalist form of institutions.[16]

Beadle[17] rejects Moore's arguments: the first on the grounds that, unlike other practices, 'business qua business' does not exist as a separate entity from the actual *area* of business (fishing, construction, retailing, etc); neither does it exhibit unique internal goods, other than perhaps 'customer service', and that the other internal goods Moore cites, such as 'quality' and 'the exercise of practical skills' are merely generic. Beadle views Moore's second argument as merely a consequence of his argument that business is a practice, in that any practice is subject to the risk of institutional corruption. And finally in rebutting Moore's third point in which he applies Macintyre's model to describe the positive features of managers, Beadle points out Moore does not answer MacIntyre's negative characterisation of management, which Beadle summarises as follows:

- the character of the manager eschews any substantive notion of the good, and
- the manager's role is to deploy supposedly impersonal facts in pursuit of the most effective and efficient means to achieve any prescribed ends, but
- the sort of morally neutral knowledge required to achieve such manipulation does not exist, and
- managers themselves inhabit a deep personal compartmentalisation without which their social role could not be understood.[18]

16. G Moore, 'On the Implications of the Practice-Institution Distinction: MacIntyre and the Application of Modern Virtue Ethics to Business', in *Business Ethics Quarterly* 12/1 (2002): 19–32; G Moore, 'Humanizing Business: A Modern Virtue Ethics Approach', in *Business Ethics Quarterly* 15/2 (2005): 237–255; G Moore, 'Corporate Character: Modern Virtue Ethics and the Virtuous Corporation', in *Business Ethics Quarterly* 15/4 (2005): 659–685.
17. R Beadle, 'Why Business Cannot Be a Practice', in *Analyse & Kritik 30* (2008): 229–241.
18. *Ibid*, 233.

This characterisation of management is one-sided, and while it may be an accurate description of some managers, could hardly be called normative. It overlooks the role that virtues in the character of a well-functioning business manager play in enabling the effective performance of the role, in relation to balancing the varying interests and concerns of the main stakeholders of the business: clients, employees and shareholders in particular. It is in relation to the form of capitalism and business espoused by economists such as Milton Friedman[19] where the interests of shareholders dominate those of other stakeholders, that MacIntyre's characterisation of business management is most relevant, in an environment where the external goods almost always dominate the internal. But this extreme form of stockholder capitalism does not represent the whole picture, and the development of stakeholder capitalism in recent decades provides an environment in which the internal goods of business management can flourish, although this cannot be assumed because such businesses generally have to operate competitively. While there are many examples from corporate scandals (such as Enron) and the Global Financial Crisis of 2007–8 that would back up MacIntyre's jaundiced view of business and business management, there are also many from the more social and ecologically entrepreneurial sectors that do not.

Accepting that *caveat emptor* is a factor in the basis upon which much business is conducted, the manager who displays *no* substantive notion of 'the good' will generally encounter considerable difficulty in agreeing deals with other managers and especially potential clients. Further, many able managers, if under pressure from their organisations to engage in a *deep personal compartmentalisation* in their private and business ethical lives, would choose, if able, to work instead for alternative organisations which expect them to behave with consistent high standards at all times, and hence the latter organisations should be able to retain higher calibre staff.

McCann and Brownsberger discuss the role of business management in an insightful article which assesses the implications of Peter Drucker's understanding of management in debate with MacIntyre.[20] According to

19. For example, M Friedman, 'The Social Responsibility of Business is to Increase its Profits', in *The New York Times Magazine*, 13 September 1970.
20. D McCann, & M Brownsberger, 'Management as a Social Practice: Rethinking Business Ethics after MacIntyre', in *Annual of the Society of Christian Ethics* (1990): 223–245, edited and reprinted in M Stackhouse, *et al*, editors, *On Moral Business: Classical*

McCann and Brownsberger, Drucker, in his business classic *The Practice of Management*[21]

> defines management teleologically as 'the dynamic, life-giving element in every business' and as the 'specifically economic organ of an industrial society' whose functions are:
> 1. economic performance: 'managing a business',
> 2. the transformation of human and material resources: 'managing managers', and
> 3. organisation of productive activities: 'managing workers and work'.

The first function, economic performance, differentiates business enterprises from all other institutions serving society, and requires them to be designed to produce goods and services as efficiently as possible. The *purpose* of business, however, is not to make a profit but to 'create a customer'; the *function* of profit is to be "the test of [the] validity" of the organisation's activity. Thus Drucker, in defining

> the function of economic performance in terms of creating a purposive relationship between market institutions and their customers gets to the heart of MacIntyre's distinction between the goods of excellence and the goods of effectiveness. For creating a new form of association for economic betterment, rather than merely maximising profits, suggests that managing such relationships not only might have its own characteristic form of moral excellence, but also that as such it would qualify as a social practice . . .[22]

So management could be regarded as a practice if the *telos* of society, the common good, is furthered through it, and/or this practice of management can only be achieved through its appropriate internal good. In Drucker's other two functions of management, the transformation of human and material resources, and organisation of productive activities, this

---

and Contemporary Resources for Ethics in Economic Life (Grand Rapids: Eerdmans, 1995), 508–513.

21. P Drucker, *The Practice of Management* (Oxford: Butterworth/Heinemann, 1954/2007).
22. McCann & Brownsberger, *op cit*, 509f.

telos is confirmed, as the manager's remit must extend beyond a narrow focus on effectiveness, to development of and partnership with staff, especially empowerment of the worker to self-management. Managers have a responsibility towards the people they manage, beyond the relationship of integrity underlying every occupation—such as the lawyer to her client or the grocer to his customer—more like being a parent or a teacher, requiring personal integrity beyond honourable dealing.[23]

Thus the answer McCann and Brownsberger believe Drucker would give to their question 'Is management a social practice, in MacIntyre's sense of the term?' would be 'How could it not be a social practice?', and that the relevant internal good would be 'service', understood as a form of empowerment. Beyond their very different overall attitudes to business, Drucker parts company with MacIntyre in his appeal to customer sovereignty as the ultimate purpose of business, against MacIntyre's overriding neo-Aristotelian notion of the common good, raising the question of the applicability of MacIntyre's overall model to a philosophically liberal approach to a market economy. (511) An interesting (and frequently divisive question) for Christians is whether the more communitarian approach to business of MacIntyre's approach can be held together with Drucker's more liberal understanding. However we agree with McCann and Brownsberger that service *does represent a genuine internal good, whose moral characteristics entitle us to qualify managing a business as a social practice.*[24] Clearly, however, the scope for corruption of this internal good is ever-present; the question remains whether it is always due to institutional factors or whether internal conflicts within the array of internal goods can also play a part.

Brewer also attempts to show that it is business management which is the practice, rather than business itself, inter alia on the grounds that that business management as a practice has as its first internal good the 'enabling of employees'.[25] Beadle, in an earlier paper, dismisses Brewer's attempt as failing to question why employees might need to be enabled in the first place, as well as Brewer's not relating management to MacIntyre's discussion of manipulation. However Beadle seems to overlook the important role of leadership by the manager in coordinating employees' efforts into an effective team, thereby 'enabling' them to function in the

23. *Ibid*, 510.
24. *Ibid*, 511.
25. K Brewer, (1997) 'Management as a Practice: A Response to Alasdair MacIntyre', in *Journal of Business Ethics* 16 (1997): 825–833.

great majority of tasks and operations which require the efforts of more than one individual. But to MacIntyre the critical issue is the *telos* of business, and we think Beadle has got him right—emotivist managers do use virtues as means to the end of profit. So, frankly, do many Christian business people and apologists, as well as 'spirituality of work' gurus, who say that fostering virtues will lead to greater productivity and profit.

Warren makes the point that MacIntyre's theme of the necessity of virtue in the creation of internal goods means that corporations are (or we would argue, can be) types of moral incubator in which individuals learn the worth of virtue.[26] Beadle rejects this argument on the grounds that it fails to address MacIntyre's argument that the logic of business organisation rests on a notion of effectiveness whose content is determined not by virtue but by power.[27] Beadle asks how an organisation fostering virtue could survive in a market economy, a point we have already addressed by pointing out that there are benefits in clients and other organisations dealing with ethical organisations, and in able and employable staff in working for them.[28] Our conclusion is supported by Dobson, who addresses MacIntyre's argument that business is morally indefensible because it privileges external over internal goods and hence corrupts practices (and by extension the virtues which support the latter). Dobson concludes that MacIntyre's critique, while partly valid, is a sweeping overgeneralisation, and that business need not of necessity be antithetical to individuals' pursuit of internal goods within practices.[29]

MacIntyre's view of business, rooted in the Aristotelian deprecation of business as conducted by lawless wandering merchants, outside the control of the *polis*, is incompatible with modern, regulated capitalist society and business.[30] But MacIntyre notes that the institutional context of the social practices and virtues changes, from Homeric war-like martial virtues to the democratic virtues of Athens. It is arbitrary, and contrary to MacIntyre's historical view of the development of institutions and virtues,

26. R Warren, 'The Empty Company: Morality and Job Security', in *Personnel Review* 25/6 (1996): 41-53.
27. R Beadle, 'The Misappropriation of MacIntyre', in *Reason in Practice*, 2/2 (2002): 51.
28. A good example of an organization behaving ethically was Johnson & Johnson, withdrawing Tylenol from sale when it discovered product tampering; when tamper-proof packaging was developed, the company recovered all of the lost market share, and became an 'employer of choice'. See http://en.wikipedia.org/wiki/Tylenol.
29. J Dobson, (2009) 'Alasdair MacIntyre's Aristotelian Business Ethics: A Critique', in *Journal of Business Ethics*, 86/1 (2009): 43–50.
30. McCann and Brownsberger, *op cit.*

to assume that business and corporations cannot evolve into incubators for the virtues also. But such an evolution of the corporation cannot be taken for granted—it can go either way.[31]

So although we find Beadle's arguments persuasive in relation to Moore's and others' attempts to apply MacIntyre's framework (exactly as described in AV), it is not because we disagree with the more moderate views of business and the role of management of several writers (Moore, Drucker, McCann and Brownsberger, and Dobson in particular), and business's potential to exhibit and/or foster certain virtues and arguably internal goods, for example service. Rather, these attempts to apply MacIntyre's framework fail in relation to business, primarily because his distinction is too sharply drawn as between the more virtuous and altruistic but potentially corruptible virtues and hence internal goods of a practice on the one hand, and the less virtuous, self-interested and potentially corrupting external goods fostered by the institution in which the practice resides, which he admits, albeit reluctantly, are necessary for institutions and social practices to survive, on the other.

In MacIntyre's discussion of the nature of practices he states that '[any particular practice] involves standards of excellence and obedience to rules as well as the achievement of goods' (AV, 190). Thus it seems to us that some of the virtues through which the internal goods of a practice are achieved, such as say truthfulness or courage, may need to be tempered in their single-minded application due to the necessary compromise between competing ethical principles, which from the viewpoint of a determined protagonist of one of the competing virtues and/or internal goods, might be argued to be corrupting. The tension between and among different ethical principles[32], and the differing emphases given to them by different individuals in a social enterprise, means that tolerance of the conscientiously held views of others is a virtue essential to the achieve-

---

31. For a very negative view of corporations as psychopathic see the book (also a documentary) J Bakan, *The Corporation: The Pathological Pursuit of Profit and Power*, (New York: Free Press, 2005). For a more positive view see M Stackhouse (1995) 'Introduction: Foundations and Purposes', in M Stackhouse *et al* editors (1995) *On Moral Business: Classical and Contemporary Resources for Ethics in Economic Life*, Grand Rapids: Eerdmans, 1995), 10–34; and M Novak, *Towards a Theology of the Corporation* (Washington: AEI Press, 1990).

32. The classic example is the competition between ends and means, where two potentially equally valuable goods conflict, and a compromise has to be arrived at. See J White, 'Ends and Means', in J Macquarrie, & J Childress, *A New Dictionary of Christian Ethics* (London: SCM, 1986), 181–182.

ment of the internal goods of many such enterprises, business being a common example. Not all such protagonists would agree that tolerance is an equivalently valid virtue, but its importance and intrinsic value as an essential element in the achievement of a range of internal goods in a business operating in a multicultural world, characterised by diverse and frequently strongly held opinions, seems self-evident. Conversely, the external goods (such as profit or status) which according to MacIntyre have the potential to corrupt, can equally have the potential to empower and ensure the practical application of what would otherwise remain little more than a forlorn hope.

Hence, at least in the context of attempted application of MacIntyre's model to business, our concern is with the appropriateness of his tight distinction between the roles and natures of internal and external goods. Despite this concern we nevertheless argue that with appropriate modification, the model potentially provides a useful means of describing business in a way which is not unaware of its corrupting potential and the need for the business environment to be appropriately regulated, while not rejecting the capitalist framework (contra MacIntyre). This appropriate modification would involve nuancing the understanding of both internal and external goods, largely as regards resolving tensions between and within each; however a full discussion of these modifications is beyond our present scope.

And what about the framework's application to professions?

The Aristotelian concept of *practice*, developed by MacIntyre, has an immediately appealing application to professions. Strenuous efforts have been made to apply the concept to various contexts, some generally accepted as professional. In this brief discussion, we shall look at aspects of various attempts to apply MacIntyre's structure in the medical area, the financial sector, public administration, journalism, and finishing with a brief comment on its relevance to education. The increasing 'corporatisation' of many professional areas of activity tends to raise similar questions to those we have already discussed in the business context, and to which we will return in the conclusion, addressing the three questions raised in the introduction to this article.

Medicine: Hoyt-O'Connor examines developments in the application in medical ethics of virtue theory in the light of AV.[33] He points out that practices in most medical areas are essentially cooperative endeavours, and cites in support of the good of cooperative human activity, and MacIntyre's communitarian approach, Bernard Lonergan's 'good of order'.[34] Medical practices have increasingly become a whole series of specialities and sub-specialities, with professionals needing to interact and cooperate in increasingly complex ways. At the same time the relationship between the medical practitioner and the patient is highly personal, and as it is a *person* rather than just a body the practitioner is treating. Hence the increasing complexity and specialisation of medical practice makes the proper exercise of the virtues of medical practice, such as honesty and trustworthiness, fortitude and justice, and wisdom and integrity, more difficult in their practical application. (Sellman, in a paper on the professional practice of nursing identifies open-mindedness as a key virtue of that medically-related profession.[35])

These high expectations are not always met, due to either individual irresponsibility or, worse, systemic corruption. Practices are not always instituted for desirable ends; at issue is not only the rightness of particular actions but also the legitimacy of a practice itself. Lonergan helpfully distinguishes minor and major inauthenticity, the former being failure to live up to the ideals of a tradition, versus the latter consisting of living up to a tradition in need of serious reform or even condemnation. This distinction significantly blunts some of the criticism leveled at MacIntyre's account of the virtues. Failure of the individual practitioner to live up to the

33. P Hoyt-O'Connor, *Virtue and the Practice of Medicine*, Paper presented at PAIDEIA, the 20th World Congress of Philosophy in Boston, Massachusetts, USA, 10-15 August, 1998; accessed 31 January 2012 at www.bu.edu/wcp/Papers/Bioe/BioeHoyt.htm.

    For other attempts at relating MacIntyrean virtues to the tension between medical and market imperatives see G Preece, (2011) 'Healthy, Wealthy and Wise? Business Ethics and Healing Professions', in *Luke's Journal* 30, 16/1 (April 2011): 28–30; H Reinders (20,02) 'The Commodity of Care,' *Zadok Papers* S 117, Autumn 2002; and M Byrne, & M Cunningham (2000) 'Health Care and the Market' in S Longstaff & G Preece editors, 'Compassion, Charity, and Conscience', *Interface* 3/2 (October 2000): 50–69.

34. B Lonergan, *Method in Theology* (New York: Seabury Press, 1972), 48–50, also *Collected Works of Bernard Lonergan* Volume 3 Insight: *A Study of Human Understanding*, (Toronto: University of Toronto Press, 1992), 619–621.

35. D Sellman, 'Alasdair MacIntyre and the Professional Practice of Nursing', in *Nursing Philosophy*, 1/1, (2000): 26–33.

highest ideals of his/her professional calling is one thing, systemic failure of the institution in which the individual practices his/her profession, or of a whole profession (for example through a code of professional conduct which protects the professional's interests at the expense of properly serving the patient or client), is quite another. Practitioners in medically-related areas can desire the good of the patient as a whole person, but need to recognise where their professional expertise stops and their role as just another human alongside the patient being starts; medical professions increasingly now recognise to a greater extent than previously that they have no special expertise when it comes to answering life's great questions.

Finance: The actuarial profession presents some interesting opportunities for reflection on the ethical significance of the institutions engaging actuaries, because for the Australian profession's first century (approximately mid- nineteenth to mid-twentieth centuries), the great majority of actuaries were employees (often very senior ones) of life insurance companies and mutual societies. Insurers exercised considerable control over the fledgling profession—for example in 1950 a job advertisement for an actuary was circulated over the name of the then president of the actuarial professional body, who was threatened with dismissal by the autocratic chairman and managing director of his company for encouraging the defection of valuable employees.[36] Similar practices continued for some years, no doubt limiting the growth in actuarial salaries which would otherwise have occurred. The growth of actuarial consulting firms, actuarial work for general insurers and independently managed superannuation funds, plus academic appointments of actuaries has meant that the close control exercised by life insurers over the profession has weakened very considerably. However as late as 1972, an actuarial academic at Macquarie University publicly attacked the life insurance industry for secrecy about the level of its reserves and its inefficiency. The situation became heated after various related incidents, culminating in the academic and a colleague announcing in the financial press the establishment of a consultancy to advise the public on the purchase of life insurance products, at which point the professional body warned them for the apparent breach of the ban in the profession's code of conduct against advertising. The point of mentioning these examples is to show that unless a professional body is able to protect its independence from the interests and control of its major

36. C Bellis, *The Future Managers: Actuaries in Australia 1853–1997* (Sydney: Institute of Actuaries of Australia, 1997), 113f.

clients, especially if they employ most of the professional body's members, it is at considerable risk of its integrity being damaged.

Over time a profession develops traditions, often codified in rules of conduct and professional standards, which, as well as maintaining ethical and work quality standards, protect the profession and its members from undue pressure from institutions and clients to whom they provide services. These traditions of ethics may not always be continuous from the past—not all professional or business activities can look back to their development over decades. For example, financial planning, which aspires to professional status, but where many of its practitioners have their roots in selling financial products such as life insurance, usually on a commission basis, which have not infrequently led to mis-selling abuses, has made considerable strides in improving its ethical standards in recent years.[37] And many businesses, with their origins in a more free-wheeling, entrepreneurial mentality, seek greater social responsibility and ethical methods as they grow, develop and mature. However it is also true that businesses (or for that matter, professional practices) founded by strongly ethical individuals can become less ethical as the founders move on and the businesses become more corporatised and institutionalised, or the environment in which they operate changes (for example, the shift in ethos in 'Big Five' accounting firm Arthur Andersen after the death of its highly ethical founder, and the shift from auditing to the more lucrative consulting, leading to its being disbarred due to criminal destruction of documents associated with Enron and other unethical clients).[38]

As an example of the application of MacIntyre's framework to a profession in the finance sector, Francis suggests five possible virtues that could be unique to the practice of accounting: honesty, concern for the economic status of others, sensitivity to the values of cooperation and conflict, communicative character of accounting, and dissemination of economic information.[39] It is interesting that in the collapse of Andersen, all five of these virtues could be said to have been violated.

Public Administration: Cooper discusses in some detail, with some examples, the sorts of pressures on officials exercising the responsibilities

37. See, for example Financial Planning Association of Australia Code of Professional Conduct July 2011, accessed 2 February 2012 at http://www.fpa.asn.au/media/FPA/FPA%20Standards/CodeofPractice_July%202011.pdf.
38. See D Hawkins & J Cohen, 'Arthur Andersen LLP', Harvard Business School, 9-103-061 http:/www.hbsp.harvard.edu
39. J Francis, 'After Virtue? Accounting as a Moral Discursive Practice', in *Accounting, Auditing and Accountability Journal*, 3 (1990): 5–17.

of public administration within hierarchical institutions, where the perceived needs of protection or even preservation of the institution are in conflict with the fearless exercise of those responsibilities.[40] He specifies an illustrative MacIntyrean framework for the internal goods and virtues of public administration in the US context, in three 'realms', as follows:

Realms of Obligation and Virtue	**Internal Goods**	**Virtues**
Obligation to pursue the public interest	Beneficence for citizenry Justice	Benevolence Courage Rationality Fairmindedness Prudence
Obligation to authorizing processes and procedures	Popular sovereignty Accountability Due process	Respect for law Rationality Prudence Honesty Self discipline Civility
Obligation to colleagues	Enhancement of standards of excellence Contribution to achievement of internal goods	Fairmindedness Trustworthiness Respect for colleagues Responsibility for practices Civility Honesty Prudence Rationality Independence

Cooper argues that his tentative framework could provide a more rigorous basis for establishing the relevant code of ethics for public administrators in the USA.

Journalism: In an article which takes a much more nuanced position about the applicability of MacIntyre's ideas to his profession of interest—journalism—Lambeth nevertheless sees much in MacIntyre's work to stimulate those concerned with the ethical future of that profession.[41] He cites a number of outstanding examples of American investigative journal-

40. T Cooper, 'Hierarchy, Virtue, and the Practice of Public Administration: A Perspective for Normative Ethics', in *Public Administration Review*, July/August (1987): 320–328.

41. E Lambeth, 'Waiting for a New St Benedict: Alasdair MacIntyre and the Theory and Practice of Journalism', in *Business & Professional Ethics Journal*, 9/1&2, (1990): 97–108.

ism, and in some cases the corrupting influences (often by governments or other powerful institutions wanting to maintain secrecy, and occasionally the media organisation employing the journalist(s) concerned). Perhaps consistent with the 'hard-nosed' reputation of journalism, Lambeth's assessment of the relevance of MacIntyre's message to the profession at the end of his article is that '. . . the trumpet sounded by MacIntyre awakens, even though we cannot tell whether the message is reveille or taps' (106).

Education: Finally, Hager reports that MacIntyre himself and others have debated inconclusively whether education is a practice. Hager has modified MacIntyre's account of practice so it will apply to teaching and a range of other activities. [42]

Overall: These accounts from a selection of professions indicate that significant efforts have been made in a number of professions to apply MacIntyre's framework, despite the negative view he takes of the capitalism and business environments in which they generally operate. This suggests something of a philosophical vacuum in the ethical principles underlying most professions (a diagnosis which we imagine would accord with MacIntyre's view). Some of the accounts also give an indication of the corrupting pressures applied by the institutions within which and for which professionals work. In this regard, an interesting contemporary case study would be an analysis of the source of the corrupting pressures on the journalists who were involved in phone hacking while employed by the *News of the World*; availability of relatively objective data probably needs to await the report of the Leveson Inquiry.)

Conclusion

We return to the original questions raised in the introduction, and offer some brief conclusions on where our discussion has led us.

Is professional practice anything more than a business? Our straightforward answer is 'yes', but it is probably also true that, in many cases, professional practice is more like a business than it once was. The contemporary interest in codifying the ethical principles underlying professions has its counterpart in many parts of business, but generally with a somewhat greater focus on client and community service, and environmental care, than in the business case. Professional practice and business have distinc-

42. P Hager, 'Refurbishing MacIntyre's Account of Practice', in *Journal of Philosophy of Education*, 45/3 (2001): 545–561.

tive practices of accountability, but with an overlapping core. However, as professional firms have corporatised, have admitted owners beyond the active professionals, and in some cases have listed on stock exchanges, the distinctions between professionalism and business have reduced.

Can business management be a profession? Our answer here is a tentative 'yes', but corrupting institutional pressures are often much harder to resist for business managers than for many other professionals, particularly if the organisation is operating in a highly competitive business environment or sector, or if, as is more often the case, its goals and employment commitments are increasingly short term.[43] However in the case of organisations where the capital and other commitments are very long term (such as mining), the need to retain high calibre, socially aware people can mean management as a profession is a more realistic possibility, particularly if the governance board has high integrity and is supportive of management making a career with the organisation.

Do MacIntyre's concepts of virtues and practices illuminate these questions? MacIntyre's jaundiced view of capitalism and business cannot be summarily dismissed in the attempt to apply his concepts of virtues, goods and practices to professions and business. We nevertheless conclude that the structure is helpful in the ethical analysis of both. Thirty years ago, when *After Virtue* was written, it was simpler to apply MacIntyre's understanding to professions rather than to business, but as the two areas of activity have generally moved closer together, as well as the differences becoming less, interestingly the overall task has become more complex and difficult. To apply these concepts in the context and environment of many professions and businesses today would particularly require nuancing of MacIntyre's model. The main concerns are with his overly tight distinction between the roles and natures of internal and external goods and his association of the latter with business in a negative and static Aristotelian sense that idealises the Greek *polis* over against more modern institutions like corporations; however we believe they could be modified to resolve tensions within and between them when applied to many contemporary businesses and professions.

43. R Sennett, *The Corrosion of Character* (New York/London: Norton, 1998), 22–27.

PART C
PUBLIC LECTURES

Interface Vol 15 1&2/2012

The Bible Hits the Streets[1]

David R Wilson

Senior Consultant, Sophia Think Tank
Bible Society Australia
Melbourne
Victoria

Introduction

The Book of Proverbs in the Bible talks about wisdom having a public face. It declares that 'wisdom shouts in the streets wherever crowds gather in the market places and near the city gates (1:20)'. Wisdom is crying out in the streets to be heard but who is listening?

The King James Bible was first published in 1611 and Bible Society Australia celebrated the 400th anniversary of that publication in 2011 with a travelling Exhibition of rare Bibles, including an original 1611 Pulpit edition of the KJB. In the month of October the Exhibition came to Melbourne and opened in the City Library. The weekend of the Exhibition opening there was a celebration in St Paul's Cathedral after which the Bible was released from the 'clutches' of the church into the streets of Melbourne. Let me explain some background before telling you more of the story.

The KJV Bible became known as 'The People's Bible' as it was translated into the language of the people so that the 'common' people might be able to access it and understand it. Before this time the church had 'owned' the authority of the Scriptures and the right of interpretation and

1. This article is taken from a public presentation by the author in various church gatherings in November and December 2011.

application belonged to its hierarchy. But now the Bible was set free and once again the 'common people heard it gladly'.

In planning the celebration of 400 years of the Bible for the people it was decided to have a church based service of thanksgiving. At the end of the service a number of church leaders of Melbourne, Canberra, and Sydney paraded an original copy of a 1611 Bible down the aisle of St Paul's cathedral and into the streets of Melbourne. Much of the congregation then joined the procession through the streets of Melbourne to the City Library where the KJV Bible was placed in a public exhibition, in the midst of the Library, for the month of October.

As I walked with this very public airing of such ancient wisdom I noticed all the sectors of Society we were passing by and I started thinking about what wisdom was calling out to each of these sectors. The Bible has so much to say to the City. What are some examples?

Wisdom Cries Out in the Streets of Melbourne

The sectors, or Drivers, of Society that we work with in Sophia Think Tank are Arts, Business, Community Services, Education, Health, Justice, Law, Media, Politics, and Sports. As we walked together we passed by a branch of the Commonwealth Bank, one of the Business drivers of the City. I imagined the Bible calling out, perhaps a passage from Deuteronomy 15: 'No one in Israel should ever be poor. The Lord your God is giving you this land and he has promised to make you very successful, if you obey his laws and teachings that I am giving you today . . . There may be poor people in the town where you live. If there are then don't be mean and selfish with your money . . . Instead, be kind and lend them what they need . . . There will always be poor people among you. That's why I am commanding you to be generous with them.' Biblical wisdom reminds the City that there is enough to go around as long as people are not greedy in their approach to wealth. The business driver needs to contribute to such wealth sharing for the wellbeing of the City

We walked on a bit further and passed a busker on the sidewalk, a representative of the Arts driver. The Arts play a major part in the life of a city like Melbourne and the Bible has much to encourage and guide it. Exodus 31 states 'Then the LORD said to Moses, [2] "See, I have chosen Bezalel son of Uri, the son of Hur, of the tribe of Judah, [3] and I have filled him with the Spirit of God, with wisdom, with understanding, with knowledge and with all kinds of skills— [4] to make artistic designs for work in gold, silver and bronze, [5] to cut and set stones, to work in wood, and to engage in all kinds of crafts.' Biblical wisdom calls out to the Arts in the City to encourage and affirm its expression as being from God, inspired by God, and enabled through God's Spirit.

There was a medical clinic over the street, a part of the Health driver, and I recalled the clear connection between spiritual, moral and physical health that a passage like Proverbs 3:7–8 announces: 'Do not be wise in your own eyes, have reverence for the Lord and shun evil. This will bring health to your body and nourishment to your bones.' This is a connection that contemporary health services are once again seriously exploring.

Sport is a powerful driver in Australia and there's no greater event in Australian Sports than the AFL Grand Final. This was the weekend of that event and both celebration and despair were in the air as the memories of the game the day before where Geelong beat Collingwood to win the premiership for 2011 lingered. Fans of both persuasions, dressed accordingly, let their presence be known as they passed by this strange procession with a huge Bible out front. I later thought of 1Timothy 4:8–9 which states 'Exercise is good for your body, but religion helps in every way. It promises life now and forever. These words are worthwhile and should not be forgotten.' I think the religion Paul is referring to here is something other than the religion that AFL can become to its followers but he is reminding us that although exercise (Sport?) is good we have to keep all things in perspective and recognise priorities.

A part of the popular media for public transport users is the MX newspaper. As we progressed on our short journey to the City Library we passed by an MX paper stand. A part of the Media driver, perhaps the most powerful of all the ten drivers. There is much in the Bible that addresses the importance of Media and that gives guidance to its proper conduct. This is especially so if the Prophets of the Old and New Testaments are seen as media professionals. I have often wondered how different the Media would look if it adhered to the call of Philippians 4:8: 'Finally my friends, keep your minds on whatever is true, pure, right, holy, friendly, and proper. Don't ever stop thinking about what is truly worthwhile and worthy of praise'.

As we approached the corner of Flinders Lane I looked ahead and noticed the grandeur of the Melbourne Town Hall, symbolic of the politics driver for this capital city. When I think about Politics I think about leadership and leadership models and Jesus' teaching on the stark contrast between religious and political models of leadership in His day and the leadership that He was proposing. This comes out clearly in Mark 9:35–37: 'Sitting down, Jesus called the twelve and said, "Anyone who wants to be first must be the very last, and the servant of all." He took a little child whom He placed among them. Taking a child in His arms, He said to them, "Whoever welcomes one of these little children in my name welcomes me; and whoever welcomes me does not welcome me but the One who sent me"'. Imagine the difference if Leadership in our cities and our nation took this seriously! Not just political leadership but leaders in all the drivers. This is truly transformative.

We turned into Flinders Lane and passed a *Big Issue* seller. The *Big Issue* is a part of the Community Services in Melbourne where people experiencing homelessness sell these high quality newspapers and earn a portion of the profit for themselves. A whole lot more dignity in that than begging and a great service to the City as well; a win all around. There are numerous community service agencies doing good work for all types of marginalised people in the City. What would the Bible be calling out to them? Affirmation, as they carry out the work of mercy and justice that is high on God's agenda. Community Service Organisations are helping to fulfil the vision that God gave Jeremiah when He told the people to 'seek the peace and prosperity of the city to which I have carried you into exile. Pray to the Lord for it, because if it prospers, you too will prosper' (29:7).

We continued our journey down Flinders Lane and passed the Melbourne East Police Station on the right. The police force is part of the Law driver and I heard the words of the Apostle Paul as he wrote to Timothy: 'We know that the law is good if one uses it properly. We also know that the law is made not for the righteous but for lawbreakers and rebels, the ungodly and sinful (1Timothy 1:8–9).' Our cities would be a lot worse off if we were left without those who help to enforce the law but we are reminded here that the law must not be abused or misused. It is indeed a good thing when it is used properly.

On our left was Ross House, a Centre for a varied lot of Community and Justice Organisations. It was here that the Federation of Community Legal Centres of Victoria got its start and it is home to such groups as the Disability Discrimination Legal Services and the Thai Information and Welfare Association, to name just two of many community and justice groups. I am reminded of the words of James: 'You will do right, if you obey the most important law in the Scriptures. It is the law that commands us to love others as much as we love ourselves. But if you treat some people better than others, you have done wrong, and the Scriptures teach that you have sinned' (2:8–9). This is just one of over 2,000 passages in the Bible that cry out for Justice and where Organisations are fighting for such the Bible passes by and cries out 'well done good and faithful servants'.

Education is the driver that is represented by the Council of Adult Education where the City Library is housed. The CAE and the Library itself are founded on the principles of all of life education and this is applauded in the Bible by such passages as Deuteronomy 6:5–9 where education of and in the everyday is espoused: 'Love the Lord your God with all your heart and with all your soul and with all your strength. These commandments that I give you today are to be on your hearts. Impress them on your children. Talk about them when you sit at home and when you walk along the road, when you lie down and when you get up. Tie them as symbols on your hands and bind them on your foreheads. Write them on the doorframes of your houses and on your gates.'

Our short journey through the streets of Melbourne comes to an end as we place the 1611 KJB in its resting place for the coming month, the centre of the Bible exhibition in the City Library, an exhibition that celebrates the history of the Bible in Australian society and the ongoing relevancy of its wisdom for today.

On our journey we have passed by representatives of each of the ten drivers of society and we have recalled what the Bible could be calling out to them as we pass by. We have heard the voice of public wisdom as it affirms, encourages, challenges, and rebukes various aspects of the life of the City today.

We have seen that the Bible is indeed relevant to all the sectors of modern society as we encounter it in the City today. I am reminded again of a passage relating the words of Jesus: 'But you rich people are in for trouble. You have already had an easy life! You well-fed people are in for trouble. You will go hungry! You people who are laughing now are in for trouble. You are going to cry and weep. You are in for trouble when everyone says good things about you. That is what your own people said about those prophets who told lies' (Luke 6:24–26).

Jesus is here talking on core values, telling the people what not to hold onto as priorities in their lives. Such things as riches, food, happiness, and popularity don't make for good priorities. They will all be seen as shallow at some point. These are to be contrasted with the values that Jesus prioritises throughout His teaching, such values as love, mercy, justice, humility, and service. Biblical Advocacy finds out what the Bible has to say about such values and priorities and then seeks to live it and speak it into the public space. Our public space is saturated with the core values of riches, food, happiness, and popularity. We have a radical ethic of difference to proclaim which is challenging but filled with incredible possibilities for transforming society, changing culture, and helping cities to find wellbeing.

How can this Voice be Heard?

But our world is not listening. As I walked with that procession through the streets of Melbourne and 'heard' the voice of wisdom calling out to the drivers, the city remained unchanged. Big business still made huge profits at the expense of the everyday citizen, the homeless lady was still homeless, the Media continued to say some really unwise things, the need for justice organisations still existed and they remain incredibly poorly resourced . . . And so it goes on. We cry out with the sentiment that Jesus had as he overlooked His City of Jerusalem and wept. Melbourne, oh Melbourne, how we have longed for you to hear the wisdom that could truly set you free, but you would not listen . . .

There are at least three ways that this voice of wisdom can be heard.

1. Public voices that are already respected are 'out there' and speaking Biblical wisdom into the public space. People such as Tim Costello, Phillip Freier, George Savvides, Ian Harper, Simon McKeon, Bryan Patterson, Barney Zwartz, Greg Clarke, Simon Smart, Hugh DeKretser, Gordon Preece, Denise Cooper-Clarke and Penny Mulvey are just some examples that come to mind. May their minds and hands be strengthened.
2. Public access media is growing in power as a way of letting our voice be known. Such avenues as letters to the Editor, Twitter, Facebook, Blogging, On Line Groups and Media outlets are some examples. This is the 'Market Place' and the 'City Gate' of today. I am reminded again of Proverbs 1:20–21: 'wisdom shouts in the streets wherever crowds gather . . . in the market places and near the city gates.'
3. The most powerful way of letting Biblical wisdom be known is through everyday life across all the drivers of society. In all these drivers there are people who are committed to understanding Biblical values and priorities, to live them and to speak that wisdom into everyday life. In this way they will be 'people of Sophia'. We are called to be such people of wisdom by knowing the values and priorities that God desires, under-

> standing the times in which we live, and looking for ways to apply that wisdom. As Paul said in his letter to the church in Ephesus, 'Be very careful, then, how you live—not as unwise but as wise, making the most of every opportunity, because the days are evil. Therefore do not be foolish, but understand what the Lord's will is' (5:15–17).

In Conclusion

The Bible is a relevant source of wisdom for today's society. It has healthy application across all the drivers of society and can be instrumental in the transforming of our cities, the repairing of our social environment.

People of wisdom are called to use every opportunity available to live and speak this wisdom that the world might be changed. As we do we are reminded that we are in very good company indeed. William Wilberforce did it. John Wesley did it. William Booth did it as did Martin Luther King, Desmond Tutu, and Johnny the bag boy! (Johnny the bag boy: who's that? I hear you ask. Google it and listen to a powerful story about how you can make a difference no matter who you are.)

I will let the last words be those of Desmond Tutu: 'There's nothing more radical, nothing more revolutionary, nothing more subversive against injustice and oppression than the Bible. If you want to keep people subjugated, the last thing you place in their hands is a Bible.'

Wisdom and Transformational Leadership[1]

George Savvides

Managing Director
Medibank
Melbourne
Victoria

Spirituality is a Part of the Human Experience and it is the Source of Inspirational Leadership.

It may sound odd, having spent twenty years as a Chief Executive Officer but I am even more passionate now then ever about the subject of leadership, in particular inspirational leadership capable of producing community and organisational transformation. I think we all would agree the world is in desperate need of leaders, leaders who leave their assignment in better shape than what they started with, not a leader defined by 'what I control' but 'what I created or enabled to happen'.

I am not talking about good management, or cost cutting, I am talking about business or organisational renewal. I have often had times when I was confronted with what seemed insurmountable business challenges including questions not answered due to unique circumstances and pressing needs. Corporate leaders are not the only people that are confronted with difficult problems. Just listen into the stories of one of the chaplains here tonight and we find many challenges calling on them to draw upon deep

1. This talk was an address given in August 2011 to an Access Ministries dinner to support the deployment of Chaplains in secular contexts. This speech represents the personal views of the author.

personal courage to assist young people with the challenges that come into their lives.

Transformational leaders make real and direct connection in relationships. They have distinctive characteristics typified by courage, inspiration or deep conviction that provides the strength to take on the harder challenge, to lead renewal, to be transformational, whether they operate at a corporate, societal, community or individual level.

I think its interesting that in the corporate world, when leaders engender a strong sense of purpose in their business, and deep engagement with their staff, where the job becomes mission, and the corporate values call for a total team commitment to accountability, integrity and respect to realise organisational purpose, such achievements are applauded as 'great'. So what are these characteristics of greatness in organisations or their leaders? My interest in this area has helped me a great deal so let me share with you what I found. But before I do I have to declare another variable, my cultural frame of reference that sits behind my Sydney birthplace, and that is my Greek Cypriot upbringing and the Greek Orthodox foundation that came with it. So my enquiry into inspirational leaders, their character and motivation found me drawn to authors who held both a practical demonstration of leading change linked to a world view that allows room for the unexplained, the unquantifiable and the spiritual dimension to life and vocation. This dimension is not new, or unusual, if you know anything about a Greek village, you will know that Sunday and Monday are well connected, belief is as natural as the air you breathe, as is the contest for hospitality and generosity.

As an aside, on the theme of connecting Sunday to Monday, faith inspired organisations continue to provide value in our society. My company Medibank contracts around twenty-five per cent of its $4 billion per annum of hospital services from faith based hospital providers. Catholic Healthcare is but one example. Australia's formation since European settlement has greatly benefited from faith based agencies in social welfare, humanitarian aid, hospitals and schools. In fact eighty per cent of humanitarian aid and social services to needy and disadvantaged Australians come from faith based agencies, and those agencies started by Christians with a faith inspired motivation . . . or should I say inspiration.

Modern Leadership Studies

So it is no surprise that I am attracted to modern leadership studies such as Jim Collins' *Good to Great* in which Level Five leaders are coaches rather than captains, with a humble but deep resolve to realise the vision and resist the temptation of complacency. The enemy of being great is to be satisfied with being good. Leaders who leave behind something that's better, or even transformed, and better still, sustainable and relevant are great leaders; Patrick Lencioni's *Five Dysfunctions of a Team* where we wrestle with the discipline of team over individual is another interesting study; Nikos Mourkogiannis' book *Purpose*, which reveals the creative and enduring power of companies or movements that retain a deep sense of purpose for why they exist; and the more confronting Arbinger Institute's narrative in which leadership and self-deception point to the blinding power of self absorption that often captures the leader; they become blind to self and blind to the needs of others, addicted to their 'me' agenda, sucked into their vortex of vanity.

The Bible and Leadership

Arguably the most profound book on human character and leadership celebrates its 400th anniversary in 2011, the King James Bible, often referred to as the AV or Authorised Version. Its influence on the English language, our values, imagination and culture has been profound. A friend and colleague, Peter Corney, has said it well:

> From William Blake's poetry and Steinbeck's *East of Eden* to a recent work, *Atonement* by the novelist Ian McEwan, and the film that followed, the influence continues. To fully appreciate the poetry of John Milton or TS Elliot requires an understanding of the Bible. It is also hard to read the words of the Prophet Micah (6:8) or Mary's song (Luke 1:46–55) or Jesus' manifesto of his ministry (Luke 4:16–21) without being inspired about justice, fairness and equality!

The inspiration drawn from the biblical narrative is evident in the overwhelming volume of human creativity unlocked in literature, art and music when human spirituality is stirred. That same inspiration has lifted leaders to move beyond their own agendas and be truly transformative.

Other inspirational leaders include people like Dr Martin Luther King who prayed a week before the protest in Montgomery that went onto to become a march that changed a nation, 'Lord, I hope no one will have to die as a result of our struggle in Montgomery he prayed, certainly I don't want to die, but if anyone has to die, let it be me'. What an example of grace!

Even voices which are critical, such as Richard Dawkins, has said, 'You can't appreciate English literature unless you are steeped to some extent in the King James Bible . . .not to know (it) is to be, in some small way, barbarian.' Andrew Motion, former British Poet Laureate and self-confessed non-believer, in an interview in *The Guardian* laments the widespread ignorance of the Bible today. He recommends that all children should be taught the Bible in school since, without it, they cannot hope to understand history and literature. Melvyn Bragg, in his recent *The Book of Books—the radical influence of the King James Bible*, outlines its deep and positive influence on English speaking culture, society and politics. It has, he says, 'driven the making of that world over the last 400 years'.

Many of the critics forget the essential role the Bible has played in forming the very liberal freedoms they espouse so loudly. It is ironic that the secular beneficiaries' of this legacy now want to exclude its study from our schools. When the first King James' Bible was printed 400 years ago, like the internet, it empowered new generations of people, giving them open access and freedom to know the source documents that framed their religious and faith experiences and heritage, without the distortion of religious power brokers.

What earthly reason, says Nick Spencer author of *Freedom and Order*, is there for a ruler to surrender himself to the same laws as his subjects? It seems so obvious to us now. But it remains far from obvious to a host of North African dictators who have recently fallen, and was certainly not obvious to the innumerable kings and emperors of the past. The Western political tradition was profoundly influenced by the biblical ideal that the law was over everyone (Deut 17: 14–29) and Kings were ultimately accountable to God. We find this interpretation down through the ages; Shakespeare for example frames his narratives with the assumption that the King is appointed through God's consent and is accountable to the same.

The Biblical narrative can bring to young students an understanding of human behaviour—pride, jealousy, greed, desired humility, compassion, selfless service and other admirable qualities—presented in a context of mankind's search for meaning and purpose. It's strange to say this but in the corporate world we want people and organisations that reflect these qualities.

Gravity and Grace

I really admire the work of the French philosopher, Simon Weil, who died at just thirty-three, a member of the French resistance and a Jew who followed Christ. She described human nature in an interesting way: I like her clarity maybe influenced from the context of a world at war when she writes:

> Two great forces rule the universe, gravity and grace. Gravity attracts to itself, enlarging more and more into itself. It is in us, this face of self interest, self absorption, to accumulate, to store treasures, security increased, success, popularity, all about us . . . All natural movements of the soul are controlled by laws analogous to those of physical gravity.

Well, is she right? Read our newspapers, watch the news. Even a Global Financial Crisis did not prevent bonuses being paid to investment bankers who sold synthetic instruments, instruments that ultimately broke the economies of nations, destroyed millions of jobs and wiped out household savings. We watched this gravity play out before our eyes. Philip Yancey reminds us that grace is Christianity's best gift to the world, a spiritual nova in our midst, exerting a force greater than vengeance, racism, hate.

Some may scoff and say we can fix this gravity through tougher laws and better education, the force of legislation or a broader investment in ethics; all helpful ideas but don't hold your breath – the markets continued to crash last week, but the bonuses will continue to flow to those that sold the cancerous bonds. We can see in the News Corporation media revelations in the United Kingdom in the last few years which show how deep journalists powered by gravity (self absorption) could not draw the line between black and white invading the personal privacy and in some cases grief of families. This gravity is powerful stuff. There is nothing unique about gravity, but it needs more than ethics, legislation or education to contain it.

He said it a long time ago but the gravity of self-absorption caught the eye of Sir Francis Bacon: 'If money be not thy servant, it will thy master. The covetous man cannot so properly be said to possess wealth as that maybe said to possess him.' The problem is not that we stash our treasurers away but rather the delusion that there is comfort in such accumulation. The U2 song by the Irish band, U2, rings in my head with the words from one of their songs, 'I still haven't found what I am looking for'.

Adaptive Leadership guru, surgeon and classical pianist Ron Heifeitz says you can fix the heart but you cannot change the heart, citing the eighty per cent of relapse to smoking within twelve months of heart bypass surgery. The problem I am referring to is not about morality, it,is about a deep transformation more powerful than logic or intellect. On the other hand in grace, which requires a step of faith and humble self acceptance, we see the power to turn the self interest vector around making it possible to serve the interests of others, or better still, reach out and care for others, with a compassion and conviction to address injustice and oppression, and more broadly, a world in need. We see the very best of human expression when 'Grace' overcomes 'Gravity'.

The creative genius Tolkien, inspired by the biblical narrative, had his own metaphor for Gravity (self-absorption) and Grace. His inspiring characters in *Lord of the Rings* reflect a humble generosity of spirit. Frodo provides inspiration through his courage and a sacrificial friendship which eventually restores order in middle earth, or should I say his leadership is transformative. The wisdom of the narrative constantly reminds us of the danger of gravity represented in the power of the Ring—'precious'—says the tragic Gollum caught and captured by forces against which he has no defences.

I recall, as I reflect on my twelve years on the Board of World Vision, some of the wonderful examples of very ordinary people working in the most difficult settings of human poverty. I found here in the most remote and difficult parts of the world young leaders inspired by grace, buying into the faith conviction of the organisation which inspired them to overcome their own self orientation and the gravity of self-interest and instead reach out to a humanity desperate to receive compassion, kindness and justice .

Whilst every job has an implied obligation to the employer, when an employee is inspired and engaged, a job turns to vocation; it is what Frederick Buechner meant when he said, 'The place God calls you to is the place where your deep gladness and the world's deepest hunger meet'.

When I hear the stories of the impact that chaplains have I can begin to understand the depth of commitment, empathy and compassion they bring to their vocation (obviously more than a job) often at a significant personal cost. It is then that I reflect on Buechner's words.

Inspiration is more than simply logic or rational intelligence. Its source is deeper and more resilient and springs from the human need for meaning and significance. When I say more than rational, I am not advocating irrational behaviour. Rather I am advocating for inspired behaviour and leadership. They are not opposites, they are both and. Its analogous to the leadership wisdom of Jesus when he said if anyone wants to sue you and take you shirt let him have you coat also, or if someone forces you to go one mile, go with him two (Matt 5: 40, 41). Not logical but inspirational.

Ask a chaplain how often they have to go an extra mile to help a young person or community. If leadership is only framed by logic or status and position or power or the authority of office, it will not be sufficient to deliver sustainable change. Leading from the head and not the heart will not unlock an extraordinary effort from the team or inspire creative innovation. This will be different for everyone, because inspiration is something that originates from a deep sense of calling and purpose in our lives, it's the realm of the spiritual in all of us, the place of unanswered questions.

I have always admired the eighteenth century collaborators called the Clapham Sect, originally labelled as Christian humanists. They were genuine transformational leaders inspired by their faith but convicted by the biblical call for justice and compassion to all. They pursued causes such as the abolition of the slave trade and did so even though it was opposed by the government and church authorities of the day. I am reminded of their example as I listen to the stories from school principals of the work of chaplains, that through their accredited role as pastoral carers there are inspiring stories of humble role models with a deep sense of calling and the desire that all people, in particular children who have challenges in their lives, be supported with kindness and compassion. These values and beliefs drive them to make themselves available for helping others at times when great sorrow, fear or grief impacts the life of a child.

Was DL Moody describing a chaplain when he said 'A holy life will produce the deepest impression. Lighthouses blow no horns, they only shine'. Mother Teresa continued this theme: 'I am a little pencil in the hand of a writing God. God is sending a love letter to the world'.

Many more inspirational leaders came from this collaboration, the Clapham Sect. William Booth who founded the Salvation Army; John Newton; William Wilberforce; Robert Raikes (Schools); Elizabeth Fry; George Williams (YMCA); Anthony Ashley-Cooper, the 7th Earl of Shaftesbury. Between them, they founded seventy-five per cent of the 500 British charitable institutions formed during the eighteenth century. Five of them were elected to parliament. Together they pursued reform, tackled the debtors' prisons releasing 14,000 prisoners and rallied public support for public education, housing the poor, help for the disabled and stopping child labour.

Many are quick to criticise the place of spiritual search or motivation. But it is more normal than many make it out to be—most of the world expresses its humanity with spiritual enquiry or faith conviction. And yes, we should beware of radical fundamentalists, whether they are atheists or whether they are religious leaders obsessed with forcing rules or constraints on others and not seeking the genuine transformation where Gravity is displaced by Grace. But when service and personal sacrifice flow through compassion and calling, we see love conquer greed, justice overcome evil, and, yes, Grace overcome Gravity.

I have referred to historical examples of Inspiring leadership, the influence of the Bible publication and mass distribution, the examples of political leaders like King or Wilberforce (and we could add Gandhi and Mandela as well) but what about modern leadership thought?

A Model from Oxford

I recently attended a leadership program in Oxford run by the United Kingdom's leading business school. I was not sure what to expect but what I found was a surprise. They took thirty Chief Executive Officer's of which I was one, on a journey of discovering inspirational leadership covering leadership case studies from Shakespeare in Henry V, who is confronted with defeat and the dark night of the soul, to Plato's cave and the question of what is real, to a new metaphor of leadership, not a coach but a conductor and in our case the Oxford choir. The conductor has no voice and no assurance the choir will follow his lead. His assignment is to produce a beautiful song from his team, to make possible through his leadership the expression of the team's individual talents through a harmonious tune that the audience (customers) will love. There is more grace than gravity in this model of leadership.

We studied leadership in the context of a failed mission where the leader remains loyal to the mission and those that depend on them despite the failure of sponsors and stakeholders to remain faithful. And yes we found that spirituality is still a recognised powerful force that overcomes gravity and releases extraordinary conviction and purpose producing the fruit of grace in the world . . . kindness and justice through humility. This suggested model of leadership serves the mission by serving the team, not self.

Wisdom and Leadership

Knowledge is not wisdom. Knowledge is the domain of science and intellectualism. Wisdom, on the other hand, goes beyond self awareness. Wisdom permits us to interpret the rational and the non-rational. Wisdom speaks to deeper truths, relevant in our moments of deepest despair or greatest joy. Wisdom finds a home in reflective meditational and religious reverence.

So what does this wisdom of Jesus look like? How does it make the world a better place? His parables in Luke 15, the lost coin, the lost sheep, and the two lost sons, reflect his deep love for the lost and those seeking return home. In God's economy the humble widow's two copper coins are worth more than the gold ones given by the proud wealthy priest.

For women, the Middle East in 30 AD was oppressive. There was no equality or discrete identity, yet Jesus in his encounter with a Samaritan woman at the well of Sychar (John 4) and the Woman about to be stoned by her religious male accusers for her adulterous indiscretion (John 8) was lovingly wise. Both women find grace not judgement, they are engaged in a compassionate conversation with Jesus who shows against the cultural backdrop of the day a respect and dignity for these women as equals. They experience justice and compassion and these stories need to be told to our young men even in this well educated generation.

The parable of the talents (Matthew 25) gives the invitation to live life fully with courage using your gifts to make a difference in the world. The powerful story of the Good Samaritan (Luke 10) deals with the questions of who is my neighbour and how do we treat a stranger? And doesn't the world need that attitude and respect for humanity today! The Sermon on the Mount (Matthew 5 – 7) includes the teaching that the search for happiness or meaning is not found in possessions, or worrying, but more in generosity to others and a grateful heart. The story of Zachaeus (Luke 19) shows how anyone, even an unlovable rat bag (or thieving skunk), gets a chance to change, to be made right and whole. Forgiveness is the new dimension in a postmodern epoch. These are but a few examples of the wisdom Jesus taught as he walked this earth.

The Chaplain as Transformational Leader

Our world needs leaders inspired by this wisdom to release more grace in the world. Karl Bath stated 'Jesus' gift of forgiveness (grace) is more astonishing than Jesus' miracles. Those miracles overpowered the physical laws of the universe.' But in Jesus gift of forgiveness we see grace that broke the judgemental legalism. Grace overpowered the gravitational field of self absorption.

If God is real in the human journey, let the wisdom, and truths from the biblical narrative speak for themselves. They will evoke the human hunger for spirituality and for God. Bertrand Russell wrote 'Unless you assume a God, the question of life's purpose is meaningless.' But we all search for meaning. Everyone has to believe in something. It is right to give people, especially children a choice to learn, to know and to choose.

It is therefore healthy to have this contrasting world-view taught to children. The world-view that inspires transformational leaders to change the world, to pursue noble causes, and to create a civil society which we value and which sustains our humanity. And how much more important is it when most other voices and most other world-views default to gravity and self interest. Without Christ's grace and the light it brings, the world would collapse under the smothering gravitational weight of self-interest.

CS Lewis wrote 'I believe in Christianity as I believe the sun has risen, not only because I see it, but because by it I see everything else.' The biblical narrative calls us to deeply commit to building a better world for the good of others. It forms as a centre-piece of the prayer Jesus taught us to pray: Thy will be done on earth.

And so the chaplain is called to service. This is how they serve. We can only but admire their example and contribution, helping young kids make a better future for themselves and our country. We should be thankful and applaud the inspiration and hope that chaplains bring to our society. Life is more than material, more than logic, it is spiritual as well. When meaning in grief or melancholy is lost, we need help to reconnect with the source of meaning and inspiration in our lives.

This life context with meaning can lift us and encourage us to love and care for others extending beyond the gravitational field of our own self interest. In doing so, we too are transformed to make our communities feel more human, more caring, like that Greek village I keep dreaming about.

Contributors

Paul Babie is Associate Professor, Adelaide Law School, and Director, Research Unit for the Study of Society, Law and Religion, both at The University of Adelaide. His teaching and research is in the areas of property law, property theory, legal theory, and the relationship between secular and non-secular legal systems, especially as they deal with property.

Clive Beed and Cara Beed are, respectively, retired Senior Lecturer in Economics, University of Melbourne, and retired Lecturer in Sociology, Australian Catholic University. They have published in a variety of academic journals on the relation between theology and economics, and in 1997 were awarded a Templeton Prize. A number of their papers were consolidated into a book in 2006, titled *Alternatives to Economics: Christian Socio-Economic Perspectives*, published by the University Press of America. Married since 1961, they have two married children and two grandsons, and enjoy a rich family life and church worship. Currently, they are Fellows, Centre for Applied Christian Ethics, Ridley Theological College, University of Melbourne, and Fellows, Australian Catholic University. Cara is also involved in the Boston-based, Theology of Work project.

Brian Edgar is Professor of Theological Studies at Asbury Theological Seminary (USA) although primarily resident in Australia. His interests lie in public theology and the integration of theology with other disciplines, especially science. He is a Fellow of the Institute for the Study of Christianity in an Age of Science and Technology. He is the editor of the on-line peer-reviewed journal *Crucible: a Journal of Theology and Ministry* and the author of a number of books and articles including *The Message of the Trinity* (IVP). Numerous articles can be accessed at his Public Theology page http://brian-edgar.com/

Brian Hill is Emeritus Professor of Education at Murdoch University, Western Australia. His doctorate was from the University of Illinois. He has authored many articles and books in the areas of philosophy and ethics of education, including *Education and the Endangered Individual* (New York: Teachers College Press, 1973), The Greening of Christian Education (London: Paternoster, 1985), *Values Education in Australian Schools* (Melbourne: ACER, 1991) and *Exploring Religion in School* (Open Book, 2004—now available through Australian Church Resources).

Nadirsyah Hosen is a senior lecturer at the Faculty of Law, University of Wollongong (Australia). He completed his first PhD (Law) at the University of Wollongong and a second PhD (Islamic Law) at the National University of Singapore. He is the author of *Shari'a and Constitutional Reform in Indonesia* (Institute of Southeast Asian Studies, Singapore, 2007), a co-editor (with Joseph Liow) of *Islam in Southeast Asia*, 4 volumes, (Routledge, London, 2009), and a co-editor (with Richard Mohr) of *Law and Religion in Public Life: The Contemporary Debate* (Routledge, London, 2010).

Gordon Preece is Director of ETHOS: EA Centre for Christianity and Society and vicar of Yarraville Anglican Church. He is also Ethicist for Christian Super (Sustainable Fund of 2008—Ethical Investor; Infinity Award 2010) and adjunct lecturer at Ridley Melbourne and Macquarie University School of Applied Finance. Gordon is an international leader in workplace theology. He is a prolific writer as author or editor of 11 books, many articles and of Zadok Perspectives. He is currently writing a book on the Global Financial Crisis and editing a book on Bonhoeffer.

Bernadette Richards is a senior lecturer at the Law School, University of Adelaide. Bernadette's research focus sits at the nexus of ethics and the law in the context of medical treatment, with a particular emphasis on consent to medical treatment. She is the co-author of *Tort Law in Principle*, (5th ed, Lawbook Co 2009), and co-editor of *Issues at the Borders of Life* (ATF, 2010). She also contributed to *Health Law in Australia* (ed Ben White, Fiona McDonald and Lindy Willmott, Lawbook Co, 2010) and is Editor in Chief of *Ethics: Contemporary Perspectives* a new journal launched by ATF and the University of Adelaide's Research Unit for the Study of Society, Law and Religion (RUSSLR) in 2012. Bernadette is also an Associate Editor of the *Journal of Bioethical Inquiry* and a committee member of Australian Association of Bioethics and Health Law (AABHL).

George Savvides is the Managing Director of Medibank, Australia's largest health insurer. George has lead the organisation since 2002, and prior to that had health sector CEO roles with Sigma and Smith & Nephew. He trained as an Industrial Engineer (UNSW) and later an MBA with UTS. He is passionate about the agenda of transformation and leadership in both societal and business contexts. He Chairs Arrow Leadership and is a board member of World Vision and the International Federation of Health Plans.

Benny Tai is Associate Professor of Law at The University of Hong Kong. His research fields include comparative constitutional law, administrative law, law and religion, law and public theology, law and politics of constitutions, rule of law, development of constitutionalism in China, law and governance.

Chris White is a retired actuary who spent most of his career consulting and in mangement with Towers Perrin (Human Resources & Actuarial Consultants) and predecessor firms. His final role was Managing Director UK & Regional Manager Europe. Since retirement he has studied and taught Christian and business ethics, and been on a number of boards of both for-profit and not-for-profit organisations (including currently Chair of Ethos, an ethics centre which is the primary ongoing activity of the Evangelical Alliance and the Zadok Institute). His present research interest is in the relationship between Christianity and economics.

David R Wilson has training in Theology, Psychology, and the Social Sciences. His experience covers drug and alcohol counselling, lecturing at a tertiary level, academic administration, and involvement in various not for profit organisations in management and governance roles. He was an elected Councilor with the City of Melbourne (2004 – 2008) with the portfolio of Community Services and Arts and Culture, and is currently Senior Consultant with Sophia Think Tank, an initiative of Bible Society Australia in Public Theology. David is married to Debbie and they have four adult children and 12 grandchildren. He comes with a passion for social justice, the importance of equality and inclusiveness, and the application of the Bible to everyday life.

CPSIA information can be obtained at www.ICGtesting.com
Printed in the USA
BVOW021711170213

313488BV00001B/12/P

9 781921 817779